The Author

WILLIAM RIGGAN is Associate Editor
of *World Literature Today* at the University of Oklahoma. He received the
Ph.D. degree in comparative literature
from Indiana University. He has trans-
lated Ulrich Weisstein's *Comparative
Literature and Literary Theory*.

Pícaros, Madmen, Naïfs, and Clowns

The Unreliable First-Person Narrator

Pícaros, Madmen, Naïfs, and Clowns

The Unreliable First-Person Narrator

By William Riggan

UNIVERSITY OF OKLAHOMA PRESS : NORMAN

PN
3383
.P64
R5

Library of Congress Cataloging in Publication Data

Riggan, William, 1946–
Pícaros, madmen, naïfs, and clowns.

Bibliography: p.
Includes index.
1. First person narrative.   I. Title.
PN3383.P64R5   809.3'923   81-2791
                                 AACR2

For K. and K.

Contents

Preface

THE IMPETUS FOR UNDERTAKING the following study was given by Professors Dorrit Cohn and Eva Kagan-Kans, whose seminars in world literature at Indiana University in the early 1970s frequently took up problems of narrative technique, in particular the role and nature of the narrating voice. Portions of Chapter 3, on the picaresque narrator, were published in 1975 in *Orbis Litterarum* as "The Reformed Pícaro and His Narrative." The research and writing of that essay and of the entire study were carried out between September 1973 and January 1977 at the Universities of Indiana, Hamburg, and Oklahoma, with the year abroad financed by a fellowship from the Deutscher Akademischer Austauschdienst.

Reference to cited materials from primary texts is by chapter or by book and chapter, where possible, as a convenience to the reader in consulting whatever edition he or she may have at hand. In works lacking such units or containing unusually long divisions, page numbers of the cited editions are used. The cited editions of the primary and secondary works, and the translations of the primary texts, are the most authoritative ones which were available at the institutions listed above. With only two or three noted exceptions, the translations from secondary sources are my own.

The selection of individual works for discussion was made on the basis of two considerations. The primary criterion was a formal one, limiting the choice to those which are narrated in the first person by the protagonist, as will be noted toward the end of the Introduction. The second consideration was linguistic in nature, restricting the selection to works written in languages accessible to me—namely, English, German, Spanish, French, Russian, and Latin. Works in these last five languages are cited here in English translation, but in each case the original was consulted for verification. Only in discussing Persian novelist Sadegh Hedayat's *The Blind Owl* do I rely solely on the English version. Lastly, though a number of French novels are referred to in passing, none fell sufficiently within the framework of the study to warrant individual analysis and discussion. I also came across many reviews and essays indicating the existence of a large number of unreliable first-person narratives from the literatures of Italy, Scandinavia, the East European countries, Anglophone and Francophone Africa, and Latin America; but my lack of close familiarity with the writers and works in question, as well as demands of space, time, and resources, necessitated the exclusion of all but an occasional token reference to these items.

I would like to express my thanks to several individuals for their advice and encouragement in this project: to Professor Breon Mitchell for his prodding guidance; to Professors Joseph Ricapito and Eva Kagan-Kans for their expert counsel on the picaresque novel and on the Russian writers respectively; to Professor Peter Boerner for his instructive critiques; to Tom Sauer for his frequent assistance in obtaining research materials; and to Michael Beard for his helpful comments on Hedayat.

Pícaros, Madmen, Naïfs, and Clowns

The Unreliable First-Person Narrator

CHAPTER 1

Introduction

I know what some would think, they would think my behaviour peculiar. I know most men would only have thought of taking an unfair advantage and there were plenty of opportunities. I could have used the
[chloroform] pad. Done what I liked, but I am not that sort, definitely
not that sort at all. She was like some caterpillar that takes three months
to feed up trying to do it in a few days. I knew nothing good would come
of it, she was always in a hurry. People today want to get things, they no
sooner think of it they want to get it in their hands, but I am different,
old-fashioned, I enjoy thinking about the future and letting things develop all in good time. Easy does it, as Uncle Dick used to say when he
was into a big one.

What she never understood was that with me it was having. Having
her was enough. Nothing need doing. I just wanted to have her, and
safe at last.

THE SPEAKER OF THESE LINES is the young ex-clerk and amateur
entomologist Frederick (alias Ferdinand) Clegg in John Fowles's
novel *The Collector*.[1] Even devoid of context, the curious in-
cohesion and nervous self-defensiveness of his words, the bizarre
mixture of reverence and possessiveness shown toward the young
woman in question, betray a mind which is at least slightly unbalanced and a narrative voice whose judgments create suspicion
in the reader. Several questions naturally arise: What has Clegg

[1] John Fowles, *The Collector*, pp. 100–101.

3

done to make him feel that others might find him peculiar? How is his "different" and "old-fashioned" nature, his not being "that sort," good in comparison to the nature of other men? What does he understand by "just having" the girl without "doing"? And is he as saintly as his prudishly euphemistic language would lead us to believe? In brief, an unsettling distrust of the speaker is felt.

In context, of course, after one hundred pages of Clegg's "observations diary" (if that is indeed what we are reading),[2] we know that he has abducted an attractive young art student named Miranda. We also know that he has placed her in captivity in an escape-proof cellar room in an English country house and now hopes to live with her for the rest of their days, blissfully content just to have her, like some prize specimen, in his possession. The premise is an appalling one in itself, to be sure, and pronouncements such as that quoted above serve only to reinforce the reader's revulsion at a criminally disturbed mind which never fully realizes or admits the extent of its perversity in perpetrating such a violation of another human being. I can scarcely imagine anyone's readily accepting Clegg's account of his elaborate two-year preparations for his "guest," his expressed failure to understand why she never conforms to his expectations, or his self-righteous outrage at the fact that she tries to escape, tries even to bludgeon him with an ax. Surely, too, few will condone his chloroforming her, then taking lewd ("artistic") photographs of her, and later letting her simply die of pneumonia rather than facing the possible consequences of having her seen by a doctor. The disparity between the horror of Clegg's behavior and the self-involved coldness of his attitude toward those events is simply too enormous not to spark at least some degree of loathing in the reader. What is being read cannot be taken as anything other

---

[2] Clegg mentions his observations diary once on the first page, but there is no further concrete reference to indicate that what we are reading has been written by his own hand. The vocabulary and syntax are his, but the many anticipatory remarks at the outset— "those days (after the ones I'm going to say about) are definitely the best I've ever had"— are out of place, unless we are reading entries written after the entire affair is over and as Clegg is planning his next abduction.

4

than a madman's attempt at self-vindication for crimes resulting from his madness.

The portrait of Clegg is so vividly revealing of the workings of his deranged mind that a trace of pitying though horrified sympathy for the man is possible in the reader. And it is also quite possible that Fowles—or rather that projection of himself which implicitly informs the novel with a set of values contradictory to Clegg's and more approaching normalcy, namely the implied author of the work[3]—has had the narrator reveal himself in such significant detail precisely to evoke such a reaction. But surely this possible trace of sympathy is the only conceivable link between Clegg and the Fowles we presume to be standing behind the actual narration of the novel. In all other respects—intelligence, emotional and moral substance, responsible social behavior—the two are starkly separated, if only because Clegg is so far removed from any semblance of normalcy in these areas and from any values which an author could reasonably expect to be shared by more than a few isolated individuals.

The result of this distancing is a classic and even exaggerated example of unreliable narration: that is, the norms propounded and exemplified by the narrator through his words and actions are at variance with those norms held by the implied author of the work and expected by him to be comprehended and largely shared by readers of the work. To apply Wayne Booth's comments on the Jason episode of Faulkner's *The Sound and the Fury*, "We watch with [the author] while this Vice reveals himself for our contempt, our hatred, our laughter, and even . . . our pity."[4] Clegg's excuses ("It was not my fault. How was I to know she was iller than she looked. She just looked like she had a cold"), vin-

---

[3] Wayne C. Booth, *The Rhetoric of Fiction*, pp. 73–75. The term "implied author" is used by Booth to subsume such various terms as "style," "tone," and "technique," or "meaning," "theme," "symbolic significance," "theology," or "ontology"—in short, "the norms which the reader must apprehend in each work if he is to grasp it adequately. . . . The 'implied author' chooses, consciously or unconsciously, what we read: we infer him as an ideal, literary, created version of the real man; he is the sum of his own choices."

[4] Ibid., p. 307.

dications ("I am not really that sort and I was only like it that night because of all that happened and the strain I was under"), and judgments ("Of course she wasn't really [stupid], it was just that she didn't see how to love me in the right way") cannot be accepted by any socially responsible person. His tortuous, awkward account can only serve to reveal him for the horribly and pitiably deranged individual that he is, as the author in his implied presence here realizes and expects the reader to realize. Out of his own mouth Clegg condemns himself.

The opening paragraphs of the novel record how Clegg watched Miranda continually, either on the street or from his office window, and finally decided that "she was the only one." Immediately thereafter he adds, in his own defense, "Of course I'm not mad, I knew it was just a dream and it always would have been if it hadn't been for the money" (he won £73,091 in a lottery). Yet, as if the mere recorded workings of Clegg's mind were not sufficient to place the reader squarely against him from the very beginning, fully half the text is devoted to a diary kept by the captive Miranda. After more than two weeks of imprisonment she writes:

October 24th. Another bad day. I made sure it was bad for Caliban [Clegg], too. Sometimes he irritates me so much that I could scream at him. It's not so much the way he looks, though that's bad enough. He's always so respectable, his trousers always have creases, his shirts are always clean. I really think he'd be happier if he wore starched collars. So utterly not with it. And he stands. He's the most tremendous standeraround I've ever met. Always with that I'm-sorry expression on his face, which I begin to realize is *actually* contentment. The sheer joy of having me under his power, of being able to spend all and every day staring at me. He doesn't care what I say or how I feel—my feelings are meaningless to him—it's the fact that he's got me.

I could scream abuse at him all day long; he wouldn't mind at all. It's me he wants, my look, my outside, not my emotions or my mind or my soul or even my body. Not anything *human*.

He's a collector. That's the great dead thing in him. [P. 171]

6

Such passages furnish the reader with a direct link to the values propounded by the novel's implied author, whose title for the novel is echoed in Miranda's words here.[5]

Several psychological and situational factors work to render her account not totally reliable, for some of her observations clearly stem from differences in class and education. Still, Miranda's literate and certainly more normal perspective on the events at the country house and on herself and her captor provides an explicit statement of the work's base of values and indicates in clear terms how the reader is to judge Clegg's character, actions, and attitudes. Her retelling of several incidents and her assessments of Clegg's conduct and motives either directly refute Clegg's own assertions or expose his frequent distorting of events and glossing of his own aberrant behavior. Miranda thus explodes even the minuscule possibility that a reader might temper his judgment of Clegg with too much sympathy or easy credulity. What Clegg states in almost blissfully reverent terms, Miranda places in its cruel and pathetic perspective:

[CLEGG] She made me wait about ten minutes and then she came out. You could have knocked me down with a feather. . . . It really amazed me what she could look like when she wanted. . . . Of course, she made me feel all clumsy and awkward. I had the same feeling I did when I had watched an imago emerge, and then to have to kill it. I mean, the beauty confuses you, you don't know what you want to do any more, what you should do. [Pp. 83–84]

[MIRANDA] I am one in a row of specimens. It's when I try to flutter out of line that he hates me. I'm meant to be dead, pinned, always beautiful. He knows that part of my beauty is being alive, but it's the dead me he wants. He wants me living-but-dead. . . . He showed me one day

---

[5] Compare ibid., p. 198, n. 25: "It is interesting to note how much more importance titles and epigraphs take on in modern works, where they are often the only explicit commentary the reader is given: *Portrait of the Artist as a Young Man, The Sun Also Rises, Vile Bodies, A Handful of Dust, Brave New World, Antic Hay, The Sound and the Fury*—strange titles these for a literature that rises unauthored from the waves of art."

7

what he called his killing-bottle. I'm imprisoned in it. Fluttering against the glass. Because I can see through it I still think I can escape. I have hope. But it's all an illusion. [Pp. 217–18]

Clegg's self-righteous moral indignation is revealed as the probable product of sexual problems and an inferiority complex:

[CLEGG] I felt happy, I can't explain, I saw I was weak before, now I was paying her back for all the things she said and thought about me. I walked about upstairs, I went and looked at her room, it made me really laugh to think of her down there, she was the one who was going to stay below in all senses and even if it wasn't what she deserved in the beginning she had made it so that she did now. I had real reasons to teach her what was what. [P. 114]

[MIRANDA] I felt sorry for Caliban this evening. He will suffer when I am gone. There will be nothing left. He'll be all alone with his sex neurosis and his class neurosis and his uselessness and his emptiness. He's asked for it. I'm not really sorry. But I'm not absolutely unsorry. . . . He is absolutely inferior to me in all ways. His one superiority is his ability to keep me here. That's the only power he has. He can't behave or think or speak or do anything else better than I can—nearly as well as I can— so he's going to be the Old Man of the Sea until I can shake him off somehow. [Pp. 208–209, 238]

And the captor's self-serving accounts of particular occurrences are corrected and augmented:

[CLEGG] She was still out, on the bed. She looked a sight, the dress was all off one shoulder. I don't know what it was, it got me excited, it gave me ideas, seeing her lying there right out. It was like I'd showed her who was really the master. The dress was right off her shoulder, I could see the top of one stocking. I don't know what reminded me of it, I remembered an American film I saw once (or was it a magazine) about a man who took a drunk girl home and undressed her and put her to bed, nothing nasty, he just did that and no more and she woke up in his pyjamas. [P. 91]

[MIRANDA] When I came round from the chloroform I was in bed. I had my last underclothes on, but he must have taken everything else off.

I was furious, that first night. His beastly gloating hands touching me. Peeling my stockings off. Loathsome.

Then I thought of what he might have done. And hadn't. I decided not to fly at him. . . .

Since then I've thought two things.

First: he's weird enough to have undressed me without thinking, according to some mad notion of the "proper" thing to do. Perhaps he thought I couldn't lie in bed with my clothes on.

And then perhaps it was a sort of reminder. Of all the things he might have done, but hadn't. His chivalry. And I accept that. I have been lucky.

But I even find it frightening that he didn't do anything. What is he? [Pp. 237–38]

Through the intimacy gained via the long personal contact with the victim of Clegg's derangement, whatever inkling of credibility the abductor may have had with some readers is destroyed. Miranda's diary is clear evidence of the implied author. It is a device which in this case serves not only to heighten the pathos of the work, but also to convey attitudes and judgments espoused by that implied author and, again, expected to be shared or accepted by the reader.[6]

The case for unreliable narration in *The Collector*, then, seems substantiated not only by the performance of the novel's hopelessly disturbed narrator, but also by the presence of the victim's diary. I have belabored this gripping but transparent work somewhat here at the outset of this study precisely because of the obviousness of its unreliable narration and in order to establish a sound point of departure for a discussion of unreliable narrators. With a narrator such as Clegg, counterweighted by Miranda's account, even the most casual reader will doubtless recognize what

---

[6] Clegg finds Miranda's diary, reads it, and keeps it. But, as he notes at the novel's conclusion, he hides the diary along with a lock of Miranda's hair in a deed box in the loft. The diary's inclusion in the account we read can therefore only be the work of the implied author.

is meant here by unreliability of narration and will thus have a grasp of the concept which is to be the subject of this study.

Obviously, the case for unreliable narration is not always so clear-cut from the outset as it is with Clegg, and rarely is it so strongly and exhaustively reinforced by a counter-voice such as Miranda's. Occasionally a title will give some indication of the seriousness with which a reader is to view the narrator-protagonist.[7] The indication may be direct, as in Nikolai Gogol's "Diary of a Madman" and Thomas Mann's *Confessions of Felix Krull, Confidence Man*; oblique, as in *The Sound and the Fury*, with its Shakespearean reference to "a tale told by an idiot"; or facetious or ironic, as with Fielding's *The Life of Mr. Jonathan Wild the Great*.[8] Then, too, multiplicity of narration often affords the reader more information and perspective with which to make his own evaluation of persons and events than is possible for any of the individual narrators in the work in question; it thus frequently exposes unreliability in one or more of these speakers. The epistolary novel, for instance, with its several correspondents, is a natural vehicle for revealing the villainy and deviousness of individuals such as Lovelace in Richardson's *Clarissa*.[9] Modern stream-of-consciousness novels such as Faulkner's *As I Lay Dying* and Virginia Woolf's *Mrs. Dalloway* also delve into several minds in a single work and provide, through their very multiplicity of

[7] Booth, *Rhetoric*, p. 198, n. 25. See note 5 supra.

[8] Fielding's purpose in this novel is made even more explicit by his own remarks on the work, which are summarized as follows in *The Cambridge History of English Literature*: "The confusion of greatness with goodness is common. 'Bombastic greatness,' therefore, is to be exposed by dealing with its qualities as if, indeed, they were the qualities of goodness; and, since 'all these ingredients glossed over with wealth and a title have been treated with the highest respect and veneration' in 'the splendid palaces of the great,' while, in Newgate, 'one or two of them have been condemned to the gallows,' this kind of greatness shall be taken as it is seen in Newgate, glossed over with no wealth or title, and written as if it were the greatness of Alexander, Caesar or—as we of a later time might add—Napoleon" (vol. 10, p. 27).

[9] However, as has frequently been argued, the extent of our direct contact with Lovelace and the rich, complex psychological portrait of him rendered through his letters make him in our minds perhaps not quite the totally heartless villain Richardson presumably intended.

10

first-person voices, a comparative basis for discerning the varying degrees of perspicacity and reliability of these individuals. In
cases such as *The Sound and the Fury*, moreover, this kind of
novel occasionally even includes a section of straightforward
third-person narration which serves as a corrective to the subjective views rendered through the minds of characters such as the
three Compson brothers.

Nonepistolary prose may contrive such multiplicity of narration as well. In E. T. A. Hoffmann's *The Life and Opinions of
Kater Murr* a printer's error mixes Murr's autobiography with a
biography of the composer Johannes Kreisler. (Murr uses the
backs of the pages of Kreisler's biography to write his own work;
hence the understandable mix-up at the printer's.) The resulting
double narrative renders the preening, posturing, egotistical Murr
ridiculous in contrast to the sensitive, talented Kreisler and places
him squarely at the negative pole of Hoffmann's philistine / artist
dichotomy. In Lawrence Durrell's *Alexandria Quartet* the young
English teacher and aspiring novelist Darley narrates what is to
all appearances a reasonably reliable account of events and characters in Alexandria in the first volume of the tetralogy, *Justine*.
But the fabric of reliability begins to come unraveled in the second volume, *Balthazar*, wherein a large portion of space is given
over to a secondary narrator of sorts: the physician Balthazar,
whose written and oral critiques of the *Justine* manuscript point
out to Darley numerous factual and judgmental errors which he
has made. The third volume, *Mountolive*, goes even farther and
adopts a neutral, third-person omniscience which reveals a wealth
of information, heretofore totally unavailable to Darley, about
the clandestine political intrigues and amours of the various characters within the first two volumes' purview. The revelations also
undercut the authority and reliability of what modest sources and
talent Darley thought himself to possess; they expose the inau-
thenticity of Justine's diary, propound the worthlessness of her former husband's novel about her, and stack the neophyte writer up
against the more experienced and capable novelist Pursewarden.

In the fourth volume, *Clea*, Darley again narrates, but now with a wider temporal perspective and with the benefit of accumulated insights, particularly those gained through Balthazar's critiques and Pursewarden's diary (which comprises an entire chapter of this volume). That the events which he narrates here have now mostly surfaced and been concluded, aids him as well, as does his own growing maturity as an artist and an individual.

Thus, by means of a complex palimpsest (the word occurs frequently in the tetralogy itself) of documents, revelations, and narrators, Darley's unreliability as the narrator of *Justine* is exposed layer by layer and made apparent not only to the reader but to Darley as well. The result is to bring him—and the reader—ultimately to a point of some clarity about the nature of the events and characters comprising the *Quartet* and to a full realization of his previous failings as a perceiver and writer. This new Darley would presumably now no longer be such an unreliable chronicler of his experiences of these events and among these people in Alexandria; but the Darley of the first three volumes of the tetralogy is indeed most unreliable as a narrator until the force of all these revelations begins to take effect and he himself realizes the extent of his mistaken facts and judgments. As Bertil Romberg notes:

Through layer upon layer of printed, hand-written, orally narrated, recollected "truths" and descriptions, the narrator has thus at last worked his way up to a starting-point for a final view of the reality which it is his intention to depict. And when he has finished with these preliminaries, the suite of novels is also finished.[10]

Each of the novels mentioned thus far, then (Durrell himself, by the way, notes in a brief prefatory remark to *Clea* that the *Quartet* is "intended to be judged as a single work"),[11] offers distinct indications of the unreliability of the respective narrator or

---

[10] Bertil Romberg, *Studies in the Narrative Technique of the First-Person Novel*, trans. Michael Taylor and Harold H. Borland, p. 290.

[11] Lawrence Durrell, *Clea*, p. 7.

narrators. In a few works the key is provided internally and correctively, as in the case of Darley, who is subjected to the critiques by Balthazar and Pursewarden, and to a lesser extent in the case of Clegg, who finds and reads Miranda's diary but who does not visibly profit in any sense by this reading. In others it is given externally and in corroborative fashion for the reader, as in the cases of Kater Murr, who does not read Kreisler's biography, and of the Compsons, whose "narratives" are supplemented by the neutral, straightforward narrative of the fourth section, to which only the reader is privy. A secret communion of implied author and reader is thereby created behind the narrators' backs, so to speak.[12]

Most often, however, such direct support or correction is absent, thereby rendering the question of a particular narrator's reliability as a source of values and judgment and as the purveyor of a factual account more problematical, even when the narrative voice belongs to an unbalanced, scurrilous, or patently prevaricative individual. Critical discussion of narrators such as Humbert Humbert (Vladimir Nabokov's *Lolita*), Oskar Matzerath (Günter Grass's *The Tin Drum*), Holden Caulfield (J. D. Salinger's *The Catcher in the Rye*), Felix Krull, and Dostoevsky's Underground Man is frequently complicated precisely by the often ambiguous nature of these characters' reliability and by the intricate ironies at work between their own accounts and the attitudes espoused by the implied authors of these works. For both the critical and the casual reader, the literacy, cunning, and seductiveness of these narrators often pose considerable problems for comprehension and interpretation of the works in which they appear. How else to explain the freshman's sympathetic view of the Underground Man, the small-town school board's banning of *Lolita* from its English classes as the vile product of a perverted mentality? How else to comprehend the numerous exasperated cries from critics over Tristram Shandy's "inability" to tell his life story properly, when in fact—as Booth points out[13]—he tells precisely the com-

<hr/>

[12] Booth, *Rhetoric*, pp. 159–60.
[13] Ibid., p. 231.

ically chaotic and inconsequential cock-and-bull story which he set out to narrate in the first place? It is possible that many readers fall victim to a lack of experience or attention or sophistication in reading, resulting in a too-ready identification of narrator and author and a condemnation of, say, Nabokov for advocating the ravishing of nymphets. But a more likely explanation of these reactions is that the readers are taken in through a sort of benevolent gullibility in combination with the natural sympathy imparted by long acquaintance with an entertaining and at least superficially candid narrator.

For better or worse, those trends have seemingly given way to an overly ironic attitude on the part of critics and scholars and perhaps many general readers as well in the face of the twentieth century's "barrage of ironic works," yielding a situation wherein "many of us . . . can't accept a straight and simple statement when we read one."[14] Such a "pervasive irony hunt" also contains certain dangers for reasonable interpretation of modern literature; but at least it bears witness to the fact that scholars and readers are coming to terms with the modern novel on its own ground and are accepting the burden of confidence placed in their perceptiveness and superior judgment as readers by the "exit author" trend of writers who have followed in the path of Gustave Flaubert, Henry James, and James Joyce. Isolated articles dealing with unreliable narration in works such as James's *The Sacred Fount*[15] and as exposed, for example, in Durrell's *Mountolive*[16] are now appearing on occasion. Countless articles and books on writers such as Joyce, Samuel Beckett, Thomas Mann, André Gide, and Albert Camus deal with these authors' works in terms which fully accept the unreliability or fallibility of the characters who narrate the novels. And most importantly, Booth's *Rhetoric*

[14] Ibid., p. 367.

[15] Philip M. Weinstein, "The Protective and Exploitative Imagination: Unreliable Narration in *The Sacred Fount*," in *The Interpretation of Narrative: Theory and Practice*, ed. Morton W. Bloomfield, pp. 189–210.

[16] Alan Warren Friedman, "*Mountolive* and the Unreliable Narration of Facts," in his *Lawrence Durrell and the Alexandria Quartet: Art for Love's Sake*, pp. 111–35.

of Fiction has placed the concepts of "implied author" and "unreliable narrator" fully into the canon of critical thought.[17]

Following these trends, the present study intends to make a systematic investigation into the operation of unreliable narration in several works by many of the above-named authors and others and to analyze in some detail one specific genus of the unreliable narrator: namely, the fictional autobiographer who recounts his own life, or a portion thereof, in his own voice and in a conscious act of writing. The abundance of novels and novellas within this one sphere alone makes the task rather formidable purely in terms of quantity and variety of material to be covered. Necessarily excluded are other kinds of narration such as the report of the dramatized biographer-chronicler (Serenius Zeitblom in Thomas Mann's *Doctor Faustus*), the secondary-participant narrator (Nick Carraway in Scott Fitzgerald's *The Great Gatsby*), or the disembodied and anonymous speaker (the satirical voice in Mikhail Bulgakov's *Heart of a Dog*), the "spoken" account (Clamence in Albert Camus's *The Fall*), the interior monologue (Hans Schnier in Heinrich Böll's *The Clown*), and also third-person narration closely linked in scope and point of view to one central consciousness or "reflector" (James's "The Liar"). Each of these types may also evidence considerable narrative unreliability, and initiatives have been taken in the study of each by critics such as Margrit Henning and others.[18]

For the present investigation, however, the focus will be solely

---

[17] Mention should also be made of Ivo Vidan's *Nepouzdani pripovjedač: Postupak i vizija u djelima triju modernik generacija* [The Unreliable Narrator: Procedure and Vision in Works by Three Modern Generations] (Zagreb: Matica Hrvatska, 1970), although the collection includes a number of essays not directly related to the topic of unreliability. To date, the work is available only in Croatian, but a review in English is provided by S. Bašić in *Studia Romanica et Anglica Zagrebientia*, 33–34 (1972–73), pp. 876–80.

[18] Margrit Henning, *Die Ich-Form und ihre Funktion in Thomas Manns "Doktor Faustus" und in der deutschen Literatur der Gegenwart*. On secondary-participant narrators, for example, see E. Duncan Aswell, "Reflections of a Governess: Image and Distortion in *The Turn of the Screw*," *Nineteenth Century Fiction*, 23 (1968–69), pp. 49–63; Gideon Shunami, "The Unreliable Narrator in *Wuthering Heights*," *Nineteenth Century Fiction*, 27 (1972–73), pp. 449–68; James C. Bruce, "The Equivocating Narrator in

on the unreliable fictional autobiographer and the nature of his narrative. Attention will first be directed to the nature of first-person narration and the phenomenon of unreliability as it is bound up with this narrative form. Chapters 3–6 will examine four distinct types of unreliable first-person protagonist-narrators—the *pícaro*, the clown, the madman, and the naïf—with discussion of individual works centering in each case on the techniques by which the unreliability of the particular narrator is established in each work and on the effects of this unreliability on the work as a whole. The final section will then summarize the results of the foregoing investigations and offer some general conclusions and observations on the nature of unreliable first-person narration.

Günter Grass's *Katz und Maus*," *Monatshefte*, 58 (1966), pp. 139–49. On Bulgakov's short novel, see Ellendea Proffer's dissertation, "Mikhail Bulgakov: His Life and Work," and her recent book, *Mikhail Bulgakov* (Ann Arbor, Mich.: Ardis, 1979). On "The Liar," see Booth, *Rhetoric*, pp. 347–54.

CHAPTER 2

First-Person Narration and Unreliability

THE TERM "first-person narration" can of course cover an immense range of prose works (poetry, too, as in the mariner's tale within the frame of "The Rime of the Ancient Mariner"). It can stretch from the archetypal autobiographical situation—whether real or fictional—of the subject's sitting at his desk composing his memoirs (*David Copperfield*) or recounting a portion of his life (*One Day in the Life of Ivan Denisovich*), through an array of witnesses, chroniclers, and secondary characters as narrators (Ishmael in *Moby Dick*, the nameless provincial chronicler in Dostoevsky's *The Brothers Karamazov*, Nick Carraway in *The Great Gatsby*), to the anonymous but largely omniscient and ever-present controlling "I" of novels such as *Tom Jones* and *Vanity Fair*. It can extend to those largely effaced narrative voices who directly intrude into their novels and stories only rarely with fleeting references to "our hero" or with remarks like "as we shall see" (*Berlin Alexanderplatz*); and it may even include diarists (Roquentin in *Nausea*), letter-writers (Werther), and the various secondary and tertiary voices of fictional editors, researchers, publishers, auditors, estate executors, and trusted friends who publish and comment upon some work which has purportedly come into their hands (*Moll Flanders*, the frame narrators of many German *Novellen* such as Theodor Storm's *The Rider on the White Horse*). Moreover, the form is as extensive in chronological terms as it is in breadth, spanning from the most ancient extant works of civilization (the narrative "I" singing the praises of Gilgamesh ca. 2500 B.C.) through the present day (William Styron's *Sophie's Choice* and André Brink's *A Dry White Season*, to name but two first-person novels published in 1979). Countless fairy tales, adventure stories, fables, anecdotes, exemplary stories, novels, diaries, epistolary works, and "most unforgettable experiences" have been couched in the "I"-form or a weakly derivative "we"-form for centuries and continue so with every month's new publications of books and journals. In short, the first-person form of narration is one of the most natural and pervasive modes in which to cast a story of any sort. Robert Scholes and Robert Kellogg, in *The Nature of Narrative*, remark that

> One of the most striking aspects of the new narrative forms which emerged in vernacular literature with the Renaissance is the appearance of the eye-witness narrator in contexts as different as Dante's *Commedia*, Cellini's *Autobiography*, and the picaresque tale of *Lazarillo de Tormes*. New stories, personal stories, stories with unusual pretensions to actuality tend, in both the ancient and modern world, to take the form of eye-witness narrative. We can almost go so far as to say that the natural form of mimetic narrative is eye-witness and first-person. Circumstantiality, verisimilitude, and many more of the qualities which we recognize as identifying characteristics of realism in narrative are all natural functions of the eye-witness point of view.[1]

First-person narration thus carries with it an inherent quality of realism and conviction based on a claim to firsthand experience or to a source of such firsthand experience and knowledge (folk myths, the traditional epics of the Greek poets, Cervantes's Cid Hamete Bengali, and so forth). The very fact that we have before us, either literally or figuratively, an identifiable narrator telling us the story directly, possibly even metaphorically grabbing us on the arm, gesturing to us, or addressing us individually or collectively from time to time, imparts a tangible reality to the narrative situation and a substantial veracity to the account we

[1] Robert Scholes and Robert Kellogg, *The Nature of Narrative*, p. 250.

are reading or "hearing." When the account is rendered in good style, with flair and interest and with at least a modicum of realistic description or explanatory detail, that veracity is enhanced all the more. And unless obvious errors of fact, outlandishly absurd occurrences, or physical impossibilities enter unexplained into the narrative, our natural tendency is to grant our speaker the full credibility possible within the limitations of human memory and capability. The greater the personalization of this "I" who is regaling us and the more intimate our contact with him on such an armchair-to-sofa level, the greater is this tendency to grant him such credibility in human terms. The less the personalization and the more anonymous and disembodied our host becomes, the weaker grows such human contact; such a narrator must then draw his authority solely from the sheer range and depth of his knowledge about the events he narrates, a phenomenon approaching the limited or full omniscience of, say, the Tolstoyan voice in *War and Peace*.

Leaving aside these anonymous and depersonalized presences who occasionally speak in the grammatical first person and also the personable but larger-than-life "Fieldings" and turning instead to the personalized or dramatized narrators, a second axiomatic principle must also be introduced concerning first-person narratives: precisely because of these narrators' simulated humanness and because of the realism inherent in the situation of a character's speaking to us directly, the natural limitations of human knowledge and judgment and memory come into play—a phenomenon which Henry James terms the *inconscience* of a narrator or reflector. Thereby any possibility of absolute reliability with regard to all facts and facets of the events and characters within such a narrative is canceled.

First-person narration is, then, always at least potentially unreliable, in that the narrator, with these human limitations of per-

---

[2] It is for reasons of this natural credibility of first-person narration and for its pronounced illusion of reality that Hildegard Zeller, in *Die Ich-Erzählung im englischen Roman*, p. 8, terms the technique well-suited for tales of the marvelous, for adventure tales, or for *Lügenromane*, literally "lie-novels."

ception and memory and assessment, may easily have missed, forgotten, or miscontrued certain incidents, words, or motives. Furthermore, precisely because the narrator sits before us as a human being—albeit a fictionalized one—we naturally react to him in varying degrees in human terms and not just as a disembodied voice providing us with information.[3] Much of what he tells us also gives us an idea of what he himself is like and has "a certain characterizing significance over and above its data value, by virtue of the fact that he is telling it to us."[4] His narrative cannot be accepted purely in absolute terms of true or false, probable or improbable, reliable or unreliable, convincing or unconvincing. Emotional ties also enter into such assessments and reactions on our part as auditors and readers of his account:

No narrator or central intelligence or observer is *simply* convincing: he is convincingly decent or mean, brilliant or stupid, informed, ignorant or muddled. Since there are few such qualities that even the most tolerant of us can observe in full neutrality, we usually find our emotional and intellectual reactions to him as a character affecting our reactions to the events he relates.[5]

The archetypal first-person narrative situation thus involves two sets of subjective and therefore humanly fallible elements: the narrator's memory, selective processes, and attitudes in the

---

[3] It is for this reason that Käte Hamburger, in *The Logic of Literature*, trans. Marilynn J. Rose, p. 313, places first-person narration outside the bounds of *das Fiktive* or "fiction" and instead into the category of *das Fingierte*, "the simulated" or "the feigned": "The concept of the feigned, which is also essential in defining the role poem, designates that place in the system of literature where the first-person narrative is to be found. . . . The concept of the feigned designates something pretended, imitated, something inauthentic and non-genuine, whereas that of fiction designates the mode of being of that which is not real: of illusion, semblance, dream, play." And it is also for this reason that David Goldknopf, in "The Confessional Increment: A New Look at the I-Narrator," pp. 13–21, speaks of first-person narration as "rupturing the mimetic membrane" from within by taking cognizance of the reader in the real world and therefore "drastically reorganizing the normal psychological topology."

[4] Goldknopf, "Confessional Increment," p. 20.

[5] Wayne C. Booth, *The Rhetoric of Fiction*, p. 273.

telling of his story; and the auditor's assimilation, comprehension, and retention of what he hears, in conjunction with his own human reactions to the storyteller as an individual. The situation is consequently a natural spawning ground for unreliability engendered through inherent fallibility on both sides of the narrative act and through the discrepancies in understanding and perception which can so easily arise when two subjects interact in such fashion:

> By definition narrative art requires a story and a story-teller. In the relationship between the teller and the tale, and that other relationship between the teller and the audience, lies the essence of narrative art. The narrative situation is thus ineluctably ironical. The quality of irony is built into the narrative form as it is into no other form of literature. . . . Irony is always the result of a disparity of understanding. In any situation in which one person knows or perceives more—or less—than another, irony must be either actually or potentially present.[6]

This ironic gap was of course easily bridged by the largely omniscient "Fielding" type of narrator, in his close association with the actual or implied author of many a work. It is still often bridged, moreover, by personalized narrators who propound norms already shared by a majority of their audience or whose sincerity, soundness of judgment, and power of persuasion can move us to accept their norms in their respective works. Still, the very fact that an individualized, dramatized narrator distinct from the author or implied author of a particular work stands before us and narrates in his own voice and in a fictionalized facsimile of a real-life narrative situation always carries with it the very real possibility of irony and divergence of understanding and hence the possibility of unreliable narration in a fuller sense than mere inconscience: being a distinct individual, the narrator may well represent values not in accord with those of the implied author, and his values may not be shared or understood or accepted by the individual reader. As Scholes and Kellogg note:

[6] Scholes and Kellogg, *Nature*, p. 240.

21

In any example of narrative art there are, broadly speaking, three points of view—those of the characters, the narrator, and the audience. As narrative becomes more sophisticated, a fourth point of view is added by the development of a clear distinction between the narrator and author. Narrative irony is a function of disparity among these three or four viewpoints. And narrative artists have always been ready to employ this disparity to make effects of various kinds.[7]

In the case of the dramatized chronicler who does not recount his own life but rather the life of a friend or the activities of a group of acquaintances, both of these factors—the narrator's human fallibility in terms of memory and interpretation, and the subjective disparity between the narrator and the effaced implied author—are very much at work. Such a narrator can only report to the best of his ability and recollection the overt words and actions in his protagonist's life and draw from these his inferences and interpretations concerning the inner nature of that protagonist. He is incapable of penetrating directly into the psyche of the protagonist or of any other character within the chronicle. He may draw upon a number of aids in gaining access to that psyche—to the extent that these aids are available to him—by incorporating diaries, letters, testaments, and the like from the hand of the protagonist, and these will in most cases strengthen his attempts at revealing the whole figure about whom he writes. Yet even the presence of such aids cannot guarantee more than a limited amount of reliability in the narrator's assessment of his subject. His judgment is still humanly fallible, his intellect may well not be up to the task of treating a particularly unusual or complex character, and his own psychic makeup may well contain certain preconceptions and prejudices—both in general and concerning his protagonist in particular—which inform his portrayal of the protagonist and thereby lead either to distorted or even outright false interpretations of that subject. One need only look at Serenius Zeitblom's lengthy chronicle of the life and work of his composer friend Adrian Leverkühn in Thomas Mann's

[7] Ibid.

22

Doctor Faustus, with its rather pedestrian and limited under-standing of the central figure's monumental, demonic stature, or at the disillusioned Nick Carraway's moody and sobered account of Jay Gatsby to see these factors in operation. An even more graphic illustration is Julio Cortázar's long story "The Pursuer," wherein the music critic Bruno chronicles the last weeks in the life of the jazz saxophonist Johnny Carter but makes him by and large into a vehicle for his own ideas on music, art, and the psy-chology of the artist so as to further his own career. As Johnny remarks at one point concerning Bruno's forthcoming biography of him: "It's very good, your book. . . . But in reality, it's like in a mirror. . . . There're things missing, Bruno. You're much better informed than I am, but it seems like something's missing. . . . What you forgot to put in is me."[8] Such accounts of course gain important dimensions through the subjective coloration of a dis-illusioned Nick Carraway, the limited sensibility of a Zeitblom, or the intellectual preconceptions of a Bruno, but they do so at the sacrifice of totally reliable narration and of a clear statement of the values and opinions held by the implied author.

In the case of the fictional protagonist-narrator—the subject of the four following chapters of this study—the problem of access into the mind of the protagonist is not present, whether the nar-rator tells his story entirely in retrospect or in the more immedi-ate form of a diary or letters or notes. Here narrator and subject are identical, and the narrator can of course report on his own thoughts, attitudes, and motivations as they occur or can recall them to the best of his ability. With such a narrator it is the sec-ond factor—the subjectivity of his narrative and therefore its po-tential discrepancy from the norms and attitudes of the implied author—which is of prime importance. The protagonist-narrator or fictional autobiographer is, to be sure, subject by nature to human limitations in recalling events and words and in delving into other characters' minds. Still, his narrative is mainly con-cerned with himself and his own inner and outer life and with his

<hr>

[8] Julio Cortázar, "The Pursuer," in his *Blow-Up and Other Stories,* trans. Paul Black-burn, pp. 207, 212.

own evaluations of that life. That life he will naturally know very intimately, and the chief interest in his account for us will therefore be the roles played by his subjective selection of data from that life and by his subjective conclusions based on these data. Because the narrator stands before us as a dramatized individual distinct from the implied author whose attitudes are those of the novel as a whole, he is potentially unreliable in both phases of this subjective process. The problem for the reader is how to recognize where and when and in what way such a narrator's account is unreliable, especially in the complete absence of counterweights to the protagonist's narrative such as that provided by, for example, Miranda's diary (*The Collector*), Balthazar's critique of Darley (*The Alexandria Quartet*), or the authorial epigraph and concluding remark to *Notes from Underground*. What is of main interest, after all, in autobiography—whether genuine or fictional—is the composite portrait of the subject, that is, the man as he now exists before us in the present and how he developed into this man: "Autobiography is . . . an interplay, a collusion, between past and present; its significance is indeed more the revelation of the present situation than the recovering of the past."[9] Hence virtually everything which the narrator relates has value not only as information about his past but also as a characterization of the present individual. The information itself may tell us a good deal about the man's development, but the very selection of this information and any evaluation or commentary passed on it by the narrator also provide definite insights into his present nature. The telling as well as the tale reveals to us the character of our narrator.

A second basic feature of autobiographical narration is the inherent narrative distance between the narrator as narrator and the narrator as protagonist. In the standard epic situation[10] of autobiographical narrative the older man tells us of the experiences

---

[9] Roy Pascal, *Design and Truth in Autobiography*, p. 11.

[10] "Epic situation" is Bertil Romberg's term for describing the actual circumstances under which a narrator writes or tells his story. See *Studies in the Narrative Technique of the First-Person Novel*, trans. Michael Taylor and Harold H. Borland.

of his earlier days, covering either his entire life or a portion thereof. The narrative distance is thus most commonly a chronological one ranging from several days to several decades. Also common are distances in maturity, intellect, and weltanschauung attained by the narrator either over the course of the years or as a result of one or more particularly dramatic experiences. And even in the cases of those individuals who seem at forty years of age or more to have no significantly greater maturity than they did at ten, the very fact that they are telling their stories in retrospect with full awareness of the outcomes and consequences of all they recount distances them from the earlier selves whose stories they narrate.[11] In brief, even though the autobiographer tells the story of his own life, his narrative situation is one which very nearly approaches that of the subject-object distinction in narratives told by one individual about another.

Thus even with the advantage of firsthand access to his own former thoughts and attitudes through memory, the protagonist-narrator is susceptible to most of the pitfalls and limitations common to the witness, the chronicler, or the secondary character as narrator. In speaking of confessional autobiographical narratives such as Rousseau's *Confessions*, Scholes and Kellogg note:

> In the confession, the subject and the narrator are literally the same person. One of the many lessons that Rousseau taught subsequent novelists was that even with the literal identity of subject and narrator, the mere span of time separating the two provides sufficient distance to allow for all the potentially ironical divergence in point of view between character and narrator that a novelist could require. Time became a significant dimension in the conception of character.[12]

Add to this fact the natural tendency of the individual to give himself the benefit of any doubt in cases of questionable deeds or

---

[11] Compare Scholes and Kellogg, *Nature*, p. 256: "To the extent that the narrating character is differentiated from the author one ironic gap opens up, and to the extent that the narrating character is differentiated from himself as participant in events another ironic gap appears."

[12] Ibid., p. 257.

decisions, to overlook or play down incidents which reveal some painful negative quality about himself, and to seek at least some self-justification for his life, and autobiographical narrative too becomes a likely spawning ground for narrative unreliability. These are tendencies which only the most candid and conscientious fictional autobiographers—a David Copperfield, perhaps—can begin to overcome.

The likelihood of some degree of unreliability in genuine autobiography and in thinly disguised fictional autobiography based on the actual author's life, then, is quite strong. In the case of the fictional autobiographer totally distinct from the author or implied author, that likelihood is stronger still, simply by virtue of the fact that the gap now opened up between implied author and narrator allows for a much broader type of unreliability than mere human fallibility, self-interest, or inconscience. Here the author's purpose in writing in the person of another individual is usually to satirize or expose this individual (or the type he represents, as in Swift's "Modest Proposal"), to provide a vehicle for social satire or commentary (for example, the alien's report on thinly disguised strange worlds as in *Gulliver's Travels*), to convey a novel and unique view of familiar historical occurrences or contemporary reality (as in Grass's *The Tin Drum*), or simply to explore and work with some particular type of mind, be it that of a genius, a rogue, a pervert, a fool, or some individualized variant of these or other possibilities:

By turning the direction of the narrative inward the author almost inevitably presents a central character who is an example of something. By turning the direction of the narrative outward the author almost invariably exposes weakness in society. First-person narrative is thus a ready vehicle for ideas.[13]

Moreover, no matter which of these purposes may be evident or implicit in a given work, the fictional autobiography, with its intrinsic cleft between implied author and narrator, again carries

[13] Ibid., p. 76.

26

with it by its very nature the strong likelihood of unreliable narration in the fullest sense—that is, not only in terms of human fallibility, self-interest, and inconscience, but also in the possible divergence between those norms propounded by the narrator and those held by the implied author.

Fictional first-person narration is a relatively modern phenomenon, dating back to the Spanish picaresque tales of the sixteenth and seventeenth centuries. Until that time—with only two or three possible exceptions in the Egyptian *Story of Sinue* (ca. 2000 B.C.),[14] Petronius's *Satyricon* (ca. A.D. 50), and Boccaccio's *Fiammetta* (ca. 1345)—autobiographical narrative was used primarily for the recounting of travels and adventures, for allegory, or for providing a frame for tale-telling, and the narrator was closely and often even expressly identified with the author. Lucius Apuleius leads us through his "metamorphoses" in *The Golden Ass* in his own person (albeit transformed into an ass for the better part of the work); Augustine writes of his own life at great length in his *Confessions*; the figure of Dante himself travels through the Inferno and Purgatory to Paradise in his *Divine Comedy*; and Chaucer appears as a traveler among the group of pilgrims in the *Canterbury Tales*. The nearest thing to fictional autobiography before the sixteenth century—aside from the three notable exceptions mentioned above—is found in the many tales of fantastic travels and adventures where the first-person voice is used solely to provide a formal framework of credibility with little or no real characterization of the narrator. It is not until such Spanish *pícaros* as Lazarillo de Tormes, Quevedo's Pablos (*The Scavenger*), and Mateo Alemán's Guzmán de Alfarache emerge in the sixteenth and early seventeenth centuries to tell their own stories that the fictional first-person form begins to be used with any frequency and literary skill in fully and distinctly characterizing the individual performing the narrative function. The picaresque tale even then germinated relatively slowly and flowered only sporadically by modern standards. But it did so effectively

---

[14] Whether this work is fictional or genuine autobiography is still a matter of speculation, as Romberg notes on p. 311 of *Narrative Technique*.

nonetheless in works such as Nashe's *The Unfortunate Traveller* (1594), Kirkman's *The English Rogue* (1665–71), and Grimmelshausen's *Simplicius Simplicissimus* (1668), until its full bloom in the early eighteenth century in the hands of Lesage (*Gil Blas*, 1715–35), Defoe (*Moll Flanders*, 1722), and Smollett (*Roderick Random*, 1748).

The eighteenth century also introduced a significant variant of the fictional autobiography in Sterne's complex and comically chaotic *Tristram Shandy*, as well as groundbreaking works in other first-person forms such as the epistolary novel (Richardson, Rousseau's *Julie*, Goethe's *Werther*) and the confession (Rousseau). Romanticism introduced the fictional first-person narrative of the sensitive and/or troubled soul, often with an infusion of the Rousseauian confessional element (Tieck's *Peter Lebrecht*, Constant's *Adolphe*, Chateaubriand's *René*, Lermontov's *A Hero of Our Time*), and the ironic or expressly comic figure's account (Hoffmann's *Kater Murr*, Chamisso's *Peter Schlemihl*, Eichendorff's *Memoirs of a Good-for-Nothing*). Realism added little to the genre except for works such as Dostoevsky's viciously satirical *Notes from Underground* and Twain's gently comic *Huckleberry Finn*; instead its preferred forms of first-person narration were the only partly fictionalized autobiography (*David Copperfield*, Tolstoy's *Childhood, Boyhood, Youth*, Keller's *Green Henry*) and the witness or secondary character's chronicle (*Moby Dick*, Dostoevsky's *The Possessed* and *The Brothers Karamazov*, Butler's *The Way of All Flesh*, Grillparzer's *The Poor Fiddler*).[15]

The late nineteenth and twentieth centuries, however, along with their radical experiments in third-person narration (Flaubert, James, Kafka, Joyce), not only initiated and cultivated such first-person techniques as stream of consciousness and extended interior monologue but also introduced or reintroduced an almost limitless range of highly individualized narrators, many of them a far cry from the reasoned and comfortably respectable voices in earlier autobiographies. Older types such as the con-

[15] See ibid., pp. 311–19, for an outline of the history of first-person narration in general.

fidence man (Felix Krull), the madman (Sadegh Hedayat's *The Blind Owl*, José Donoso's *The Obscene Bird of Night*), the traveler (Conrad's Marlow), and the secondary character as narrator (Zeitblom, Nick Carraway) reappear enriched and enhanced by stylistic experimentation; and the technological advances and concomitant disruption of many traditional bases of value and belief and social order bring in their wake a host of alienated (Roquentin, Meursault), demonic (Clamence), traumatized (Dowling in Ford Madox Ford's *The Good Soldier*), unscrupulous (Jason Compson), and brooding (Joseph in Saul Bellow's *Dangling Man*) narrators often possessed of considerable intellect and occasionally reminiscent of some of those loners, tortured souls, and ironic types of the romantic era. In only slightly oversimplified terms, then, social and technological progress's gradual depersonalization of modern life has occasioned an intensified focus on the individual in literature in an apparent effort to counter or humanize or merely come to grips with the modern world; and stylistic and formal developments in literature and an increased awareness of psychoanalytical terminology and methods have enabled the modern writer to couch these efforts in a far more complex fashion than was previously the case.

For the modern reader, the product of these two trends is an often confusing, challenging, ambiguous, and sometimes even disturbing array of self-portraits painted by what must frequently seem to be totally aberrant or absurd types with whom no more than a few isolated readers can comfortably or fully identify. Only rarely in serious literature does a reasonably normal, earnest soul like Dr. Rieux in Camus's *The Plague* tell us somehing of his life or experiences, and even he harbors considerable doubts about his subjective status as narrator and about his understanding and evaluation of his shattering ordeal. These doubts make him cast his narrative in as neutral and objective a fashion as possible in the hope of giving the most faithful and least distorted or refracted rendition of what he has lived through during the plague in Oran—he does not reveal his identity as narrator until the conclusion, speaking of himself in the third person before that point.

29

Most narrators in modern fiction are themselves at a loss to explain or clarify or come to terms with their particular experiences or situations or states of mind. And since the author or implied author is often nowhere visibly present to offer solid value bases or explicit solutions, the reader himself is forced to share the narrator's quandary or find his own path out of the narrator's dilemma, depending upon the narrator's degree of reliability in conveying the implied author's view of the world comprising the particular work in question.

The implied author may, of course, on occasion be in general sympathy with the plight of his narrator in such works, as is seemingly the case in Sartre's *Nausea* and Camus's *The Stranger;* but the very fact that the narrator himself is such a confused, alienated, and troubled individual inevitably compels the reader to question the reliability of this narrator's account at every point and in every respect:

The reliable narrator of an older work like *Great Expectations* could provide a secure haven for the erring Pip, but there is no secure haven for Paul Morel or Stephen Daedalus. In this respect as in so many others, modern fiction has tried to move closer to life itself than was ever attempted by earlier fiction. Leave the reader to choose for himself, force him to face each decision as the hero faces it, and he will feel much more deeply the value of the truth when it is attained, or its loss if the hero fails.[16]

Moreover, the confused narrator or reflector in modern fiction is not alone in his unreliability, for even the reasonably well-adjusted and controlled narrators portrayed writing the very works in which they narrate are revealed either directly or indirectly as fallible and unreliable in their accounts:

There have been, it is true, many self-conscious narrators in modern fiction, but they have almost all been dramatized as unreliable characters quite distinct from their authors. The narrators of Mann's *Doktor*

---

[16] Booth, *Rhetoric*, p. 293.

Faustus and *The Holy Sinners,* of Gide's *Les faux-monnayeurs,* and of Huxley's *Point Counter Point* all engage in strongly implied praise for the works *they* are writing: but despite their pretensions, they are writing works rather strikingly different from the actual novels of Mann, Gide, and Huxley.[17]

In sum, the twentieth century has largely adopted unreliable first-person narration—and unreliable narration in general—as its own special child. In what has so often been termed an ever more confusing and complex modern world, traditional concepts of reality have been rejected or are seen as no longer applicable:

We have already seen something of the fun Sterne could produce by confusing the reader about the kind of book he was writing. Many modern works use the same kind of confusing, unreliable narration in a deliberate polemic against conventional notions of reality and in favor of the superior reality given by the world of the book.[18]

In addition, the producing of an illusion of such traditional reality has been largely abandoned in favor of a focus on the struggle of the individual to perceive some sort of reality or to comprehend the modern world:

Modern narrative prose has to a great extent departed from the issue of authority and no longer shows such an ardent solicitude to verify its facts for the sake of the illusion of reality; but it has deepened and brought into sharper focus the study of the mind or minds which form the centre in the story.[19]

Also, explicit generalization of such individual perceptions of reality is eschewed:

Reliable narration is often not allowed in modern works, almost never does one character know enough about the meaning of the whole to go

[17] Ibid., p. 205, n. 28.
[18] Ibid., p. 288.
[19] Romberg, *Narrative Technique,* p. 100.

31

beyond his personal problems to any general view. . . . The task of generalization may be left entirely to the reader. . . . No narrator's voice extends the significance of *The Sun Also Rises*—except, of course, to provide the generalizing title and epigraphs.[20]

Any attempt to present an individualized narrator with some claim to authoritative truth concerning his life and the world in which he lives is immediately held up to serious question:

The narrator does not need to be dramatized for the modern audience so much as he needs to be relativized. A narrator who is not in some way suspect, who is not in some way subject to ironic scrutiny is what the modern temper finds least bearable. . . . By giving himself a fictional shape [the author] has entered the ironic gap, which now lies not between author or narrator and characters but between limited understanding which is real, and an ideal of absolute truth which is itself suspect. This irony cuts in two directions simultaneously. The reader who tries to reduce a story like *The Good Soldier* to a single absolute meaning becomes himself a victim of one blade of this irony. His only other choice is to accept a limited resolution of the work's meaning, holding part of this meaning in his mind as an unresolvable ambiguity—which is to enter the ironic gap, shake hands with Dowell and say, "I don't know either."[21]

The authoritative presence of the implied author is most often no longer available to provide a convenient guide to the novel's attitudes and judgments:

The reader of Wayne Booth's *The Rhetoric of Fiction* . . . will see how the traditional ironic narrator, a Fielding or an Austen, has evolved, by way of the Flaubertian or Jamesian impersonal ironic narrator, into the narrator who has entirely abandoned any obligation to guide the judgment of his reader, and by so doing has become the modern counterpart of the old Greek "eiron."[22]

[20] Booth, *Rhetoric*, p. 198.
[21] Scholes and Kellogg, *Nature*, pp. 276–77.
[22] D. C. Muecke, *Irony*, p. 15.

The consequence of this development is the placing of a tremendous responsibility on the reader's abilities of perception and evaluation:

The unreliable or semi-reliable narrator in fiction is quite uncharacteristic of primitive or ancient narrative. The author of an *apologia* is expected to be presenting himself in the best possible light, and thus is to be taken *cum grano salis*, but the idea of creating an unreliable fictional eye-witness is the sophisticated product of an empirical and ironical age. Unreliability itself requires a fairly thoroughgoing conception of reliability before it can be recognized and exploited in fiction. Its frequent use in modern fiction is also an aspect of the modern author's desire to make the reader participate in the act of creation. The Renaissance allegorist expected his readers to participate strenuously in his work, bringing all their learning and intellect to bear on his polysemous narrative. Similarly, the modern novelist often expects just such intense participation, but being empirically rather than metaphysically oriented he makes the great question that of what really happened inside and outside the characters he has presented; whereas the allegorists made the question of what these characters and events signified the primary question for their audience.[23]

The reader's task in taking up this burden is twofold. First, he must come to terms with the nature of the narrative voice confronting him:

Though it is most evident when a narrator tells the story of his own adventures, we react to all narrators as persons. We find their accounts credible or incredible, their opinions wise or foolish, their judgments just or unjust. The gradations and axes of approval or condemnation are almost as rich as those presented by life itself, but we can distinguish two radically different types of reaction, depending on whether a narrator is reliable or unreliable. At one extreme we find narrators whose every judgment is suspect (the barber in "Haircut"; Jason in *The Sound and the Fury*). At the other are narrators scarcely distinguishable from the omniscient author (Conrad's Marlow). In between lies a confused

[23] Scholes and Kellogg, *Nature*, pp. 264–65.

variety of more-or-less reliable narrators, many of them puzzling mixtures of sound and unsound. Though we cannot draw a sharp line between the two types with any great confidence, the distinction is not arbitrary: it is forced upon us by our recognition that we have, in fact, two different kinds of experience, depending on which kind of narrator is in charge.[24]

And second, if that narrator proves partly or wholly unreliable, the reader must discover or discern "which values are in abeyance and which are genuinely, though in modern works often surreptitiously, at work"[25] in order to gain full enjoyment and comprehension of the work. Except in the most obvious cases of scurrility (Jason Compson), madness (Clegg), inconscience (Darley), or ridiculousness (Kater Murr), these tasks are rendered difficult by the very sympathy naturally arising through sustained intimate contact with the individual addressing us and through the credibility one is naturally inclined to grant any speaker.[26] This sustained intimacy with the narrator is particularly seductive and perilous for the reader, as Booth takes pains to point out more than once:

Objective narration, particularly when conducted through a highly unreliable narrator, offers special temptations to the reader to go astray. Even when it presents characters whose conduct the author deeply deplores, it presents them through the seductive medium of their own self-defending rhetoric. It is consequently not surprising that reactions to such works have been marked with confusion and false accusations.[27]

Failures of understanding, communication, et cetera, in many novels come from the reader's inability to dissociate himself from a vicious center of consciousness presented to him with all of the seductive self-justification of skillful rhetoric.[28]

[24] Booth, *Rhetoric*, pp. 273–74.
[25] Ibid., p. 144.
[26] Compare ibid., p. 352: "To read [James's 'The Liar'] properly we must combat our natural tendency to agree with the reflector. He wins our confidence simply by being the reflector, because in life the only mind we know as we know Lyons's is our own. Yet it is this very appeal which makes him dangerous; his touch will be fatal to certain effects."
[27] Ibid., pp. 388–89.
[28] Ibid., p. 390.

Complicating the problem further is the fact that with some narrators this sympathetic effect may well be the primary intent of the implied author in an effort to make the reader share the plight or confusion of a narrator with whom this implied author is in general agreement—narrators such as Marlow, Meursault, Roquentin, and Marcher in James's "The Beast in the Jungle." In this kind of narration "even though the narrator may, like Miranda [in Katherine Anne Porter's *Pale Horse, Pale Rider*], have serious faults, we are scarcely aware of them" simply because of the implied author's silent concurrence with his narrator's plight.[29] Such narrators are therefore not unreliable in the full sense of the term, owing to this sympathetic link with the implied author.

With most modern fictional autobiographers, however, this link between narrator and implied author is not present. Rather, the link intended is one between implied author and reader:

A second kind of effect requires a secret communion of the author and reader behind the narrator's back. . . . Though the narrator may have some redeeming qualities of mind or heart, we travel with the silent author, observing as from a rear seat the humorous or disgraceful or ridiculous or vicious driving behavior of the narrator seated in front. The author may wink and nudge, but he may not speak. The reader may sympathize or deplore, but he never accepts the narrator as a reliable guide.[30]

This link may be either an intellectual one or a moral one or a combination of the two. When the link is intellectual, the narrator most often trips himself up by simple inconsistencies of fact, by inconsistencies between facts and conclusions, or by obviously or surreptitiously revealing a low level of intelligence; also, indirect information within his own narrative or direct information parallel to that narrative may expose to the reader facets of the narrator which the latter himself either ignores or fails to realize.

[29] Ibid., p. 300.
[30] Ibid.

35

On the moral plane the narrator's unreliability is most often revealed by a facetiousness of tone, by a gaping discrepancy between his conduct and the moral views he propounds,[31] by an insufficiency or a fallaciousness of foundation for his moral philosophy, or simply by the unacceptability of that philosophy in terms of normal moral standards or of basic common sense and human decency: "Though the narrator may frequently trip himself up, the reader will know that he has done so only if his own sense of what is sane and sound is better—that is, more nearly like the departed author's—than is the narrator's."[32]

The result of both types of discrepancy is the creation of a community of implied author and reader, making the narrator the butt of obvious satire or of a complex and sustained irony[33]—assuming of course that the reader perceives these discrepancies and the satiric or ironic nature of the narrative. When this perception does take place, the resulting collaboration is a highly rewarding and enjoyable activity for the reader and certainly one of the most exciting aspects of modern fiction:

On this moral level we discover a kind of collaboration which can be one of the most rewarding of all reading experiences. To collaborate with the author by providing the source of an allusion or by deciphering a pun is one thing. But to collaborate with him by providing mature moral judgment is a far more exhilarating sport.[34]

The dangers of excessive ambiguity on the implied author's part, of overinterpretation on the reader's part, and of an overly snobbish pleasure in collusion on the part of both are certainly ever-present and are considerable in such fiction.[35] If, however,

---

[31] On this point compare Romberg, *Narrative Technique*, p. 92, where he mentions the tension created by certain narrators between their roles of raconteur and moral teacher (Moll, Apuleius, Simplicissimus, and others).

[32] Booth, *Rhetoric*, p. 240.

[33] Compare ibid., p. 304; Romberg, *Narrative Technique*, p. 126; Scholes and Kellogg, *Nature*, p. 263.

[34] Booth, *Rhetoric*, p. 307.

[35] Compare ibid., pp. 315, 391.

the author has done his job well in surreptitiously ironizing his narrator, and if the reader goes about his task of interpreting the work with due attention and discretion, these pitfalls may be avoided and the resulting pleasure may be legitimate. Readers and critics who favor the delights of straightforward, traditional narrative may view the subtleties and complexities and the consequent difficulties of unreliable narration with disapproval or dismay; but such narration exists throughout literary history and has become part and parcel of modern literature, offering its own very definite rewards and delights when dealt with reasonably on its own terms. In the chapters which follow, the analyses of four kinds of unreliable first-person protagonist-narrators will attempt to reveal some of the specific methods by which the implied author carries out his task and how the reader may carry out his in order to attain these pleasurable and rewarding ends.

CHAPTER 3

The Pícaro

As is the case with any generic entity, definition of the precise nature and characteristics of the picaresque novel is confounded by a wide array of opinions and approaches. Greater diversity exists perhaps only in efforts to define the even more generalized categories of, for example, "the modern novel," "the realistic novel," or "the novel" itself. The historical approach views the picaresque as the descendant of Greek adventure tales, Roman comedy and satire, Dance of Death stories, fabliaux and animal-rogue narratives, tales of popular pranksters such as Till Eulenspiegel, and Boccaccio's stories of astuteness and deceit. This viewpoint also sees the emergence of the picaresque novel as the antithetical reaction to the "lovely edifices of enchantment" represented by the chivalric and pastoral romances of the late Middle Ages and the Renaissance.[1] The historical perspective often blends with a sociological one which finds the picaresque a natural outgrowth of late sixteenth-century Spanish society—declining political power, widespread poverty, stark class distinctions, religious persecution, Counter-Reformation doctrine, and a supposedly inherent Castilian pride mixed with an equally charac-

---

[1] Compare Frank Wadleigh Chandler, *Romances of Roguery*; and Ronald Paulson, "Picaresque Narrative: The Servant-Master Relation," in his *Fictions of Satire*, pp. 58–74.

teristic loathing for honest toil—and later, of European-wide war and the rise of capitalist enterprise.[2]

The analytical approach singles out as salient features of the picaresque a loosely jointed episodic structure, a wide-ranging social and geographical ambience, an emphasis on action and adventure, a tone of raucous and often vicious humor, a wealth of realistic and occasionally naturalistic detail, strong elements of social satire and critique sometimes augmented by explicit moral sermonizing, an open narrative form corresponding to a chaotic world order in contrast to the ordered and unified world of romance, and particular focus on the life of a single *pícaro* (or *pícara*), who in most cases tells the tale himself.[3]

For many critics, this last feature—the first-person narration by the *pícaro* himself—is the major and even indispensable element which a work must contain if it is to be qualified as a fully picaresque novel or tale.[4] For them, third-person narratives such as *Tom Jones* are, at best, works with picaresque qualities but not fully admissible within the canon of picaresque novels per se—a canon which stretches from *The Golden Ass* of Lucius Apuleius (ca. A.D. 150), through the Spanish works *Lazarillo de Tormes* (1554; anonymous), *The Scavenger* (1626; Quevedo), and *The Rogue, or The Life of Guzman de Alfarache* (1599, 1604; Mateo Alemán), to Germany and England in *Simplicius Simplicissimus* (1668; Grimmelshausen) and *Moll Flanders* (1722; Defoe), to name but six of the most prominent pre–twentieth-century works. The point is a good one. For only if the *pícaro* himself handles the entire narrative load will the account be imbued with

[2] Compare Chandler, *Romances of Roguery*; Robert Alter, *Rogue's Progress*; and Alexander Augustine Parker, *Literature and the Delinquent: The Picaresque Novel in Spain and Europe 1599–1753.*

[3] Compare Alter, *Rogue's Progress*; Parker, *Literature and the Delinquent*; and especially Stuart Miller, *The Picaresque Novel*; and Claudio Guillén, "Toward a Definition of the Picaresque," in his *Literature as System*, pp. 71–106.

[4] E.g., Parker, *Literature and the Delinquent*; Miller, *Picaresque Novel*; Guillén, *Literature as System*; Amado Alonso, "Das Pikareske des Schelmenromans," in *Pikarische Welt*, ed. Helmut Heidenreich, pp. 79–100; and Hans Robert Jauss, "Ursprung und Bedeutung der Ich-Form im *Lazarillo de Tormes*."

39

a unified and completely "picaresque" point of view and thus be wholly "picaresque."[5] The presence of a "Fielding," while immensely enjoyable in itself, precludes the possibility of a reader's ever experiencing the ups and downs of Tom's peregrinations from Tom's own vantage point and turns the work instead into a marvelously witty and urbane epic tale with a number of picaresque elements—riotous set-to's, travels, disguised identities, social climbing, moral lapses, and social satire. But *Tom Jones* is not a true picaresque novel, since the picaresque viewpoint is eschewed in favor of the omnipresent and omniscient epic narrator. Only the *picaro's* own narrative can provide this picaresque viewpoint.

This assertion naturally begs the question of the nature of the *picaro* himself, however, and this question must be taken up briefly before the actual nature of the picaresque narrative and specific examples of such narratives can be explored. Fortunately, while English renderings of the word *picaro* have ranged from such disparate terms as the playful "scamp" and the overly harsh "scavenger," to the more standard "rogue," and to Parker's eccentric "delinquent,"[6] the qualities of the *picaro* (or "picaroon," as some insist) are fairly well agreed upon:

The *picaro* is an anti-hero (an "unheroic" literary hero) whose parents are usually morally decadent and often occupy the lowest rung of the social and economic ladder. The *picaro's* life is governed by a general

---

[5] Compare Guillén, *Literature as System*, p. 81: "The picaresque novel is a pseudo-autobiography. This use of the first-person tense [*sic*] is more than a formal frame. It means that not only are the hero and his actions picaresque, but everything *else* in the story is colored with the sensibility, or filtered through the mind of the *picaro*-narrator. Both the hero and the principal point of view are picaresque. Hence the particular consistency and self-saturation of the style. Life is at the same time revived and judged, presented and remembered."

[6] The use of "delinquent," with its evocation of "juvenile delinquency," seems at least partly unsatisfactory, for it is fully applicable only to the young *picaro* whose story is narrated and not to the older *picaro* who actually performs the narrative function. Except in cases where the "narrating I" is still quite young (e.g., Pablos in *The Scavenger*), there is a large chronological distance between this "I" and the "narrated I," a distance which the word *picaro* can encompass but which "delinquent" cannot, despite its frequent appropriateness in regard to the young *picaro*.

deterministic principle and he never loses his negative social stigma. Heredity and environment tend to make a criminal of him. He is an occasional petty criminal, not a professional one. While many of his crimes are motivated by hunger and need, he often steals out of vengeance, or steals to get attention and approval from others he considers important. He has no particular profession and is incapable of sustained effort or purpose. The *pícaro* avoids work or does various kinds of marginal labor, but has a general disdain for manual labor. Necessity and poverty are usually his goad. The satisfaction of his basic needs, primarily hunger, takes precedence in his life over other needs. The *pícaro's* behavior is marked by rebelliousness and he gives voice to protest against the prevailing decadence of which he himself is a symptom. He embodies resentment and aggressiveness and his actions are a defense against a hostile and cruel reality. Love plays a marginal role in his life, and he is generally incapable of deep emotions. He resorts to cunning and will try to attain by trickery what others attain by hard work. Because of the inferiority he feels about his origins (social, racial, and economic), the *pícaro* strives to be accepted in a society that constantly rejects him. His world view is characterized by resignation and pessimism usually caused by adverse fortune or merely by ordinary contact with others. Within the religious and didactic purposes of the picaresque novel, he serves as an example of vice, a symbol of depravity, and an embodiment of the obstinacy of sin.[7]

Along his life's course the *pícaro* experiences precipitous rises and falls of Fate, comes in contact with a wide range of characters and social types, learns the game of survival the hard way, so to speak, and gradually develops the ability to function in almost any conceivable situation so as to turn things to his own advantage and to gain financial and/or social benefit. He becomes a master of disguise and pose and develops an often astonishing capacity for astuteness of action and adroitness of speech. Despite these cultivated talents, however, his final position is almost inevitably one of defeat in his lofty social and material ambitions: he may enjoy

[7] Joseph V. Ricapito, "Towards a Definition of the Picaresque," pp. 631–32. For more detailed description and commentary on the nature of the *pícaro*, see Chandler, *Romances of Roguery*, pp. 46–49; Guillén, *Literature as System*, pp. 80–85; and especially Miller, *Picaresque Novel*, pp. 23–88.

at best a successful station in life tinged with considerable moral compromise, may ultimately be caught and sentenced to penal servitude, may finally be cast into such despondency by ill fortune that he withdraws from the world and often into penitent reclusiveness, or he may experience some combination of these fates.

These, then, are the basic situations in which the *pícaro* usually finds himself at the end of his career and at the point in time from which he narrates his experiences: a dubious success figure, a despondent failure, a convicted felon, or a religious convert. Each of these narrative situations presents a certain problematical precondition for the conduct of the *pícaro's* autobiographical account, for each stands in rather marked contrast to the coarse, rollicking life which has preceded it and which forms the subject matter of the narrative. With the added consideration of the older *pícaro's* acquired proclivities for perpetual role-playing and verbal adroitness, this situation becomes still more problematical. Not only is the narrative situation rife with potential for dissonance between the newly-found uprightness or piety of the older *pícaro* and the roguishness of the younger one; there is also the distinct probability that long years of perpetual mask-changing and verbal chicanery have rendered the *pícaro* incapable of anything except role-playing, so that his entire narrative becomes a pose, whether consciously or unconsciously assumed. Also, with some exceptions such as Guzmán de Alfarache and Simplicius Simplicissimus, the *pícaro* is seldom a genuinely intelligent individual with more than average insight into character and motivation or pronounced sensitivity to complex situations and problems, despite his astuteness and adroitness. Just as he himself operates on a constantly changing level of appearances and verbal gloss in his roguish career, so do his perceptions of others and his grasp of events which he experiences often remain confined to the superficial or to some idée fixe such as "freedom of movement." Thus a gap is opened between his own rather whimsical and entertaining account and his self-indulgent explanations and morality, on the one hand, and the perceptions of the more sensitive author and reader on the other. His narrative situation is, then, a ready-made one for unreliable narration and narrative irony, with the *pícaro* himself as the likely unwitting butt of that irony.

As for the *pícaro's* narrative itself, a certain realism of speech predominates, at least in the older works of the picaresque canon. There the illiterate or semiliterate, lowborn rogue usually recounts his knockabout life in a chaotic, digressive, rambling, and unlettered style peppered with thieves' slang, folksy aphorisms, and sometimes—if he is a social or religious convert by the end of his adventures—bolstered with considerable doses of sermonizing. He is a boon companion who is at his lively best when regaling us about the various successful gulling escapades in his past and about the times when he rode high on Fortune's wheel. He can also wax marvelously on certain unfortunate incidents which befell him, if their consequences were not severe enough to destroy their humor in retrospect and especially if they afford him the opportunity to relate something particularly bawdy or scatological and comically shocking.

A certain fragmentation in the picaresque narrator's personality becomes apparent, however, in the contrasts between these relishingly recalled events and the accounts of occurrences which ended disastrously or which cast a strongly negative light upon his actions and character. Here a great bitterness or even rage is often evident, a deep-seated resentment at his lot and station in life, which casts its shadow on the rest of the account and sets the *pícaro's* mask of rowdy gaiety at least slightly askew. The split is also frequently evident in the prefatory and concluding stages of the accounts of those more successful times: a particularly malevolent or hypocritical master is recalled and painted in markedly vicious terms—often with vile epithets thrown in from the narrator's present, retrospective point of view—before the account turns to glorifying in the master's duping; and the account frequently concludes with yet another blast at the dupe and savors the vengeance which has been wrought upon him or at least the profits which have been gleaned from the gulling. On the surface the picaresque narrator rejoices at his success in having adapted to external realities and having turned them to his own benefit, but at the core there seems to lie a definite estrangement from, and even anger at, his fellow men and the world in general:

In its inner workings, the picaresque novel shows how a character is ensnared by life and victimized by a corrupt society. In its negative presentation, the picaresque novel displays a wish for a better world. Inherent in the novels is an interpretation of life seen as a struggle. In the picaresque novel, comic or pseudo-comic adventures seem to belie an essential concept of bitterness and a negative vision of the world.[8]

In the cases of the reformed and converted *pícaros*, especially those withdrawn into seclusion from the world, this estrangement is even more pronounced and explicit and is coupled with another split between the new piety and the old amorality. The new convert must logically condemn his own past misdeeds and be forgiving of the failings of others, yet is usually understandably unable to repress a good deal of relish in reliving old successes and considerable bias against reprehensible figures in his life. He will also not wish to eliminate too much pleasure for the reader by overloading his tale with sermonizing, lest the moral lesson sink by its own weight; nor will he wish to open himself too conspicuously to charges of hypocrisy by overly sacrificing edification to delectation. The reformed *pícaro's* narrative problems are therefore considerable, whether he is fully aware of them or not, for he must somehow strike a harmonious balance between these disparate forces within him. Given his lifelong devotion to appearances and role-playing and his frequent tendency to stress the negative qualities of others and the positive features of his own character and conduct, it is no wonder that such a task as a rule proves too much for him. This is not necessarily to question his conscious sincerity in what he says and how he narrates—though that too may well often be suspect—but rather to question his

8 Ricapito, "Towards a Definition," p. 635.

very capability of presenting a fully reliable portrait of himself, of his life, of the world through which he has made his peripatetic and roguish way, and of the values and attitudes he would have us accept.

Lucius, the protagonist-narrator of Lucius Apuleius's *The Golden Ass*, pays little attention to autobiography as such. Since he is using Egyptian paper and Nile reeds as writing instruments, he presumably composes his work while he is in Egypt attending to his duties as a priest of Osiris; yet all that he intends to do in his book is to "string together divers stories, and delight [the reader's] kindly ears with a pleasant history,"[9] that is, to write a simple "Milesian tale"[10] for popular consumption. He then continues for the greater part of his account to adhere to this aim of sheer entertainment by tossing in descriptions mainly to demonstrate his wit (for example, the den of thieves) and by switching between the comic and the tragic modes (the unhappy father) so as to provide genuine diversity for the reader. As the experiencing Lucius grows weary of his assy state, however, and as the narrating Lucius nears the point where he will recount his conversion (literal as well as spiritual in this case) and his religious initiations, a second motive becomes apparent. Throughout Lucius's accounts of the religious festival, his grievings at his sad lot, and his prayers to the goddesses a new tone of piety is assumed. The tone increases in moral fervor until the priest of Isis sets forth to Lucius (and to the reader) the explicit religious preachment of the work:

O my friend Lucius, after the endurance of so many labours and the escape of so many tempests of fortune, thou art now at length come to

[9] Lucius Apuleius, *The Golden Ass*, trans. William Adlington, bk. 1, chap. 1.

[10] Compare Ben Edwin Perry, "An Introduction of Apuleius' *Metamorphoses*," pp. 255–56: "In modern times the term ['Milesian tale'] is applied by common consent to a realistic and unmoral *novella*, such as . . . that of Philesitherus in Apuleius. . . . On the contrary, it seems very likely that by the time of Apuleius 'Milesian' was broad enough to include any kind of popular tale, provided that it was written in the style of the realistic *novella*, or that it came from Miletus."

45

the port and haven of rest and mercy. Neither did thy noble lineage, thy dignity, neither thy excellent doctrine anything avail thee; but because thou didst turn to servile pleasures, by a little folly of thy youthfulness, thou hast had a sinister reward of thy unprosperous curiosity. But howsoever the blindness of fortune tormented thee in divers dangers, so it is that now by her unthoughtful malice thou art come to this present felicity of religion. [Bk. 11, chap. 15]

Such piety is nowhere in evidence in the first nine books; and although Lucius constantly intones Providence and the gods, he never passes moral censure on himself. He applies such strictures only to the crooked Priests of the Syrian Goddess and to brigands and faithless spouses, castigating himself solely for his stupidity in trying to gain access to Pamphile's occult mysteries. The moral aspect is, then, confined to books 10 and 11, and all the foregoing is presented primarily as entertainment. No real autobiography results; for Lucius recounts only a brief period of his life, does not even portray only his own experiences or relate only tales of his own invention, and in no way presents a picture of himself with any completeness.

There seems little question but that Lucius's religious conversion is a sincere one—it originates from within Lucius (the ass) himself, in his prayer to the goddesses, and that prayer is heeded almost immediately by Juno/Isis. Furthermore, his fervor in recounting both his final metamorphosis and his threefold initiation into the various mysteries seems a genuine reflection of the fervor with which he presumably underwent those experiences. But book 11 has little if any discernible connection to anything which is narrated between the opening paragraph of book 1 and the close of book 10. The question naturally arises as to how a convert so fully steeped in the sacred mysteries and reputedly chosen by the divinities themselves for admission to those orders can so totally eschew any overt moralization when recounting his past flirtations with sorcery, how he can render with such obvious relish those lavish descriptions of Fotis's charms, how he can possibly relate with such boisterous good humor his encounter with the woman who wants to couple with him publicly while he is still an ass. His various stories of unfaithful wives and husbands (including his initially mistaken impression of the kidnapped girl's flirtation with Haemus) evince a stern morality, but it is a social morality and not that of a religious zealot. And the long interpolated tale of Cupid and Psyche has a thematic link with Lucius's own story in its rebuke and eventual redemption of the mortal who seeks direct entry into the forbidden mystery of the gods; but Lucius never makes the link clear, as he should do in such a work aimed at popular consumption.

The most plausible explanation would seem to be that the account of the conversion is merely tacked on to provide a serious counterweight to the general levity of the foregoing portions of the work and thereby "redeem [the author and] his work from the charge or appearance of absolute frivolity."[11] Ben Edwin Perry notes that Lucius's moral ending is a substitute for the burlesque conclusion of the genre's Greek model and seems to represent not only the necessary (for contemporary Roman ethics) compensation for levity but also simply one more item in a literary tour de force. The aretology of the eleventh book, then, should not be taken as the prime intent of the work for those sake the first nine and one-half books were written as mere illustration. As Perry aptly concludes:

The avowed purpose of the *Metamorphoses* is romantic entertainment . . . ; but this is not altogether inconsistent with the theory that the entertainment was intended to honey the cup of religious or moral propaganda. Nevertheless, it is hard to believe that Apuleius had any serious intention of playing the part of the good-natured physician; for he has mixed, as it were, ten parts of honey to one of wormwood.[12]

Thus, while Lucius cannot be faulted for presenting only a grab bag of loosely connected tales in the Milesian style—his purpose

[11] Ibid., p. 245.
[12] Ibid., pp. 243–44n.

was solely to delight his readers' ears through divers tales—his status as a true convert must be considered somewhat suspect, at least in terms of the fictional premise on which his narrative is conducted and his current position defined. Relegating his religious message to one-eleventh of his total work does not mark him as a devout priest of Osiris and makes the moral value of that message quite small indeed.

In *The Life of Lazarillo of Tormes* it is from a standpoint of relative affluence and newly gained respectability as town crier of Toledo that Lazarillo narrates his tale. The occasion for his telling of the story is a request by a certain august personage in the city—addressed as "Vuestra Merced," or Your Honor—for an explanation regarding town gossip about the possibility of impropriety in the relationship between Lazarillo, Lazarillo's wife, and the Archpriest of Toledo, who is an acquaintance and subordinate of the august personage. Rumor has it that the maid has been and still is the Archpriest's mistress, and the implication therefore is that the latter has tried to divert suspicion on this count by marrying the girl off to Lazarillo and has sweetened the bargain by procuring for him a "civil service" job. Lazarillo's entire narrative, then, becomes an exercise in explaining away these suspicions and in justifying his present position to Vuestra Merced and to the general reader. He recounts the hardships of his past life, invokes the dignity of the Archpriest, vilifies the gossipmongers, and swears a sacred oath as to his marital bliss, all in a concerted effort to demonstrate his triumph over adversity and to vindicate his current respectability. Nonetheless, from the very outset Lazarillo's narrative stands under a cloud of suspicion as the self-defense of an accused individual at pains to cast himself in the best possible light. That cloud throws its shadow both on Lazarillo's telling of the story and on his character and reliability as a narrator.

Other factors reinforce this initial impression of the narrative's suspect nature. In the course of his early life Lazarillo demonstrated a certain knack for imitation and dissimulation, as he himself confesses:

> With a low, sickly voice, my hands crossed over my chest, and with my eyes looking up to heaven and God's name on my tongue, I began to beg for bread at the doors of the biggest houses I saw. But I'd been doing this almost from the cradle—I mean I learned it from that great teacher, the blind man, and I turned out to be a pretty good student—so even though this town had never been very charitable, and it had been a pretty lean year besides, I handled myself so well that before the clock struck four I had that many pounds of bread stored away in my stomach and at least two more in my sleeves and inside my shirt.[13]

It is this mimetic abililty which enables Lazarillo not only to beg with great success but also to reproduce with remarkable grace the rhetorical style of an eloquent prayer and simultaneously to turn this prayer into a disillusioned complaint at his ill fortune with his current master, the squire. And it also seems to be this ability which enables him to couch his Prologue to Your Honor in terms and a style which doubtless echo those of that august personage himself. A quick tongue, a dissimulative facility, and an ability to lie convincingly (which he also admits in the same chapter) are all ingrained in Lazarillo through dint of his various experiences and must be considered as pertinent characteristics of the town crier who now recounts his tale to us. He has used them all many times before to gain certain ends and to overcome adverse circumstances; there is no reason to assume either that he is at all able to shuck them completely or that he will eschew them now that his newly acquired respectability and security are seriously jeopardized.

Moreover, the very structure of Lazarillo's narrative raises strong doubts about his complete honesty and forthrightness as a narrator. In the autobiographical portion of his tale—chaps. 1–6—the overwhelming emphasis in terms of space allotted is

[13] *The Life of Lazarillo of Tormes*, trans. Robert S. Rudder, p. 62.

placed on chaps. 1, 2, 3, and 5. The first three recount his times of adverse fortune and his own roguish activities of theft and beggary, alternately reveling in successful displays of ingenuity and groveling in past miseries; and the fifth is devoted to an unabashedly admiring account of the corrupt pardoner. Lazarillo's times of relatively good fortune, decent employment, and financial security—with the friar, the artist, and with a small-town priest—on the other hand, are glossed over in two chapters of less than a page each (4 and 6). Given Lazarillo's avowed purpose— and his virtual necessity—of showing himself to be a basically decent citizen, this emphasis on knavery seems strange indeed. For, far from proving Lazarillo's moral uprightness and constancy, it presents a soul which, though now nominally reformed, is still far more closely attuned to the amorality and occasional vindictiveness of the young *pícaro* than to any respectable standards of conventional morality. Despite the seventh chapter's tone of self-righteous and affronted dignity and the oath on the Holy Spirit that all is as it should be in Lazarillo's married life, the protagonist's narrative reveals a heart which still seems to go out to the picaresque life and thereby renders those outcries ineffective.

Either Lazarillo has willingly entered the arrangement with the maid and the Archpriest with some awareness of the real situation and thereby gained a measure of security in typically picaresque fashion, or he has naïvely agreed to the bargain solely for that security and has later acquiesced in the affair despite the nagging suspicions which he himself admits but can nonetheless tolerate as long as no real threat to that security exists. Either way, his attempts to justify the "case" ring hollow, and he stands exposed as a *pícaro* at heart play-acting the role of decent citizen. The invisible implied author's sarcastic juxtaposition of Lazarillo's arrival at the "safe haven" of his present state and the victorious Emperor's triumphant entry into Toledo only adds the final, definitive touch to a "portrait of dishonor and shame."[14] The result of Lazarillo's efforts is not the intended portrayal of himself as a model citizen and Christian but rather the tragicomic and

[14] Joseph V. Ricapito, "Introducción," in his edition of *Lazarillo de Tormes*, p. 81.

ironical depiction of a basically unreformed *pícaro* pinioned in that role by his own testimony.[15]

Guzmán de Alfarache is much more exhaustive and candid in recounting his life story than is Lazarillo. Because of the incomplete state of Alemán's novel, however, Guzmán never comes to give an explicit statement of his intentions in writing of his past; all that the reader has to go on are the opening and closing remarks of the existing parts of the novel. Besides simply wanting to relate his adventures, Guzmán intends to provide considerable background and secondary diversions, as indicated by his anecdote about the two painters in the opening chapter.[16] He also has a moral lesson in mind, as implied by his concluding remarks:

And heere (gentle Reader) doe I put a full point to these my mis-fortunes. I have given thee a large account of my lewd life; it is truely summ'd up unto thee. What it is hereafter, thou shalt see in my third and last Part, if God shall give me life: and that I doe not first exchange this transitorie one, for one that is eternall, which is the hope and life of the faithful.[17]

Guzmán, as he constantly reminds us, is never prudent or frugal enough to rest content with the considerable fortunes he occasionally gains through various stratagems (as in the case of the Milanese banker) and outright theft (for example, from the Ma-

[15] For other approaches, textual analyses, and critiques which reach this same conclusion, see especially Frank Durand, "The Author and Lázaro: Levels of Comic Meaning"; L. J. Woodward, "Author-Reader Relationship in the *Lazarillo de Tormes*"; R. W. Truman, "Parody and Irony in the Self-Portrayal of Lazarillo de Tormes"; and Francisco Rico, *La novela picaresca y el punto de vista*. See also the entries by Bataillon, Carey, Gilman, Guillén, and Tarr listed in the bibliography at the end of this study.

[16] Two painters are commissioned to paint a horse. The one who most pleases the patron will receive a generous bonus. One produces a perfectly lifelike picture of the horse, the other a fine portrait with an extensive and detailed background of landscapes and riding accouterments. The patron rewards the former, evoking the indignation not only of the second artist but of Guzmán as well.

[17] Mateo Alemán, *The Rogue, or The Life of Guzman de Alfarache*, trans. James Mabe, pt. 2, bk. 3, chap. 9.

drid apothecary), but his constant goal is nonetheless a state of relative affluence and security. The first real leanings toward a serious conversion are the consequence of crisis and punishment and possess materialistic overtones. The threat of death through a violent storm at sea on a voyage from Genoa to Barcelona brings to the surface the first genuine indications of a latent sense of guilt in Guzmán for his actions (in this instance, the gulling of his own relatives in Genoa): "It was not the Sea, but the shame, that wrought upon me. This was it, that made me say to my selfe, when I saw how the winds blew, and the Seas raged, that all the rest did fare the worse for my sake, and that I was that Jonas, for whom this tempest was rais'd, that it might raise me up to repentance" (Pt. 2, bk. 2, chap. 10). His liberation from the galleys for helping abort a prisoners' mutiny seems to Guzmán to be Heaven's just recognition that he has suffered sufficiently and learned his lesson, for Heaven itself placed him in a position where he had to be taken into the mutineers' confidence. Hence his resolution to reform.

There is in Guzmán's attitude and account, however, a certain dualism which casts doubt on the genuineness of such a conversion. First, the betrayal of his fellow prisoners is as much a pragmatic act of self-preservation as it is a sign of moral reform. On the galley he has assiduously curried the favor of the cook and the captain and a knight and has incurred the enmity of a number of the ship's servants and the slaves, particularly the prisoner Soto, one of the instigators of the mutiny. His thwarting of the revolt is thus both an effort to protect his acquired position of favor with the ship's authorities and an act of revenge on Soto— who had previously stolen some parcels from him, eliciting a secret vow of vengeance from Guzmán—as well as an act of self-defense out of fear for his life at the hands of the hardened galley slaves.

Second, Guzmán's retrospective moralizations have as much basis in materialistic concern as in morality, if not more. For every recognition of his past hypocrisy, pride, and self-love there are two or more instances of self-reproach for overzealousness and unfrugality in obtaining and spending material wealth. He can periodically note that Pride is ridiculous and chameleonlike or that every criminal carries his own punishment with him in his perpetual fear of discovery; but he castigates himself much more frequently for prodigality and wastefulness, continually recalling past follies in financial matters and resolving to manage better in the future.

Third, the preeminence of materialistic concerns in Guzmán's mind is revealed by another feature of his retrospective musings: namely, the extensive efforts at justifying his continual illegal attempts to make a quick killing through some sort of ruse. These efforts are comprised in fairly equal measure of assertions of weakness and necessity. On the one hand, Guzmán claims, it is extremely difficult to shed roguish propensities—many of which, he says, are universally practiced in business anyway—and on the other, necessity often forced him to turn to theft and extortion or to moral complacency (when, for example, his second wife earned their keep through her lovers) in order to survive. He can occasionally see the immorality of his actions and allow that a punishment or banishment (for example, from the Cardinal's house in Rome) was just, but at the same time he harbors considerable vindictiveness toward the executor of that justice for casting him out from a secure and profitable position. In most of these instances the feelings of vindictiveness are those of the "narrated" rogue and not of the present narrator; but there is no indication that the present narrator has changed or overcome these feelings, no corrective moderations or judgments, and hence no firm ground for asserting that a genuine reform has taken place.

And fourth, Guzmán has already once been so down and out that he has undergone a conversion: namely, following the death of his first wife and his subsequent loss of her inheritance and dowry. But the conversion was a consciously hypocritical and self-serving one aimed solely at procuring a subsistence through becoming a priest:

I knew that this came not from my heart, for I was not ignorant of mine owne evill inclination; but he that hath no other meanes, and is put to his shifts, must doe as he may. . . . The money that I shall make of this house, will serve well enough to maintaine me as a scholler; which being well husbanded, though I should spend yearely a hundred Ducats, or a hundred and fiftie, which will be the most, (and is a good liberall allowance) I shall have store of money for that time, that I will need to continue there; so that I may live like a Duke, (if I list my selfe) and yet have wherewithall to buy me bookes, and to take some honourable Degree. [Pt. 2, bk. 3, chap. 4]

Granted, one such instance of blatant hypocrisy and simulation of piety does not exclude the possibility of a later, genuine conversion. Still, the circumstances of what seems to be Guzmán's ultimate reform are not such as to inspire confidence in the sincerity or lasting nature of that conversion or to indicate that a road-to-Damascus revelation of faith is the case with Guzmán's resolution. Guzmán has offered seemingly heartfelt thanks to Heaven on previous occasions (for example, when a kindly monk shared his food with Guzmán), then set out again with renewed hopes and no hint of roguish intentions, only immediately to turn once more to theft and trickery (following the monk's kindness, Guzmán took to cheating travelers while employed at an inn). Perhaps the galley experience has had a stronger effect upon his resolve than did earlier setbacks; but Guzmán's past retrogressions and the lack of a firm, unequivocal moral tone on the part of the present narrator provide no certainty that this has been the case and that Guzmán's reform has been a genuinely complete and lasting one.

The narrative position of the protagonist-narrator Pablos in Quevedo's *The Scavenger* is that of a failed *pícaro* at some indefinite time and place in the New World, possibly in jail, but at any rate despairingly moralistic at the course his life has taken. Here no outside force prompts the writing of the story, and no specific purpose is put forward by Pablos for the recounting of his adventures and fate. Rather, the cause for the writing seems to be that

54

very despair so evident in the final pages and particularly in the closing lines: "I made up my mind, after talking it over with La Grajal, to sail for the New World with her and there to see if a change of continents would better my luck. It turned out to be worse, as you will see, sir, in the second part, for a man who only changes his habitat and not his way of living never betters things for himself."[18] This despair seems to have moved Pablos to relate his story both as something of a warning to others and as an effort at palliating his despondency somewhat through the vicarious reliving of some of his more fortunate earlier experiences. Just as the damning rumors of compromised morality clouded Lazarillo's narrative, so does this despair cast its shadow over Pablos's tale by overlaying his narrative with the strong hint of futile effort and of moral and physical ruin.

No conversion proper is evident in Pablos; rather, there is the bitterly moralizing philosophy of defeat which in retrospect sets the entire parade of adventures into a strongly negative perspective. Pablos has, after all, been successfully driven—out of shame, fear, or despair—from Segovia, Alcalá, Madrid, Toledo, and Seville. He has engaged in beatings, parasitism, exploitation of friends and strangers alike, deceitful courtships, theft, kidnapping, and brutal hooliganism. He has been jailed once and threatened with prosecution on two other occasions, and has suffered frequent public humiliation. He has seen his attempts to enter higher social realms fail miserably, has gained and lost small fortunes, and has betrayed and then tasted the justice of the one decent individual among his string of acquaintances, Don Diego. Each separate decision to move on has been something of an admission of defeat, but always there seemed better prospects ahead. It is only with the gradual, cumulative effect of these defeats and with Pablos's concomitant descent into ever lower depths of the petty criminal's world that his hopeful, assertive outlook ultimately dims, turning into the pessimism born of despair at whatever final setbacks have been suffered in the New

[18] Francisco Gómez de Quevedo y Villegas, *The Scavenger*, trans. Hugh A. Harter, chap. 23.

World. Not a very pretty picture, and not a situation which inspires much trust in the teller of the tale.

Adding to the negative portrait of Pablos and to the reader's early distrust of his narrative is the psychology of the protagonist. Pablos's desire to leave home, to gain an education, and to rise in social standing, his toadying to the schoolmaster, and his servitude to Don Diego all appear to be part of a compensatory effort to overcome a sense of guilt and shame at his mother's whoring and witchcraft and at his father's petty thievery. This stigma, Pablos seems to feel, provokes society's continued brutal hostility toward him. He never realizes that such favor-currying on his part only perpetuates that animus and traps him in a vicious circle of moral sellouts and humiliating defeats. The only courses left open to him are despair and evasion, on the one hand, and ruthless adaptation to a harsh world on the other. The latter is of course the path which Pablos chooses in progressively worsening stages from the school rowdies to the Seville thugs; and the consequence is an ever-increasing hypocrisy on Pablos's part, as his actions and attitudes become steadily more scurrilous in his efforts to attain his goals of high social standing, respectability, and financial security, all of which in him are questionable values at best. Pablos himself seems not to discern this constantly widening discrepancy between means and desired ends and entertains no scruples about his actions. For the reader, however, the resulting portrait is an ugly one of a morally bankrupt individual whose life has brought nothing. And however pathetic that life may be in respect to its adverse beginnings and harsh turns of fate, it inspires only a kind of understanding pity and not the sympathy required to accept the moral and social attitudes espoused by Pablos himself in both word and deed.

Instead, the reader aligns himself with the values of the implied author, whose presence here is considerably in evidence, particularly in passages such as that describing the miserly schoolmaster Cabra: "His nose, which had once been a Roman one, had been worn flat by sores, from *colds*, but which one would have thought to come from the French disease except that

that illness involves the price of a girl. . . . On sunny days he wore a cap; it was riddled with holes and had a trimming of grease" (chap. 3). Here the intricate linguistic play in the Spanish original turns a fairly detailed recollection of Cabra's nose and cap into a biting indictment implying venereal disease, shabbiness, and squalor and "stretches and distorts realism into caricature, creating a grotesque world of surrealistic fancy"[19] attributable more to Quevedo than to Pablos. The novel's verbal play runs in this fashion throughout, whether focusing on a small detail such as Cabra's cap or describing at some length a scene such as the repulsive banquet of Ramplón and his cronies or the perverted Eucharist indulged in by Pablos and the Seville hoodlums. The effect is to expand what Pablos sees simply as a harsh and cruel world into a unified vision of grotesqueness revealing at once what Parker terms (in the continuation of the above analysis) "the distortions and unreality of human social life in the self-conceit and hypocrisy of men."

Thus, while Quevedo's and Pablos's views of the world and of men are both negative, the former's is of such a wider and more penetrating nature that a very distinct gap opens up between the two. Pablos is alternately funny, bitter, self-revealing, and, on occasion, superficially philosophical; but his account is ultimately only a loose series of episodes from his life. Quevedo's thoroughgoing psychological portrait and his structurally consistent pattern of biting wit together provide this episodic account with a foundation by complementing each other and thereby lending the novel a strict unity of serious satirical purpose which both pillories the depraved world depicted therein and ironizes the *pícaro* who recounts his life in that world.

Simplicius Simplicissimus gives us a highly detailed and concrete epic situation—we find a full description of him on the island where he has taken up a pious hermitage and hear how he put together his manuscript using dried palm leaves and an ink

[19] Parker, *Literature and the Delinquent*, p. 58.

made of Brazil wood and lemon juice—and is extremely conscientious in relating everything he has experienced and done.
He sounds a candid autobiographical note when he declares, "I
want to conceal my vices no more than my virtues"; yet he makes
this statement not with the primary intent of portraying his character and life as completely as possible (that is, writing an autobiography), but rather to portray for the reader the wickedness of
many who populate the world: " . . . not only because I want the
reader to know the whole story, but also so that he knows what
strange characters populate this world—characters who give little
thought to God."[20] He also adamantly denies having written a
purely entertaining series of adventures, although there is much
in his work that, he admits, is indeed pleasurable. Such entertainment is beneath him, he asserts, and he has resorted to it only
out of moral and artistic necessity:

> The reason I am presenting my story with a dash of humor is that some
> delicate tenderlings can't swallow pills that are good for them unless
> they have been coated with sugar and gilt, not to mention the fact that
> even the most sober-sided of men will put down a serious book, whereas
> they keep reading one that makes them smile ever so little every once in
> a while. [Bk. 6, chap. 1]

He goes on to conclude: "If here and there a reader is satisfied
with the husks and disregards the kernel which is hidden under-
neath, he will have a jolly story to content him, but he will miss
by far that which I had really wanted him to get. So I'll start
where I left off at the end of the fifth book." Simplicius is not
above indulging in lavish self-praise of his erudition, his musical
and storytelling abilities, his appeal to women, and even his pro-
ficiency in "foraging"; but these instances are comparatively infrequent in relation to the large amount of self-castigation more

---

[20] Hans Jakob Christoph von Grimmelshausen, *Simplicius Simplicissimus*, trans.
George Schulz-Behrend, bk. 4, chap. 10.

befitting his present pious life and frame of mind. He does not attempt to apologize for his past weaknesses and sinful inclinations and is consequently quite faithful to the autobiographical mode; but he does subordinate the autobiographical intent to a moral and therefore more general purpose.

Although Simplicius's religious convictions seem genuine in view of his strict, self-imposed regimen of intense prayer and productive labor in his island seclusion, his narrative must be viewed with some caution, for the reader is dealing here with a trained storyteller and performer. Simplicius demonstrates a healthy respect for the perspicacity of his reader by anticipating the many possible objections to his narrative (for instance, that it is often too fantastic or that it is too frivolous or indecent) and by admitting the various artistic devices which he uses (allegory, fantasy, exhaustive detail, lewd description). He justifies these narrative techniques and nonrealistic aspects by pleading their usefulness in his literary and moral endeavor: the throwaway line at the end of the account of the witches' sabbath notes that the ride on the enchanted bench is an easy means of getting the young hero from Hersburg to Magdeburg in a short time, and the extensive allegory to the pilgrims is excused because of its exemplary teachings. The lewdness he of course pardons because he must depict his (and others') former state as basely as possible, so that his conversion is all the more impressive and so that the vile nature of worldly affairs stands in marked contrast with the pious life. Still, his obvious glee in recounting the several lecherous, villainous, and scatological episodes makes any ulterior moral purpose at least a little suspect; but this tendency is largely countered by his frequent moralizations damning his vanity, his ambition, his falseness, his inclination to vice, and the general hypocrisy of men. His erudite use of mythology and of biblical lore (simultaneously comparing himself, for example, to Theseus against the Minotaur and to David with Jonathan [1 Sam. 18–23] when he first appears at court) and his sophisticated employment of character to illustrate his own nature (the contrasts between himself and the piety and evil of Hertzbruder and Oliver respectively) augment both the credibility of his moral purpose and the highly literary mode in which that purpose is couched.

Despite all the "protective smokescreen" of erudition and expressed justification of the basic unreality of much of the tale,[21] however, there emerges something of a disparity between the narrator's moral stance and what he actually narrates. Simplicius would have the reader believe that the young hero was an innately good soul who was constantly aware of moral and religious demands and whose various falls and relapses were honest failures brought on by nothing more than insufficient spiritual strength in the face of youthful proclivities and worldly temptations. Numerous soul-searchings and moments of penitence occur in the young Simplicius; but in daily confrontation with the world the youth easily forgets the fears and remorse which brought on the penitence and again yields to his more mundane stirrings, even when the penitence has been almost overwhelming—for example, when Simplicius is struck by fear of the Devil, and when he falls into a meditative state under the influence of Guevara's writings.

There seems little cause to doubt the momentary sincerity of these recurrent conversions, yet they cast a certain odd light on Simplicius's final conversion. It seems that almost any of the earlier moments of penitence might have been lasting and therefore genuine, had the youth not again been cast into the world of men, where his own tendencies and weaknesses soon led him astray once more. Even his most serious conversion (on reading Guevara) falls victim to forgetfulness, once he is back in the world—and that during a pilgrimage! Only his rekindled conversion on the desert island proves enduring, for here, after the death of his friend, he is totally isolated from the world and therefore no longer confronted with the situation which heretofore has always caused his relapse. This "true" conversion thus appears to

[21] Bertil Romberg, *Studies in the Narrative Technique of the First-Person Novel*, trans. Michael Taylor and Harold H. Borland, p. 35.

lie more in the fact that Simplicius is no longer tempted than in his having conquered the basic weakness of his character. Moreover, it is a chance occurrence (a shipwreck) and not his own resolve which initially imposes this isolation upon him. He later has the opportunity for choice when a passing ship offers him passage to Europe, but he refuses, averring that the island seclusion affords him "freedom from want and vain desires." His is, then, the safe piety of one who merely avoids all possibility of temptation, not the piety of one who conquers temptation.

Simplicius's morality thus rings a bit more hollow than he would like, for by virtue of his own example he preaches the piety of avoidance and spiritual security. Within his heart he seems sincerely devout in his religion. He does not really seem guilty of forgetting or stifling his new moral stance while narrating his story; he cannot fairly be accused of actually sensing any hypocrisy in his position and then trying to gild that hypocrisy with fervid preachings; nor is his piety predominantly dependent upon financial and physical well-being. Nonetheless, even this most pious and sincere of reformed *pícaros* is ultimately guilty of a conversion which, to the modern reader, appears second-rate at best. Beneath the breast of the convert there still beats the heart of the *pícaro*. He can be admired only for having removed himself from those situations which brought that picaresque nature to the surface, not for truly reforming or quieting that nature.

Moll Flanders, writing from the comfortably well-off position of a retired and upstanding former landowner now resettled in England, is, like Guzmán and Simplicius, extremely conscientious and candid in rendering her past with relative completeness. But like those two predecessors, she also writes for reasons other than the mere illumination of her life and personality. As she notes:

The moral indeed of all my history is left to be gather'd by the senses and judgment of the reader. I am not qualified to preach to them; let the

61

experience of one creature completely wicked, and completely miserable, be a storehouse of useful warning to those that read.[22]

Later she is even more explicit concerning her lofty moral intent—"the publishing of this account of my life is for the sake of
the just moral of every part of it, and for instruction, caution,
warning, and improvement to every reader"—and she persistently buttonholes her reader in order to whisper confidential asides or
to add a bit of rhetorical moralization. Yet, at the same time as she
expounds upon the seriousness of her task, she realizes that she is
also providing an interesting diversion for her readers in recounting the particularly scandalous portions of her life and imparting
useful information to them for self-defense against cutpurses and
the like as well. And Moll, too, like Lazarillo and Guzmán, is out
to toot her own horn—her story's full title reads "The Fortunes and
Misfortunes of the Famous Moll Flanders," and she praises her
talent for thievery ("I grew the greatest artist of my time, and
work'd myself out of every danger") as unabashedly as she lauds
her present piety and prosperity. She also takes advantage of every
opportunity to exculpate herself as much as possible by invoking
necessity and the evil proclivities "natural" to her negative heritage
and frequently adverse conditions.

Moll's story thus becomes virtually an apologia for her life, delivered not in response to the query of an august personage but to
the more general community of religious and respectable souls
whose normal reaction would be to condemn or look unfavorably
on such a life as hers. She often confesses to certain weaknesses
in matters of the flesh and the purse. She prates her basic goodness, however, and pleads necessity and circumstance for having
given in to those weaknesses and for having become hardened in
heart. There is something in these pleas (as in those of many
pícaros) that offers a key to Moll's character: Moll feels she is a cut
above the indigents from whose midst she sprang and envisions
for herself such a state of social and financial security that the

[22] Daniel Defoe, *Moll Flanders*, p. 256.

relatively good circumstances in which she periodically lands (her marriages to Robin's younger brother and to the "gentleman-tradesman") do not begin to satisfy her. "Necessity," for her, thus balloons into the all but impossible task of achieving an affluent security, not just keeping body and soul together in relative comfort.

Until such total security is attained, then, Moll will continue to go her calculating way, despite whatever innate goodness she may possess and despite whatever moral judgments she may pass on herself. It is this dualistic morality which allows her, for example, to live for six years as a kept woman ("I was not without secret reproaches of my own conscience for the life I led, . . . yet I had the terrible prospect of poverty and starving, which lay on me as a frightful spectre, so that there was no looking behind me") and to keep for so long from her brother the secret of their incestuous marriage. And it is this same dualism which is at the bottom of Moll's relapse into her hardened condition so shortly after her original conversion in Newgate: the conversion occurs when Moll is certain she is going to die on the gallows; the retrogression follows immediately upon her learning that transportation orders have been obtained for her instead, whereby she once again is made "uncertain of her condition." As the picture brightens for Moll—her material and financial stock increase through various manipulations and good fortune, she is reunited with her true love Jemy, and she finds herself suddenly prosperous in Virginia—the piety of her earlier conversion rekindles, however, and continues to grow in direct proportion to the affluence and security which she attains.

The upshot of this process is that the "sincere penitence" of the older Moll who narrates the story is virtually synonymous with, as well as dependent upon, that security of wealth and status. "Necessity" has become a thing of the past, and there is consequently no deterrent to her living out her life in pious reverence. With no call to resort yet again to the calculating life, she can safely pass judgment now on such dealings. Those judgments, however sincerely they may be felt and delivered by the old Moll, sound rather empty in light of their symbiotic relationship with Moll's purely worldly state of affairs. While Moll lauds the pious life, her story subordinates the concern with such reverence to that of obtaining a more secular security.

It is something of a commonplace to say that the twentieth century's dissolution of social and cultural order and its concomitant depersonalization of the individual have led to an ever-increasing internalization in literature and philosophy and to a concern with individualized activity and the problem of personal identity. Hence, though many modern works are spoken of as "picaresque" in nature, their debt to the tradition of those novels discussed above is often tenuous and their concerns more consciously reflective and existential, as in Ralph Ellison's *Invisible Man* (1947). Two works which do, however, stand directly and admittedly in the picaresque tradition are Saul Bellow's *The Adventures of Augie March* (1953) and Thomas Mann's *Confessions of Felix Krull, Confidence Man* (1954).

"A man's character is his fate," asserts Augie March (citing Heraclitus) at the outset of his narrative, conjuring up an image of a vast world of possibilities for making something of himself in life. But by the time he comes to write his "memoirs," he is still only "a traveling man, traveling by myself [with] lots of time on my hands," tied to a less than fully devoted wife, and engaged in less than honest work on the Continent as the agent of the shady lawyer Mintouchian, work that occasionally even touches on the sordid:

And what have I been doing? Well, perhaps I had a meeting with a person who used to be in Dachau and did some business with him in dental supplies from Germany. That took an hour or two. After which I may have gone to the cold halls of the Louvre and visited in the Dutch School . . .[23]

[23] Saul Bellow, *The Adventures of Augie March*, p. 522.

64

How dismal the contrast to Augie's initial hopes. As he himself candidly notes in a faint echo of his opening lines: "I said when I started to make the record that I would be plain and heed knocks as they came, and also that a man's character was his fate. Well, then, it is obvious that this fate, or what he settles for, is also his character." For an individual who has persistently and repeatedly removed himself from the influence of so many strong figures and has always felt a "better fate" in store for himself, this reversal is sad indeed. Augie's story suddenly assumes in retrospect at least some shadings of an account born of despair.

The revelation of Augie's final position at the time of the memoir's composition does not come as a total surprise, for his life up to this point has been in large measure the familiarly picaresque one of vicissitudes ranging from petty thievery to sponsorship by or servitude to various "masters," to opportunistic attempts at profiting from marriage or friendship, to honest and prosperous work at various jobs, to adventurous escapades in the Mexican highlands, to spontaneous and sporadic attempts at selfimprovement. Much is made of his low origins and early negative influences, which cast a pall over his chances in life:

But when there is no shepherd-Sicily, no free-hand nature-painting, but deep city vexation instead, and you are forced early into deep city aims, not sent in your ephod before Eli to start service in the temple, nor set on a horse by your weeping sisters to go and study Greek in Bogotá, but land in a poolroom—what can that lead to of the highest? And what happiness or misery-antidote can it offer instead of pipes and sheep or musical, milk-drinking innocence, or even merely nature walks with a pasty instructor in goggles, or fiddle lessons? Friends, human pals, men and brethren, there is no brief, digest, or shorthand way to say where it leads. Crusoe, alone with nature, under heaven, had a busy, complicated time of it with the unhuman itself, and I am in a crowd that yields results with much more difficulty and reluctance and am part of it myself. [Pp. 84–85]

As a result of this background, there is much rationalization on Augie's part intended to excuse such enterprises as book-stealing, illegal immigrant-running, and toadying to the wealthy, all of which are viewed—at least at the time—as means to set Augie on his feet toward better things. Like the other *pícaros*, too, Augie has a certain facility and adaptability which further such enterprises and make them successful for a time:

When I face back I can recognize myself as of this time in intimate undress, with my own and family traits of hands and feet, greenness and grayness of the eyes and up-springing hair; but at myself fully clothed and at my new social passes I have to look twice. I don't know how it all at once came to me to talk a lot, tell jokes, kick up, and suddenly have views. When it was time to have them, there was no telling how I picked them from the air. [P. 125]

He also possesses an adeptness at small-time tricks and dissemblances, which makes him a natural at, for example, shoplifting and card-sharping, and he has a number of the *pícaro's* ready-made excuses for indulging in such pastimes—wanting "a change of scene," being made by nature to "live and do as worms and beetles do," or not having "the calling" for a line of endeavor like union work. And like many of his picaresque predecessors, Augie is often too quick to go along with whatever opportunity presents itself to him at a given moment: he is "adoptable," as he is fond of saying; and he fits into other people's schemes too easily and follows their leads too readily, whether it be to rob a safe, to manage a third-rate boxer, to hunt iguanas with an eagle, or to do research for a wealthy eccentric.

At the same time, however, at least to hear Augie tell it, there are many features which counterbalance the image of him as a purely directionless drifter casting about between the good life and the bad. He feels physically repulsed at the thought of participating in a major crime such as the smuggling of illegal aliens; he insists he could never have married the rich and sympathetic Lucy Magnuson purely "to get to the objective" of financial security rather than for love; he is unable to bear a grudge, even against those who wrong him; he lacks "the true sense of being a criminal" and consequently often fails or is caught skimming store profits or cheating customers. This line of retrospective commentary could easily sound like the facile, self-serving gloss of a typically amoral rogue, were several corroborating acts of genuine human feeling not also recounted: Augie's frequent and touching visits to his nearly blind mother and his half-wit brother Georgie in their respective "homes"; his selfless loyalty to the waitress Mimi Villars during her abortion ordeal, which finally ruins his chances with Lucy; his instinctive admiration of the eagle Caligula's refusal to submit totally to human domination and to kill on command; his never once contemplating theft from the likes of the entrepreneur Einhorn, the slightly mad millionaire Robey, or the socially elite Renlings. Perhaps his most important virtue is his "opposition," his ultimate refusal to let other people "make what they wanted" of him—to let Thea turn him into a thrill-seeking outdoorsman, to let his brother Simon mold him into a ruthless businessman, to let the Renlings make a well-set young dandy of him. These actions paint him in a positive light and lend some substance to his dreams of a better fate: "I had looked all my life for the right thing to do, for a fate good enough." And Augie repeats this dream so incessantly and with such resilient enthusiasm for so long that the reader is ultimately drawn into sympathy with him when he asserts, for example:

Well, now, who can really expect the daily facts to go, toil or prisons to go, oatmeal and laundry tickets and all the rest, and insist that all moments be raised to the greatest importance, demand that everyone breathe the pointy, star-furnished air at its highest difficulty, abolish all brick, vaultlike rooms, all dreariness, and live like prophets or gods? Why, everybody knows this triumphant life can only be periodic. So there's a schism about it, some saying only this triumphant life is real and others that only the daily facts are. For me there was no debate, and I made speed into the former. [P. 194]

Because of this sympathy that Augie evokes during the course of his narrative, his occasional morose moments and hints of a creeping, negative fatalism are unsettling but by and large offset through his recuperative powers and the optimism with which he strikes forth on some new path. Once his final status is revealed, however, these fatalistic tones loom larger and cast a retrospective gloom over his memoir:

I wasn't proud of myself, believe me, and my stubbornness about a "higher," independent fate. I was no wizard, for sure, nor gazetted as anything illustrious, nor billed to stand up to Apollyon with his horrible scales and bear's feet, nor slated to find the answer to all my shames . . . There was no such first-rate thing that I could boast, and who was I, not to make up my mind and be so obstinate? [P. 424]

And this is what mere humanity always does. It's made up of these inventors or artists, millions and millions of them, each in his own way trying to recruit other people to play a supporting role and sustain him in his make-believe. . . . That's the struggle of humanity, to recruit others to your version of what's real. Then even the flowers and the moss on the stones become the moss and the flowers of a version. I certainly looked like an ideal recruit. But the invented things never became real for me no matter how I urged myself to think they were. [P. 402]

Very good and bravo! Let's have this better, nobler reality. Still, when such an assertion as this is backed by one person and maintained for a long time, obstinacy finally gets the upper hand. The beauty of it is harmed by what it suffers on the way to proof. I know that. [P. 316]

There is a darkness. It is for everyone. You don't, as perhaps some imagine, try it, one foot into it like a barbershop "September Morn." Nor are lowered into it with visitor's curiosity, as the old Eastern monarch was let down into the weeds inside a glass ball to observe the fishes. Nor are lifted straight out after an unlucky tumble, like a Napoleon from the mud of the Arcole. [P. 175]

God may save all, but human rescue is only for a few. [P. 152]

To reread or recall such statements in the light of Augie's illicit dealings and unhappy arrangement in Europe at the narrative's end is to see his career in less than the glowing colors of eternal optimism and opportunity. And further, to hear him conclude with yet another rebound into the positive affirmation of mobility, search, and endeavor is a somewhat incongruous experience:

I was still chilled from the hike across the fields, but, thinking of Jacqueline and Mexico, I got to grinning again. That's the *animal ridens* in me, the laughing creature, forever rising up. . . . Look at me, going everywhere! Why, I am a sort of Columbus of those near-at-hand and believe you can come to them in this immediate *terra incognita* that spreads out in every gaze. I may well be a flop at this line of endeavor. Columbus too thought he was a flop, probably, when they sent him back in chains. Which didn't prove there was no America. [P. 536]

The bright hope of a Columbus voyaging toward the discovery of he knows not what is an ennobling one; and as Augie has pointed out earlier, unhappy people such as Rousseau and Marx have "persisted in thinking of the best, and the best only, . . . still wanting to set themselves apart for great ends, and believing in at least one worthiness." But his own experiences offer no firm prospect that he will ever attain an America or achieve a truly better fate.

Augie's opting for "triumphant life" over the "daily facts" has effectively alienated him from reality—a fact he has failed to estimate correctly, despite his candid soul-searching and self-analysis. Even at the conclusion of his story, as he is walking across that frozen Belgian field with the maid Jacqueline, his efforts to follow her lead and sing for warmth fail dismally; and when farmyard dogs rush to greet them, he backs off in fright as they bound at the homely woman and lick her face. Augie can only retreat from such reality to the cold city of Bruges or to the cold halls of the Louvre, as always, laughing at Jacqueline and at nature. This continued refusal to believe in the reality of the human condition has in it elsewhere in the memoir a spark of something truly sublime; but in this concrete closing scene and in the face of Augie's experiences it is also supremely self-defeating both to his life and to his narrative.

Felix Krull's *Confessions* are the recollections of a congenial con artist, unfortunately never completed by Thomas Mann and covering only the early years of Krull's career. The narrative position from which Felix's delightful parade of adventures is recounted is alluded to only briefly and sporadically but is nonetheless recognizable as that of an ex-prisoner, forty years of age, living "in complete retirement" where "I no longer feel the old irrepressible urge toward the society of men."[24] The narrator is in good health, but haggard of features and "tired, so tired that I shall only be able to proceed by short stages and with frequent pauses for rest"—as he in fact demonstrates at least once when, at the outset of book 2, he allows that "indifference toward the enterprise and doubt of [his] success" have kept him from continuing his confessions, so that the papers have lain idle for at least a year.

Without indulging in fruitless speculation as to how Mann would have developed the narrative position as Felix's life progressed to the point where he actually landed in prison and then in "retirement," I think it is readily apparent that there exists a marked disparity between the worn and weary nature of the recluse and the sprightly comedy and joie de vivre which characterize his narrative: "In any event, the assertion that he is destined to enjoy good fortune sounds odd coming from a spent man who, having just been released from prison, now recalls his days of past glory."[25] The Felix of these early years lives up to his name fully, enjoying only good fortune and success, reveling in human contact, and thoroughly relishing the worlds of nature and art. The older Felix has tasted what seems to have been a serious defeat which has depleted him spiritually and physically, to judge from his few remarks on his present state. The very paucity of these remarks, coupled with the otherwise consistently sustained tone of sparkling humor and vitality, gives rise to the thought that

[24] Thomas Mann, *Confessions of Felix Krull, Confidence Man*, trans. Denver Lindley, bk. 1, chap. 2.

[25] Klaus Hermsdorf, *Thomas Manns Schelme: Figuren und Strukturen des Komischen*, p. 54. Translations from secondary sources are my own unless otherwise noted.

Felix's entire narrative is the unconsciously self-deluding exercise
of a failed and unhappy man lolling in the memories of brighter
times when his life actually did correspond to his image of himself as Fortune's favored son. He seems virtually to become as one
with that former self for long stretches of the novel through a kind
of "transfiguring sympathy":

> Perhaps this is Mann's bold epic artistic concept: Krull, who following
> his prison stay narrates his life as a lonely, tired, prematurely aged man
> (he is still only forty years old), is already so far removed from this life
> that it seems to lie in some distant, dreamlike realm, transfigured by
> memory, in which the rememberer confronts his former self with sur-
> prise, admiration and astonishment.[26]

This submersion of the present self into the past self results in our
extensive firsthand acquaintance with the thoughts, conversations, experiences, and reactions of the young Krull, while the
older narrator, when he does emerge in person, does so almost
exclusively to admire or to expound in retrospect upon his young
self—praising his looks, his air of nobility, his lovemaking, his
sensitivity—and not to indulge in any lately acquired philosophy
or morality. The epic situation is thus rife with the likelihood of
unreliable narration: the story of an amazingly successful confidence man's career, told with verve and loving wit by the rogue
himself at a time when success has crumbled so completely that
he avoids all but the most cursory allusions to the ultimate failure
of that career.

Concerning Felix's narrative itself, the old familiar features
already encountered with many of the earlier *pícaros*—verbal
adroitness, self-praise, lack of extensive education and erudition,
ingrained role-playing, and frequent superficiality of perception—once again are in evidence. In certain particulars these
traits are developed to a much higher degree than in Krull's predecessors, a fact substantiated at least in part by the long, uninter-

[26] Joachim Müller, "Glücksspiel und Göttermythe: Zu Thomas Manns 'Krull,'" *Vollendung und Größe Thomas Manns*, pg. 234.

rupted string of good fortune which Felix's talents and qualities bring him. First, he is a consummate master with words, able to produce a charming and often overwhelming line of patter with anyone from foreign whores to kings, to speak for minutes on end in tongues with which he has had only minimal contact (e.g., his conversation with the hotel director Stürzli), and to expound at length and with great ardor on subjects in which he has only the most superficial knowledge (nature, Kuckuck's cosmic history). A Parisian jewelry fence compliments Felix's "oily tongue," Stürzli raves about the "poetry" of the lift-boy's speech, the Marquis de Venosta marvels at his elegant phrasing and facility of style, the young Portuguese beauty Zouzou notes his conversational "adroitness," and Felix himself frequently refers in glowing terms to his "glibness," his ability to talk "like a book," and his often "inspired" loquaciousness in situations such as the draft-board sequence and the interview with Dom Carlos I of Portugal.

Felix's gab is all form and without substance, however, a virtuoso exercise in mimicry which is at bottom a forged reproduction of a series of styles and on a series of topics, just like his forged notes to the school authorities in his childhood days and his bogus letters to the Marquis's parents; like the elegant stage figure cut by the ugly, aging Müller-Rosé, it is in essence an elaborate masquerade. That substance is lacking in Felix's talk is readily evident through his own "misgivings" about his educational background, his only sporadic attendance at school, his ignorance of, for example, history and myth in his encounters with Kuckuck and Mme Houpflé followed by his rote references to their ideas (on "spontaneous generations" and Hermes respectively) in later instances, and his genuine lack of noble standing and cosmopolitan experience in contrast to the image he projects. His lofty philosophy and convincing shows of sickness or nobility or whatever are thus mere magnificent double-talk and sham. They are honestly believed by Felix at times, it appears, but already they constitute a "most murderous parody of the solemnity of idealism" and "a process by which the shallowness of all high-sounding principles is revealed—not by attacking them, but by professing them in all sincerity."[27]

Felix's language is, like his entire life, an elaborate and continuous form of role-playing wherein even he does not know at what point his real character ends and the assumed role begins. Preceding his account of the chance meeting with the Marquis, Felix himself says:

But I have already divulged the answer: from time to time, by way of experiment and practice in living the higher life, I would dine in some elegant restaurant on the rue de Rivoli or the avenue des Champs-Elysees or in some hotel of the same quality as my own, or finer if possible, the Ritz, the Bristol, the Meurice, and would afterward take a loge seat in some good theatre devoted to the spoken drama or comic opera or even grand opera. This amounted, as one can see, to a kind of dual existence, whose charm lay in the ambiguity as to which figure was the real I and which the masquerade: was I the liveried *commis-de-salle* who waited on and flattered the guests in the Saint James and Albany, or was I the unknown man of distinction who looked as though he must keep a riding-horse and who would certainly, once he had finished dinner, call in at various exclusive salons but was meanwhile graciously permitting himself to be served by waiters among whom I found none equal to me in my other role? Thus I masqueraded in both capacities, and the undisguised reality behind the two appearances, the real I, could not be identified because it actually did not exist. [Bk. 3, chap. 3]

This is astounding candor in a picaresque narrator and of course a perfectly accurate assessment of his position. But at the same time the analysis is an admission of Felix's inability to recognize or define his true character and virtually a confession that, at bottom, he has no character, only a wide assortment of masks, a continuous alternation of appearances: "Felix the 'clothes horse' is Proteus. . . . For his Being is no existence at all but rather remains pure *essentia*, endless possibility, freely at the disposal of

[27] Oskar Seidlin, "Picaresque Elements in Thomas Mann's Work," p. 196.

the imagination."[28] This inability further prevents Felix from recognizing, from his present standpoint, the yawning gap between his persistent vision of a Fortune-blessed life and the course which that life has taken, the cleft between the imagined appearance and the substantive reality:

The actual substance of Krull's actions stands in contradiction to his fluent, glossing commentary. The reality which constantly pierces his complacent stylization discredits his eloquence. The unconcealable difference between assertion and reality becomes the very source of the comedy—and it is of course a comedy at Krull's expense.[29]

Thus, for all his self-praise, lofty intentions (of writing a complete confessional for the perceptive and sensitive reader), and personable courting of the reader, Felix does not prove a convincing and reliable narrator:

When mention is made of memorable occurrences or of a confessional work or even of an "intellectual undertaking," an "instructional work giving an account of my life," something gives us pause to think. Such expressions sound at least pretentious and have an air of somewhat importunate *captationes benevolentiae* about them.[30]

Instead, he emerges through his own account as the butt of authorial irony. Felix has been seen as many things to the implicit presence of Mann behind the narrative: one in a line of "sons" who embody the decaying and disinherited status of a dying age; one in an equally long line of essentially useless and occasionally reprehensible artists who are variously childish or demonic but always have something of the charlatan and the failed burgher about them;[31] and at the same time a figure with some traits of

---

[28] Richard Baumgart, *Das Ironische und die Ironie in den Werken Thomas Manns,* p. 187.
[29] Hermsdorf, *Thomas Manns Schelme,* p. 59.
[30] Müller, *Vollendung,* p. 234.
[31] Compare Hermsdorf, *Thomas Manns Schelme,* pp. 45–47.

Mann himself.[32] Krull's narrative is also demonstrably many other things to the author: in its original conception (1906), the inspired fictional analogue to the memoir of the real-life con man Georges Manolescu; in its first version (1911), a satyr play to the tragedy of the just-completed *Death in Venice*;[33] a parody of the eighteenth-century autobiography, particularly Goethe's *Poetry and Truth*;[34] a burlesque of confessional literature from Augustine to Rousseau, as indicated by the title which Mann gives the novel;[35] and a fictional effort at personally coming to terms with his own artistic nature and his relationship to tradition.[36]

Through the parodic intents of the author, Felix becomes the egotistical and unreliable autobiographer who unwittingly ironizes both himself and the literary and social traditions from which he springs.[37] Yet through the personal and sympathetic bonds which link him to Mann, Felix is never damned by this multilevel irony. Instead, he remains "the most endearing product of Thomas Mann's antipathy toward satire,"[38] the issue and

---

[32] Several incidents and locales in the novel, as well as the problem of the artist as charlatan, have frequently been identified and sometimes acknowledged as autobiographical. See particularly Hermsdorf, *Thomas Manns Schelme*; Müller, *Vollendung*; and Hans Wysling, "Archivalisches Gewühle: Zur Entstehungsgeschichte der *Bekenntnisse des Hochstaplers Felix Krull*," for discussion of such elements.

[33] Compare Wysling, "Archivalisches Gewühle," p. 241.

[34] Compare Thomas Mann, *Lebensabriß*, vol. 12 (1930), p. 408: "What enchanted me stylistically was the still untried autobiographical directness, . . . and a fantastic intellectual fascination emanated from the parodistic idea of transposing an element of cherished tradition, the Goethean self-creating autobiographical element, the aristocratic-confessional line, into the realm of criminality."

[35] It is also interesting to note that Felix himself never refers to himself as a confidence man (*Hochstapler*). Hence the indication of Mann's implicit presence through the title.

[36] Mann himself says in his *Lebensabriß* that the work "may in a certain sense be the most personal one, since it depicts my relationship to tradition, which is at once loving and dissolvent."

[37] Compare Baumgart, *Das Ironische*, p. 192: "Even the narrative form of the novel comes through as a parody of the Goethean self-creating autobiographical element, . . . despite Krull's own intent. For while Proteus, this time in the role of a conservative German burgher, feels the traditional dignity of his recitational form to be thoroughly fitting and so with his 'natural gift for good form' seriously adopts it, all these stylistic means are for Thomas Mann a transparent con game and the object of secret merriment."

[38] Hermsdorf, *Thomas Manns Schelme*, p. 62.

object of a sympathetic and positive parodic bent rather than a destructive or negative one.

The *pícaro*'s fictional autobiography, then, may take any one of several forms, but almost invariably it produces a situation of narrative unreliability. Whether the rogue narrates from a standpoint of religious or moral conversion, of penal servitude, of tainted success, of dismal failure, or of some combination of these four, his epic situation in every case clashes to some degree with the subject matter of his narrative, either in logical or in moral terms. He is first of all egotistical enough to attach importance to the story of his roguish or even petty life and to cast that story in the first-person form, audacious enough to fill that story with perpetual self-praise and self-indulgence, and presumptuous enough to assert that his narrative will be both entertaining and edifying to the reader. As Oskar Seidlin notes concerning *Felix Krull*:

It is the basic implication of a first-person narrative that the world has been swallowed up, that the "I" has become the center of all things. In this very form, the form of the autobiography, lies the intrinsic ironical connotation of the picaresque novel. The discrepancy between the wretched, lowly Picaro who does not amount to anything in this world, and the effrontery with which he dares to say "I," is in itself a piece of *blague*, of persiflage and roguery. . . . In the case of Thomas Mann this persiflage, only tacitly implied in the picaresque novels by their very form, is quite conscious and one of the sources of most refined delight. That the unreformed scoundrel dares call the report on his mischievous tricks *Bekenntnisse*, thus evoking associations with two of the most profound and soul-searching literary documents of mankind, St. Augustine's and Jean Jacques Rousseau's *Confessions*, is in itself the height of impertinence, a slap in the face of anything honest, sincere, and serious.[39]

Second, the *pícaro* is often an incorrigible, ambitious, scheming, role-playing, mask-wearing, and essentially characterless

[39] Seidlin, "Picaresque Elements," p. 192.

master of physical and verbal pose whose picaresque attributes have become so ingrained that he himself has difficulty in distinguishing truth from appearance and substance from form. For that reason, again, his narrative must be viewed with a prima facie skepticism. Third, psychological forces such as shame, guilt, inferiority, vengefulness, or unfounded optimism distort the picaresque narrator's vision of his life and world and consequently exert an adverse effect on the objectiveness of his account. Fourth, the presence of the implied author's hand is always discernible behind the narrator's back—whether all but invisibly as Lazarillo scurries to defend himself against rumors of moral impropriety, whether surreptitiously through the emergence of, for example, typically Mannian themes (the charlatan artist, the Hermes and Proteus figures) or characteristically Quevedoan cynicism and verbal brilliance, or whether through direct authorial address such as that provided by Defoe's "editor" in *Moll Flanders.*

And fifth, the skepticism engendered by the above factors is increased by the retrospective vantage point from which all the picaresque accounts examined here are narrated; for each *pícaro's* final state and consequent attitudes color his entire narrative almost completely and occasion a high degree of dissonance between the robustness of many of the adventures recounted, on the one hand, and the lately acquired tone of religious fervor or despairing failure on the other. In some cases this discrepancy is apparent from the outset or at an early point: Lazarillo addressing Your Honor to defend himself concerning his "case"; Felix Krull lamenting his fatigue and implying his ultimate failure in the world; Moll, Simplicius, and Guzmán intoning explicit themes of edification and moral warning. In others the dissonance is not fully struck until late: Lucius's conversion and initiation in the final chapter of his tale; Pablos's closing references to his ignominious failures in the New World; Augie's distasteful dealings in European contraband. Whether early or late, this dissonance has the effect, on the stylistic level, of turning an episodic, digressive, entertaining, and frequently ribald tale into a solemn address or even a hortatory sermon (for example, the narratives by Lucius, Moll, and Simplicius); at the very least it adds a discordantly negative conclusion to a lively if not always flattering parade of adventures (the accounts by Pablos and Augie in particular). Given the natures of the conversions and failures producing this dissonance, the result is in each case an unsettling insecurity regarding the intent, authority, and veracity of the picaresque narrator.

The sum of these elements is a work which, to paraphrase the critic Hermsdorf, demands the unconditional independent collaboration of the reader, who must put together his own picture from the various levels of the presentation. The author does not explicitly pass judgment on the *pícaro*, but instead limits himself to guiding that judgment. The picaresque narrative unfailingly provides a largely or wholly enjoyable reading experience via its lively, raucous account of adventures or misadventures through all levels of society. But it is just as unfailingly provides serious social, moral, or cultural satire or parody in varying degrees of severity, using unreliable narration as both the means toward and the frequent embodiment of these serious ends.

CHAPTER 4

The Clown

THE ORIGIN of the fool or clown, much like that of the *pícaro*, can be traced to the social parasite of second-century Greece and to Plutarch's accounts of parasites at the courts of Philip and Alexander, as Enid Welsford relates in her exhaustive study on the subject.[1] Whether a transient or a permanent retainer of the house, such a parasite earned his keep through the amusement and diversion which his presence provided for host and guests alike. The amusement often took rather scurrilous forms such as outright raillery, lewd behavior, and obscene stories, likely as not making one or more of the guests the butt of the fun, to the great delight of the latter's co-celebrants. But most often the source of amusement was simply the generally base figure cut by the buffoonish parasite himself, whether by his very nature or by design— "that 'sudden glory at the sight of an inferior,' which Hobbes most characteristically . . . believed to be the one mainspring of all laughter."[2] Even earlier, as far back as the sixth century B.C., dwarfs, freaks, and idiots of every sort were kept at court and in the more affluent houses for the sheer physical curiosity and novelty of their appearance, speech, or antics—the more grotesque, the better—and also in the superstitious belief that the presence of such "possessed" or "afflicted" creatures was beneficial in ward-

[1] Enid Welsford, *The Fool: His Social and Literary History.*
[2] Ibid., p. 50. Welsford does not share Hobbes's view, however.

ing off evil. The babble of these genuine grotesques and half-wits was allowed virtually total impunity, of course—for who could take serious offense at the rantings of an idiot?—and this impunity was largely carried over in the later Roman period both to those freaks who did in fact not possess their wits and to more normal physical types who chose to adopt the life of parasite and buffoon. On the basis of several anecdotes in the writings of Martial, for example, it is apparent that "already in Rome a distinction was drawn between the 'artificial' and the 'natural' fool; and it is possible that occasionally the dwarf-fools were quite sane and tickled their masters' sense of humor as well as their degenerate curiosity."[3]

Thus what Pliny termed the "folly from a professed fool (*stultum a morione*)" derived from a tradition which effectively gave free rein to the wit and the imagination, a license which the fool generally used to perpetrate the most insulting and scabrous behavior for the entertainment of house or court but which also allowed some rarer types to develop the higher arts of mime and narrative invention. The resulting performances and tales by and large remained at the grosser level of the scatological, the sexual, and the exploitative from late Roman times to the late Middle Ages, and many such tales were only the embellished or even fictitious, self-serving accounts of the narrator's own purported adventures (here again the paths of the *pícaro* and the fool are joined). Nonetheless, the evolution of the "artificial" fool from insult artist and idiot-imitator to raconteur and mime did lay the groundwork for the clown-buffoon-fool's eventual transition from court and banquet hall to stage and print in the late medieval period, when he merged with another figure: the clown king of the traditional religious and fertility festivals.

By the fifteenth century the festival clown—"some honest countryman who on certain days of the year blackened his face, dressed up and talked nonsense, for no other reason except that his fathers had done it before him, and that in some undefined

[3] Ibid., p. 59.

way it would bring good luck"[4]—retained hardly any of the old religious significance, but instead afforded the designated personage "an admirable opportunity for dramatic experiment and satirical comment" which he came to use to full advantage:

He was a "Fool," the elected "King of Fools": very well, then, he would exercise the fool's right of free speech, and he would model himself on the ways of the court rather than of the country village; he would in fact adopt the dress, assume the role, and claim the privileges of the court-jester. And so the two divergent types of fool come to be reunited in the person of "the Lord of Misrule," who is none other than the traditional mock-king and clown, who has adopted the appearance and behaviour of the court-jester and in that guise exerts an influence on literature and the drama quite beyond the scope of his simpler brother.[5]

Complex socioeconomic circumstances outside the scope of the present investigation led the clergy to sanction such "intermittent public folly" as "a safety-valve, a permitted form of relief and relaxation." This approbation permitted the rise of various *sociétés joyeuses* such as the Enfants-Sans-Souci, who in their turn appropriated the idea of folly as "a mask for the wise and an armour for the critic, . . . adopting the role and tacitly claiming the privilege of the licensed court fool." In this manner

. . . the Sociétés Joyeuses undoubtedly popularized and universalized and gave significance to the figure of the court-fool. The French Lord of Misrule was in fact a middleman who conveyed the cap and bells from the shaven heads of the half-witted into the creative imagination of the philosopher, the satirist and the comic poet.[6]

From crude court buffoons and ordinary peasants in festival garb to *sottie* clowns to the subtle and masterful irony of Erasmus is therefore not such an incredible leap as it may appear. The reversal of convention which came to characterize most of the fool

---

[4] Ibid., p. 199.
[5] Ibid., pp. 200.
[6] Ibid., pp. 218–19.

societies had produced not only the spectacle of worthless knaves masquerading under the veneer of wealth, learning, and respectability, but also the "sage fool," the clown as truth-teller, "whose real insight was thinly disguised as a form of insanity."[7] Simple irony, variations of meaning, ambiguities of definition, and possibilities for reversal and counter-reversal were thus already present in the comedy of the *sottie*. Erasmus's distinction is, in Walter J. Kaiser's assessment, the fact that he was "the first post-classical author to employ irony in any *sustained* fashion and to perceive its infinite possibilities." Kaiser continues:

In much the same way, Erasmus may be said to have given Europe the paradox of the Wise Fool. For though that personified oxymoron is at least as old as Socrates and Christ, and though its medieval ancestors and apologists are legion, its first modern, and most influential, appearance is as the figure of Stultitia in the *Moriae Encomium*.[8]

Although Erasmus's *Praise of Folly* (1511) is descended directly from the unreliable-speaker traditions of the comic societies' foolish gentlemen and sage fools, the possibility of misreading the work is evident in its first critic, Martin Dorp, who harumphed that Erasmus should write a praise of wisdom as a corrective. Apparently Dorp was unaware even of the obvious reverse implications of a pronouncement by Folly herself, not to mention the "humanistically transcendent sentiments informing both overt statement and implied opposite."[9] The epistle dedicatory alone should have given the critic a clue: the absurd suggestion that the dedicatee, Sir Thomas More, of all people, should need a clarifying preface; the corollary that the ostensibly private epistle is therefore meant for public consumption; the wordplay on "More" and *moriae*; the style, with its double and triple negatives and its many qualifiers, creating confusion and ambiguity; the repeated remarks about laughter and edification; the string of con-

[7] Ibid., p. 239.
[8] Walter J. Kaiser, *Praisers of Folly: Erasmus, Rabelais, Shakespeare*, p. 21.
[9] Ibid., p. 23.

ventional rhetorical disclaimers (a scholarly thing written *en voyage* merely to pass the time); the acknowledged use of a mask. All these features should have marked *The Praise of Folly* as a game of wit, a trifle, but one with hints of serious concerns and strict formality—as both classical oratory and games in general tend to be.[10] The title too, with its Latin genitive that could be read both as objective (Praise of Folly) and subjective (Folly's Praise), should have indicated that more than mere foolishness is at work here: not only is the praise a mock encomium, but the mocking itself is mocked through its delivery by the voice of Folly. Dorp should at least have seen that it is wrong to take Stultitia literally. His missing the doubling of the irony is more excusable, for therein lay Erasmus's great innovation: the fashioning of a new kind of irony in which it is equally wrong to take as the final truth the *opposite* of what Stultitia says. The irony, in Erasmus's hands, *becomes* the meaning and does not simply affect it.[11] Kaiser explains:

In Stultitia's analysis of the true nature of prudence, we have a paradigm of the method Erasmus generally employs to effect a transvaluation of values. A value (prudence) is transvaluated by means of praising its opposite (rashness and self-deception); the fool's gold of both is refined by the alchemy of the fool into the pure gold of a new value (true prudence based on understanding). The reader is led into this transvaluation gradually and unwittingly, as satire turns to sympathy. For the Erasmian technique is to begin with satire; and on the simplest level, this advocacy of rashness and self-deception from the mouth of a fool is nothing more than satire. . . . As Stultitia begins her attack on prudence we are doubtless expected to read it as we should any other satire and reject what she ironically praises. Yet in the end the satire is spoiled, *manquée*. A humanity, a sympathy for human frailty inevitably enters in . . . and deflects the point of the satirical dagger. For rashness looked at in a certain way may actually be prudence. To live at all is a kind of rashness, but it is better to live than not to live. It is better, and finally more prudent, to accept experience and learn from it than to retreat to the so-called prudence of those who claim to learn about life in their

[10] Ibid., p. 34.
[11] Ibid., p. 38.

83

libraries. . . . By means of this argument, it is not so much rashness and self-deception that Erasmus advocates as a new kind of prudence, a prudence which is redefined and revaluated in the very process of praising, partly in satire, partly in sympathy, its opposite.[12]

Stultitia's mask does occasionally slip to reveal part of the face of Erasmus, as in her vilification of false clergymen, pompous orators, and mindless princes; but on the whole her encomium maintains the equipoise of that transcendent double irony just set forth. "The truth she derives from polar opposites is the dynamic truth Erasmus believed in, and her irony is the logical mode of expression both for a quality of mind that perpetually perceived the qualifying *but* to any argument and for an empathy of heart that participated actively in all aspects of being without committing itself exclusively to any one."[13] And the message she delivers is precisely that given by Saint Paul to first-century Athens:

"Let no man deceive himself. If any man among you seemeth to be wise in this world, let him become a fool, that he may be wise." It is this final paradox—that folly is wisdom and wisdom folly—that, with its Christian ramifications, informs the whole of Stultitia's speech. Even pleasure, which so often seems her final goal, is not an end in itself but a means to a further end, the wisdom of folly. With this paradox she begins her speech, when she claims that she is not ignorant; and with the same paradox she ends it, when she quotes a lost play of Aeschylus to say that even a fool may speak in season. It is . . . the basis of her irony, but it is also the burden of her message.[14]

Perhaps the most notable clown-narrator between Folly and her twentieth-century successors is Tristram Shandy in Laurence Sterne's *The Life and Opinions of Tristram Shandy, Gentleman* (1759–67). Dressed in cap and gown and slinging ink all about as he fights his antic battle against time and his own digressive tendencies in an ostensible effort to impart the story of his life and

[12] Ibid., p. 61.
[13] Ibid., p. 93.
[14] Ibid., p. 84.

opinions, Tristram cuts a ridiculous figure, to say the very least. To take him at his word and read on with the expectation of eventually being presented with that promised story can ultimately lead only to confusion, consternation, and such sour disappointment as that expressed by William Thackeray, who disapprovingly termed Sterne-Shandy "a great jester, not a great humourist." [15] An even ruder disappointment is experienced by the fictitious Madams and Good Sirs addressed throughout the book who alternately doze off or facetiously and piquedly ask after irrelevant realistic details, which of course are never forthcoming. The author's dedication to Pitt, like that of Erasmus to More, should have provided a clear indication to the contrary, speaking as it does of the "constant endeavour to fence against the infirmities of ill health, and other evils of life, by mirth." [16] The same applies to the first page's strong implication that Tristram's begetting was carried out in such a fashion as could only produce a creature whose "motions and activity" would ever "go cluttering like hey-go-mad" and also to his enjoinder a few pages later:

Therefore, my dear friend and companion, if you should think me somewhat sparing of my narrative on my first setting out,—bear with me,—and let me go on, and tell my story my own way:—or if I should seem now and then to trifle upon the road,—or should sometimes put on a fool's cap with a bell to it, for a moment or two as we pass along,—don't fly off,—but rather courteously give me credit for a little more wisdom than appears upon my outside;—as we jog on, either laugh with me, or at me, or in short, do any thing,—only keep your temper. [Bk. 1, chap. 6]

If these rather obvious and direct statements do not suffice to reveal the clown at work and play, then the shortly ensuing references to Don Quixote, Sancho Panza, and Yorick (of Danish extraction, no less) might key the appropriate response. And if not these, then perhaps any of a thousand things that follow: the ab-

[15] William Makepeace Thackeray, "Sterne and Goldsmith," in his *English Humourists of the Eighteenth Century*, p. 169.
[16] Laurence Sterne, *The Life and Opinions of Tristram Shandy, Gentleman.*

surd re-creation of formal rhetorical devices such as the "Virgin Dedication" or the much-belated "Author's Preface" which finally appears in book 3; the inclusion of such mock-learned apparati as medical disquisitions, the interpolated tale of Slawkenbergius, the essays upon subjects of ostensibly great import (noses, chapters), and the references to famous classics of philosophy and literature; the mad typography and the inclusion of blank pages, marbled pages, and diagrams of various ilk; the constant losing of the thread of the story of Tristram's birth; and the narrator's hilarious "forgetfulness" which leaves characters tapping ashes from pipes, listening at keyholes, or thrashing about the marriage bed for thirty pages or more before correcting the interruptus. It should also be most difficult to take seriously any narrator who speaks of his account as a smoothly rolling machine and who even diagrams his work's flow, yet originally described his technique as merely writing the first sentence and trusting God for the rest. And if anyone has the misfortune to labor through nine books without realizing that a proper story of Tristram's life and opinions will never be given here, then surely the novel's famous closing lines—spoken, appropriately enough, by Yorick, the classic jester's namesake—will tell him he's been had: "L——d! said my mother, what is all this story about?—A COCK and a BULL, said *Yorick*—And one of the best of its kind, I ever heard."

Tristram Shandy is, then, on one level an enormous and sustained leg-pull, a shaggy-dog story to end all shaggy-dog stories. And the telling of that story is the work's primary interest. Hence Tristram's interminable obsession with the business of narration, the constant worry that he will never catch up with time and bring his story up to the present, his repeated bantering with the reader over details and the progress of the story. Hence the frequent comments on what he is doing or has done or will do and on how he is doing it or has done it or will do it, and his almost equally frequent "failure" to do the thing promised or his occasional sudden "recollection" of a thing he has left in abeyance while indulging in one of his myriad "progressive" digressions.

On the surface he is the circus clown trying to negotiate the tumbling artist's trampoline only to fall repeatedly on his face, Stan Laurel attempting to close all the drawers of a devilishly self-willed bureau, Chaplin trying to cope with a seemingly malevolent conveyor belt. And as with those film clowns, the immediate result of Tristram's efforts is total farce and a comic portrait of the artist who wreaks only havoc at his attempted task.

The joke is first of all on Tristram himself, as with all clowns, for he takes nine volumes to pratfall his way through two story threads which could easily be rendered in a hundred pages or so—his birth, circumcision, and breeching, and Uncle Toby's "affair" with the Widow Wadman. A corresponding joke is on the characters of the story, who all ride their respective hobby-horses in a fashion not unlike Tristram's efforts at storytelling and who succeed only in exasperating both themselves and their fellows or sink into the blissful escape of whistling "Lillabullero."

The reader of *Tristram Shandy* comes in for his lumps too, at least to the extent that he brings with him any normal expectations of continuity, consequentiality, and coherence in the usual sense, or of any overt moral lesson imparted through readily apparent satire or parody. There is of course a great deal of satire and parody in the book—of Tristram as narrator, of numerous philosophical and intellectual traditions, of social customs, of character types—but it is all, on balance, of a sympathetic cast and really only incidental,[17] as was that of Stultitia. Its first purpose is delight and not destructive vituperation, as even Tristram himself realizes when he speaks of imparting a lesson in Shandeism, which "makes the wheel of life run long and chearfully round" and produces (he hopes) "a kingdom of hearty laughing subjects." But its second and higher purpose, again like that of *The Praise of Folly*, is implicit and instructive. Tristram is something of a "wise fool" and has inklings of a serious intent when he prays "that God would give my subjects grace to be as wise as they

---

[17] Compare Wayne C. Booth, *The Rhetoric of Fiction*, p. 230; and John M. Stedmond, *The Comic Art of Laurence Sterne*, p. 89.

87

were merry"; yet the conveying of this lesson is more a function of the competent author whose presence in the wings Tristram's clownish performance implies.[18] For Tristram's chaotic narration is ultimately indistinguishable from what he relates, so that a "seamless web of subject and treatment" is created within "a work that gives an air of complete disorganization."[19]

Tristram as clown-narrator, then, is Sterne's mask, and "the very fact of having recourse to fiction, of assuming a mask, presupposes, beyond all personal reasons for disguise, an intention of a much higher order."[20] The nature of Sterne's intention is perhaps best summarized by Ian Watt in his introduction to the Riverside edition of *Tristram Shandy*:

The members of Sterne's society, comprising both the fictional characters in the book and its circle of readers, belong, it is true, to the genus *homo ludens* rather than to *homo sapiens*. But why not? If we concede that there are games of varying seriousness, and that some of them exercise the head and heart rather strenuously, we surely have a sufficient justification for most of literature; and certainly for *Tristram Shandy*. It is through imaginative play that we learn about ourselves, and a very few authors have been as honest teachers as Sterne, though there are no doubt some lessons we have to look for elsewhere. Tristram's voice is not an interior monologue, but it is attuned to the endless dialogue within us, which is so much more inconsequential, indecent, and above all— shall we face it—trivial, than the public dialogues we can hear going on around us, or than we can find in most recorded literature; Sterne's sad recognition of this discrepancy enabled him to create a mode of speech for Tristram which compels what he most desired—our acknowledgment of intimate kinship. And once the Shandean laughter has punctured the authorized hyperboles which make it so difficult for us to recognize our real identity, the remembering mind can sometimes go on beyond this to discover that real feeling and a kind of logic somehow subsist and even trace a shadowy coherence upon the muddled and miscellaneous indignities of our personal lot. [P. xxxv]

[18] Compare Stedmond, *Comic Art*, p. 67.

[19] Booth, *Rhetoric*, pp. 223–24.

[20] Henri Fluchère, *Laurence Sterne: From Tristram to Yorick. An Interpretation of "Tristram Shandy"*, p. 342.

"Sterne's comic irony is, then, in a measure Erasmian," John Stedmond says, "though it has undergone many changes from the original. The main difficulty with Erasmian irony . . . is in trying to assess its complex significance. It cannot simply be turned upside down—both of its polar meanings must be given full consideration. The implications of Sterne's irony, like Erasmus', are not quite so obvious as some readers have assumed. Most of the characters in *Tristram Shandy* are 'fools,' though they represent different kinds of folly."[21] What Erasmus achieves on a high religio-philosophical level through his patently mock-rhetorical exercise in having Folly praise folly, Sterne accomplishes on a more general social level through a deliberately chaotic and unrealistic fictional narrative. This narrative constantly denies any suspension of disbelief and continually calls attention to its own artifice, practically pleading for an ironical attitude toward the events of the work.[22] It is this same basic approach which, with individual additions and modifications, characterizes the narratives of two clown figures two centuries later: Humbert Humbert of Vladimir Nabokov's *Lolita* (1955) and Oskar Matzerath of Günter Grass's *The Tin Drum* (1959).

"We all admire the spangled acrobat with classical grace meticulously walking his tight rope in the talcum light," says Humbert Humbert some three-quarters of the way through his narrative in Nabokov's *Lolita*. "But how much rarer art there is in the sagging rope expert wearing scarecrow clothes and impersonating a grotesque drunk! *I* should know."[23] Indeed he should. This pseudonymous narrator with the "bizarre cognomen" is admittedly "especially susceptible to the magic of games," confesses that "the artist in me has been given the upper hand over the gentleman," but also acknowledges that he has "only words to play with" now that he is locked away awaiting trial for the murder of the play-

---

[21] Stedmond, *Comic Art*, pp. 91–92.
[22] Compare Richard A. Lanham, *"Tristram Shandy": The Games of Pleasure*, p. 23; and John Traugott, *Tristram Shandy's World: Sterne's Philosophical Rhetoric*, p. 127.
[23] Vladimir Nabokov, *Lolita*, bk. 1, chap. 11.

wright and roué Clare Quilty ("guilty of killing Quilty"). And play with words he does—from the very first lines of his account:

> Lolita, light of my life, fire of my loins. My sin, my soul. Lo-lee-ta: the tip of the tongue taking a trip of three steps down the palate to tap, at three, on the teeth. Lo. Lee. Ta.
> She was Lo, plain Lo, in the morning, standing four feet ten in one sock. She was Lola in slacks. She was Dolly at school. She was Dolores on the dotted line. But in my arms she was always Lolita.

Throughout Humbert's narrative, alliteration abounds, often to comic effect, but usually nonetheless apt and precise ("Filthy fiend," "pubescent park," "zigzagging zanies," "globules of gonadal glow"); assonance does the same ("awkward daws," "torpid morning," "ugh of disgust"); and the two often combine in longer sequences of individual phonemes or entire words ("polished plop," "articulate art," "working wonder with one"). Parallelisms and reversals add to the phonic effect ("dream dad protecting dream daughter," "normal big males with normal big mates," "good lands and bad lands," "cold anger and hot tears"), as do rhyme ("grope and hope," "ads and fads") and the linguist's coupling of related consonants such as the voiced *b* and unvoiced *p* ("laboring lap," "limp limbs").[24] Such verbal and phonic play is often used to purely comic ends when, for example, it emulates ad-speak ("Papa's Purple Pills," "Dramatics, Dance, Debating and Dating") or when it concludes a passage with a punch-line effect ("my philter had felled her").

Wordplay in the traditional punning sense also characterizes Humbert's narrative ("my dolorous and hazy darling," "there was no Lo to behold"), as does its usually erotic variant, the double entendre ("the Mann Act," the book title *Know Your Own Daughter*, "provided male parts are taken by female parts"). Many puns are bilingual (*qu'il t'y* and Quilty, Blanche Schwarzmann, Avis

---

[24] Compare Carl Proffer, *Keys to "Lolita"*, pp. 81–119 passim for further examples. Proffer's book is a most valuable aid in sorting out the various stylistic devices and literary allusions used in *Lolita*.

Byrd) and involve proper names, which are far and away the greatest single source of linguistic fun in the book, whether metonymi-
cal (Mrs. Opposite, Mr. Taxovich, Mr. Junks), anatomical (Lake
Climax, Conception Park, D. Orgon, Miss Redcock), whimsical
(Aubrey McFate), anagrammatic (Vivian Darkbloom/Vladimir
Nabokov), pathetically fallacious (Killer Street, Grimm Road), or
learnedly allusive (Dr. Byron, Shirley Holmes, Dr. Tristramson).
Humbert's own name and that of his nymphet lover serve as the
source of virtually endless variants: Humbert the Humble, Hum
and Chum, Hummy and Mummy, Humbug, a Hamburger and
a Humburger, loquacious Lo, lovely Lo, lone light Lolita, Dolly's
Dell, doted on Dolly, Dolores endorsing a Dromedary. And other
names continue the narrative's phonic preoccupation: Bryan
Bryanski, Reverend Rigger (a.k.a. Rigor Mortis), Vanessa van
Ness, Lakes Onyx and Eryx.

   Literary allusions run rampant, particularly during Humbert's
"cryptogrammatic paper chase" after Quilty and Lo (Morris
Schmetterling; Arthur Rainbow; N. Petit, Larousse, Ill.; Donald
Quix, Sierra, Nev.), and direct and indirect literary references lit-
ter the rest of the novel as well, most notably to Poe, Joyce, and
Mérimée, as befits Humbert's background in English and French
literature. Though many are gratuitous and self-indulgent, some
of these references are contextual and relevant to Humbert's story:
the echoes of Poe in Hum's early lover Annabel Leigh and in his
occasional characterization of himself as a beast in a cage (recalling "Murders in the Rue Morgue"); the several associations between Hum and Melmoth the Wanderer; and the evocation of
Mérimée's *Carmen* in lines like "O my Carmen, my little Carmen" and in Quilty's signature as "Lucas Picador, Merrymay,
Pa." All point toward a tragic conclusion for poor Humbert-Poe-
Melmoth-José's love and cast a certain romantic glow over the
Humbert-Lolita-Quilty triangle.

   In Humbert's case, then, his assertion that "you can always
count on a murderer for a fancy prose style" certainly holds. A
natural question, though, is whether such a poetic and allusive
account could ever have served its original, ostensible purpose of

91

providing the trial jury with a defense of Hum's crime: "When I started, fifty-six days ago, to write *Lolita*, first in the psychopathic ward for observation, and then in this well-heated, albeit tombal, seclusion, I thought I would use these notes in toto at my trial, to save not my head, of course, but my soul." Any jury would undoubtedly take offense at such an address as "frigid gentlewomen" and at the insinuation that the gentlemen members secretly share Hum's passion, and they would take much of the rest as the alternately mawkish or absurd prattling of an effete, a pervert, or a madman.

To Humbert's credit, he abandons such self-serving intents in the course of writing ("In mid-composition, however, I realized that I could not parade living Lolita") and admits that, as a judge, he would have given himself "at least thirty-five years for rape, and dismissed the rest of the charges." Instead, his purpose evolves into a combination of artistic aims: to assuage his misery through the "melancholy and very local palliative of articulate art," to "fix once and for all the perilous magic of nymphets," and to create for Lolita and himself "the only immortality [they] both shall ever know." On the surface these goals comform somewhat to Nabokov's own espousal of esthetic bliss as the foremost criterion in the novel,[25] and there is much of Nabokov the word-master and playful man of letters in Humbert the narrator. But there is much, much more which separates the two and renders Humbert unreliable as the teller of his tale.

To begin with, there is much that is self-contradictory in Hum's narrative performance, some of it due to the midstream shift in purpose, some of it never recognized. His early assertion that he is no poet and "only a very conscientious recorder" obviously yields to the lyrical impulse in the later effort to invoke "aurochs and angels, the secret of durable pigments, prophetic sonnets" and to immortalize Lolita. The disdainful refusal to go into a "detailed account of Lolita's presumption" on the seduc-

[25] Vladimir Nabokov, "On a Book called *Lolita*," p. 316 of the Putnam edition of *Lolita*.

tion night and the expressed lack of concern with the "irrelevant matters" of "so-called 'sex'" in recounting that episode stand in stark contrast to the elaborate description of Hum's earlier self-manipulation against Lo's leg on the Haze living-room divan, which concludes in "the longest ecstasy man or monster had ever known," and also to several later less-detailed reports of activities in which Hum forces Lo to engage. The presumed haste and roughness of a first draft completed in eight weeks under observation and behind bars are belied by the intricacy of plot development, the wealth of detail, and the conscious planting of detective-story clues, for which Hum warns the reader to be on the lookout. Humbert's claims of knowing all the psychoanalyst's mumbo-jumbo to the point of being able to play games successfully with his doctors during his various stays in asylums are undercut by his confession that his story often makes his "slippery self elude [him], gliding into deeper and darker waters than [he cares] to probe." And his condemnation of himself for rape seems odd in light of his assertion that Lo actually seduced him on that fateful night at the Enchanted Hunters Lodge.

Perhaps more significantly, Humbert's lament that "we are inclined to endow our friends with the stability of type that literary characters acquire in the reader's mind" does not prevent him from himself creating an array of types and caricatures, even to the point of turning himself and Lolita into purely literary constructs retaining only "bits of marrow . . . and blood." He depicts himself as alternately monstrous, buffoonish (Harlequin and Bertoldo are both invoked for comparison), witty, brutish, tender, malevolent, and kind. And Lo is both caricatured as a gum-popping, commonplace juvenile and beatified as something which "has individualized the writer's ancient lust, so that above and over everything there is—Lolita." The real Lolita weathers the entire experience largely unmoved and unscathed, eventually settling into rather mediocre circumstances as a dumpy housewife with chapped hands; the Lolita whom Humbert hymns is a different creature altogether, one that is "totally solipsized" and recast by Hum into a vision of ethereal splendor: "What I had madly possessed was not she, but my own creation, another fanciful Lolita—perhaps more real than Lolita; overlapping, encasing her; floating between me and her, and having no will, no consciousness—indeed, no life of her own." She is but a name, a sound, a sensually esthetic experience. Lo-lee-ta, light of his life, fire of his loins, his sin, his soul.

Questions of morality thus quite naturally become unimportant for Humbert, filled as he is with such a lyrical vision of loveliness, with what he believes to be genuinely transcendent love, and with self-loathing for the conduct by which he has squandered such bliss. He can juggle literary blocks with the easy deftness of a master, yet he fails to realize that he is ultimately the duped slave of his own art:

The immortality of *Lolita*, Humbert the artist's immortality, exists in the telling, in the farce and the anguish of his narrative, and not in the bizarre facts of the story told. It is the telling that matters. . . . Nabokov is attempting to show that there is nothing *intrinsically* remarkable about an older man falling in love with a twelve-year-old girl. What happens in *Lolita* is that Humbert *makes* it remarkable by the terms he puts it in, by the telling, because he makes an art out of a perversion. Humbert's eye confronts vulgarity (his own and the world's) and converts it through imagination and subsequently language into a thing of beauty. Lolita is in reality a rather common, unwashed little girl whose interests are entirely plebeian, though, in certain respects, precocious. But the real irony is that Humbert's power to turn rough glass into sparkling crystal eventually subsumes him, and he is reduced to a servant of his art. Humbert sitting in his cage talking about the salvation afforded by the writing of his memoirs suggests, in fact, his imprisonment in art. Humbert perverts life, and art eventually perverts him because his life *becomes* art.[26]

The result of such hopeless imprisonment and solipsism is self-parody,[27] making Hum's account a "burlesque of the confessional

[26] S. Page Stegner, *Escape into Aesthetics: The Art of Vladimir Nabokov*, pp. 114–15.
[27] Alfred Appel, Jr., *"Lolita:* The Springboard of Parody," p. 205.

mode, the literary diary, the Romantic novel that chronicles the effects of a debilitating love, the *Doppelgänger* tale, and, in parts, a Duncan Hines tour of America conducted by a guide with a black imagination, a parodic case study."[28] And by definition,

. . . parody and self-parody suspend the possibility of a fully "realistic" fiction, since their referents are either other literary works or themselves, and not the world of objective reality which the "realist" or "impressionist" tries to reproduce. Only an authorial sensibility, outside the book, can be said to have ordered the texture of parody; the dizzying, multiform perspectives it achieves are beyond the capacity of any "point of view" within the book. In the terms of Henry James or Percy Lubbock, Humbert's is finally *not* a credible point of view.[29]

Much of *Lolita*'s parody, cynicism, and irony is Humbert's own: the ironic projection of himself as "nastiness" and "beastliness" personified, the many elaborate masks and voices, the subtle literary and cryptogrammatic games, the identification with and subsequent destruction of Quilty, the elegant and bemused satires of towns and travels and people. The cynicism and satire produce much of the book's humor, of course, in the descriptions of characters such as Hum's first wife Valeria and her cavalier Mr. Taxovich, Charlotte Haze, Gastin Godin, and the schoolmistress Miss Pratt, and in the accounts of such events as Charlotte's miraculously convenient demise, Hum's dyspepsia on the seduction night, the Cook's tour of American motels, and Hum's interview with Frederick Beale (the driver of the car which ran down Charlotte) while lying in his bath. Though the humor in many of these passages is vicious, a ray of sentiment, even tenderness, occasionally shines through: Humbert plots a perfect "accidental" death for Charlotte at Hourglass Lake yet closes the episode with the confession, "But what d'ye know, folks—I just could not make myself do it!"; after recounting his actions preparatory to fetching the newly orphaned Lo from camp, Hum drops the cyn-

[28] Ibid., p. 213.
[29] Ibid., p. 216.

ical tone and lets fly with an admittedly mawkish directive to the printer to keep repeating Lolita's name until the page is full; the passage describing Lo's tennis game is a rich poetic delight of genuinely lyrical feeling; and the encounter with the married and pregnant Dolly Schiller alternates between strained humor and the bathos of Hum's desperate love. With such breaks in Humbert's harsh comic mask there indeed seems some justification for viewing his character as at least somewhat decent at its deeper levels, for taking his cynical pose as, "to alter Marvell's phrase, begotten by despair upon cruel self-knowledge," [30] and for seeing the whole novel as Hum's "attempt to conceal, to distort, even to abolish his own identity, and to assert the grotesqueness of his recreated self." [31]

Within such a context Humbert's doubtlessly heartfelt confession of love and his agonized and belated realization of that love, while they do win him our sympathy to a considerable extent, prevent any conventional pity and understanding [32] and thereby lose all genuinely tragic force, becoming instead mere tragic farce. Clown Humbert's tragedy is the self-created chaos and destruction of a Harlequin, not the wrenching drama of a Pagliaccio. And fittingly, that tragic farce ends in "the turbulent fighting of fools" bringing "a jerry-built new world tumbling about their ears" (as Welsford notes concerning the *sottie* drama), with Hum and Quilty trading one-liners and rolling over each other like two goatish buffoons in a grotesquely comic parody of a suitors' quarrel, here fought over a maid whom one of them has defiled and lost and the other all but forgotten.

Nabokov the author, in his appendix to the novel, insists that *Lolita* "has no moral in tow," that he is "neither a reader nor a writer of didactic fiction." There is no apparent reason not to take him at his word here, but it is clear enough from the work itself and from Nabokov's expressed "disagreement" with his narrator

[30] E. Rubenstein, "Approaching *Lolita*," p. 363.
[31] Ibid.
[32] Martin Green, "The Morality of Lolita," p. 367.

on "many things besides nymphets" that Humbert's judgments are not to be taken as the work's final say on moral matters, that there is no final, unambiguous moral lesson. As Welsford notes concerning Harlequin:

> In spite of minor variations Harlequin's appearance is more unchanging than his character; the only qualities which remain constant through the centuries are agility, resilience and, as a rule, complete absence of the moral sense. Unlike the fool in cap and bells, he can tap no hidden source of mysterious knowledge or unworldly wisdom. . . . Harlequin . . . was wholly a creature of make-believe, without background, and therefore without either religious significance or subversive tendencies.[33]

Yet inasmuch as Humbert does personify the spirit of Harlequin or a *sottie* clown who annihilates reality, turns life into a game and the world upside down, and ends by creating chaos, there is something of a dark abyss beneath the whole elaborate joke; for the world inhabited by Harlequin and the *sottie* fool is irrational, menacing, and demonic. Hum possesses a certain resiliency and insight, and perhaps the implied authorial rejection of his paean (through the fact of Hum's imprisonment, his loss of Lo, and also his self-parodying narration) constitutes something of an implicit, positive reassertion of human values. At any rate, he is not condemned or dismissed out of hand. As in the cases of Folly and Tristram, neither the literal sense nor the mere reversal of overt statement comprises the full import of Hum's performance. Richard Pearce's conclusion is the only reasonable one:

> With his fertile and daring imagination Humbert Humbert made the ugly Lolita into a nymphet of singular beauty. He destroyed her life but also transformed her imaginatively—giving her far more value than she would have achieved on her own. In the end, he destroys his imaginative creation with the final violent shift in perspective. This final shift

---

[33] Welsford, *The Fool*, p. 303.

forces us to question not Humbert Humbert's grasp of reality but our own. Quilty dies, Dolly dies, Humbert dies, the novel is over; but like the *sottie* fools, and like the ghost of Gogol's Akaky Akakyevich, the narrator who has gleefully destroyed everything in sight continues to haunt us.[34]

Oskar Matzerath's entire life and narrative are suffused with the imagery of the clown. From age three to twenty-one he remains a three-year-old in size and appearance, a condition which he exploits fully to wreak havoc ranging from the playful to the fatal while retaining the protection afforded by his deceiving physical state to survive dangers and crises unscathed in body and conscience; and from twenty-one to his present age of thirty he is an only slightly larger hunchback whose proclivities toward role-playing and the assuming of masks continue unabated. In his narrative he invokes not only the obvious shades of Tom Thumb and the Lilliputians, but also those of Yorick and Hamlet, the court jesters and dwarfs of old, the Lord of Misrule and his classical predecessor Dionysos, the satanic clown Mephisto, the legendary holy fool Parzival, the charlatan holy fool Rasputin, and the genuine holy fool Christ, all of whom he at one time or another links with his own figure. And the acknowledged primary influence on his life is the dwarf and circus clown Bebra, whom Oskar terms his friend and master and whose advice at their initial encounter serves as Oskar's motto from that moment on: "My dear Oskar, believe an experienced colleague. Our kind has no place in the audience. We must perform, we must run the show. If we don't it's the others that run us. And they don't do it with kid gloves."[35] Under Bebra's guidance Oskar gradually evolves from the private clown who rains destruction on family, friends, and window panes to the public clown who disrupts Nazi rallies with a waltz-time drumbeat, entertains troops at the front, engineers orgies of mischief and vandalism as a wartime street-gang leader,

---

[34] Richard Pearce, *Stages of the Clown: Stages of Modern Fiction from Dostoevsky to Beckett*, p. 101.

[35] Günter Grass, *The Tin Drum*, trans. Ralph Manheim, p. 114.

and evokes catharic tears in the postwar crows at the Zwiebelkeller in Düsseldorf.

It therefore comes as no surprise that Oskar's narration takes on the character of a clown's performance. From the opening sentence he is onstage, as it were, writing from his hospital bed under the watchful eye of his keeper Bruno, whom he regularly and with considerable success regales with "made-up stories" which Bruno then appreciatively re-creates in knot sculptures. Oskar also hints that there is a touch of madness in him, wishes to maintain a certain distance from everyone, plays whimsically with words—using "virgin paper" instead of the usual white paper (compare Tristram's "Virgin Dedication")—and makes quite a fuss as to how he should go about writing his story, thus casting himself very early in the role of the conscious but somewhat suspect artist. The ensuing account of his maternal grandparents' fateful first encounter in a Kashubian potato field and his great pains to point out to the reader along the way exactly what he is doing ("If I have made a special point of my grandmother's skirt, leaving no doubt, I hope, that she was sitting in her skirts; if indeed I have gone so far as to call the whole chapter 'The Wide Skirt,' it is because I know how much I owe to this article of apparel") smack strongly of Shandean stuff, if not made up (*vorgelogen*) then certainly performed (*vorgespielt*) and imaginatively embellished to the point of assuming tall-tale or even mythic proportions, albeit with a decidedly earthy touch:

Suddenly Koljaiczek found himself short, wide, and coverless in the rain, and he was cold. Quickly he buttoned his pants, which fear and a boundless need for shelter had bidden him open during his stay beneath the skirts. Hurriedly he manipulated the buttons, fearing to let his piston cool too quickly, for there was a threat of dire chills in the autumn air. [P. 24]

A similar mixture of narration and extensive embellishment with frequent digression characterizes such later scenes as the family outing to the seashore, the Herbert Truczynski–Niobe episode,

99

and the fizz-powder sequence between Oskar and Maria Truczynski. Just as Oskar plays with photographs by cutting and rear-
ranging them into infinitely new and whimsical patterns, so does
his narrative become something of a photo album (as he himself
admits), with characters and incidents drawn from the past but in
effect totally reshaped by Oskar and with only the barest remnant
of actual reality as their basis.

A touch of Tristram, as well as overtones of the circus and
nightclub performer, is also evident as Oskar begins the account
of his own birth, questioning his drum at length about such a
seemingly irrelevant detail as the wattage of the light bulbs in his
natal bedroom and then concluding irreverently: "Well, then, it
was in the form of two sixty-watt bulbs that I first saw the light of
this world. That is why the words of the Bible, 'Let there be light
and there was light,' still strike me as an excellent publicity slogan
for Osram light bulbs." Just as an object mania characterized
much of Tristram's account—chestnuts, pipes, window sashes,
clocks, satchel clasps—so do individual objects such as the light
bulbs here serve to focus much of Oskar's narrative: matches, fizz
powder, a horse's head filled with eels, a Nazi pin, a severed finger, and the ever-present drum. To Oskar's mind, seemingly, his
fate and the course of all that has happened in his life have
turned on such small determinants. Rather than convey a genuinely historical and humanized account, however, such a re-
ductive, object-focused method again lends that account the air
variously of the comic's stage turn or the fabulist's effort at myth-
spinning.

If the idiosyncratic narration and extraordinary content to this
point in the novel have at times strained credulity, Oskar finally
steps over the line in asserting that he had no trouble in freeing
himself from his mother's womb, that he heard and comprehended all that was said by those in the room at the time, that he
noted the premonitory symbolism of a "drumming" moth around
the light bulbs, and that he made then and there a firm decision
regarding his own future: "Outwardly wailing and impersonating

a meat-colored baby, I made up my mind to reject my father's projects, in short everything connected with the grocery store, out of hand, but to give my mother's plan favorable consideration when the time came, to wit, on my third birthday." Similar pronouncements occur at two later points in Oskar's narrative: on the aforesaid third birthday he purportedly decides to stop growing and therefore contrives a severe fall down the cellar steps in order to provide his family with a plausible physical cause for that phenomenon; and over his father's grave, at age twenty-one, he ostensibly makes a decision to resume growing. In both instances blows to the head (at the funeral Oskar is struck with a rock thrown by his presumed son Kurt) and the probable resultant jostling of the pituitary gland provide the likely physiological explanation of arrested or resumed growth. Oskar's claim of personal intent as the sole cause in each case, as in that of the natal-day resolution, therefore rings of the most obvious kind of retrospective fancy.

This imposition of impossible explanations on past occurrences lifts Oskar's narrative out of a realistic framework once and for all, as far as the larger lines of character and event are concerned. Scenes of the East Prussian coast, of Danzig, of Düsseldorf streets, and of the many museum and church settings seem plausible enough; but such incredible events as the breaking of windows from great distances by a remarkably accurate and humanly inaudible scream or the drumming statue of Jesus, as well as such outlandish scenes as those in the Niobe room of the maritime museum and on the coast of Normandy, rupture the fabric of realism inalterably. They lend the account an air of surreality, of grotesqueness, of imaginative excess, and they thereby ineluctably focus attention on the telling of the tale instead of on the tale itself, on the nature of the narrative voice rather than on content alone. In the midst of the bloody siege on the Polish Post Office, for example, we watch as Oskar, oblivious to the fact that men are dying all around him, waits for the turmoil to jostle a red tin drum from a shelf and into his arms; not even from his present vantage point does he seem to sense that anything horrible was taking place. Or later, as Russian soldiers enter the Matzerath cellar, we see Oskar (again both the young protagonist and the narrator) concerned more with the fate of his father's Nazi pin and with the adaptable orderliness of a column of ants rather than with the actual death of his father or the repeated rape of the Widow Greff. We gain vivid microcosmic pictures of the Post Office siege and the Russians' arrival, but the extreme idiosyncrasy of the narrative stance and focus in each case subordinates those portraits to the perspective and the apparent concerns of the narrator himself.

Just as a sort of narrative innocence blunts all the horrors and a certain insouciance of voice robs cataclysms, death, and suffering of any direct significance, so do Oskar's incessant Shandean obsession with narration (his pen refuses guidance; he could insert whole essays on this or that subject; have we heard the story of . . . ; we must not suppose that . . . , etc.), his highly eclectic style (biblical references, literary associations, mythological allusions, puns, neologisms, digressions, town histories), and his tendency toward metonymy (triangular face, scarred back, frock coat, billowing skirts) deprive individuals and actions of any literal import. Instead, they make of Oskar an almost allegorical construct, a *Kunstfigur*,[36] a verbal clown, and they render his narrative a peformance severed from reality, an abstract and solipsistic fabrication rather than a representational historical account. Oskar himself contributes to this interpretation of his figure by frequently speaking of himself in the third person and by oscillating wildly between images of himself as Satan and Jesus, as Goethe and Rasputin, as Apollo and Dionysos, as Nazi fellow traveler and Nazi-baiter, as child and man, as spurious father and spurious son, as eminently sane and patently insane, as victimizer and victim; and Oskar's narrative bounces just as wildly from official history to scurrilous and fantastic biography to rhapsodic drumming. The clown changes hats so often that he him-

---

[36] See Manfred Durzak, "Kunstfigur und Figur des Künstlers: *Die Blechtrommel*," p. 144; and Hans Mayer, "Felix Krull und Oskar Matzerath: Aspekte des Romans," p. 40.

self seems totally unable to say which is his real self, which his real story, which his real view, which the final interpretation or import of his performance. And too, even at the end of his tale, at the point in time from which he narrates, he is still playing his drum and toying with the question of which role he will adopt in the near future upon his release from the asylum.

Full trust can therefore not be placed in Oskar's narrative. The performance nature of that narration, the vacillating roles of the narrator as observer and observed, the waverings of perspective, the alternate reductiveness and epic expansiveness of the telling—all leave no firm ground on which the reader can stand. Instead, they hint at the presence of the author behind the figure of the drumming dwarf-narrator, making Oskar as cognizant subject part of the entire objective fabric described by the implied author. [37] Two small instances of such objectification of Oskar occur within the actual narrative itself: when Bruno at one point renders a straightforward and compressed report of Oskar's flight from Danzig to the West, and when Vittlar tenders his minutely detailed deposition on Oskar's discovery of a human finger. The economy and soberness of both contrast sharply with Oskar's garrulous, self-indulgent scurrility and imaginative play[38] and thereby imply an ordering mind at work behind Oskar's back. The same authorial mind is implied in such moments as the seduction scene involving Matzerath and Maria, where the fornication enrages Oskar but the war news being reported on the radio in the background does not, although the latter is clearly perceived by the reader as the greater cause for tears. [39] "Through the imperious rat-tat-tat of his drum Oskar does achieve a form of spontaneous expression that allows him to anathematize his bourgeois milieu" and to depict in rambling microcosm something of the flavor of the prewar and war years through an account of his own life. Yet "such an organ of knowledge is not only indiscriminate-

---

[37] Alexander Gelley, "Art and Reality in *Die Blechtrommel,*" pp. 53–54.
[38] Durzak, "Kunstfigur," p. 139.
[39] W. Gordon Cunliffe, *Günter Grass,* p. 72.

ly aggressive but also self-destructive," as is seen in Oskar's collapse into fear and silence at the final approach of the dreaded "Black Witch," a figure repeatedly evoked in snatches of a children's song.[40]

Oskar's role as dwarf-clown-drummer is linked with artifice and also with impotence, with pathological self-absorption, with a total absence of human feelings, as seen variously in his encounters with Jan, Dorothea, Sigismund Markus, and his parents. His own art is thus "necessarily formed of parody and uncontrollable primitive feeling" born of desperation and a regressive "spiritual" development in the course of the novel. (One of the work's many parodistic effects, as in the case of *Felix Krull*, is an inversion of the Bildungsroman's humanistic principles.)[41] Such an art is incapable of bringing off any hard and fast epic account and is also incapable of revealing the nature of its narrative voice as anything more than a fictional device, a *Kunstfigur*, "a contrived approach which keeps itself at as distant a remove as possible from the simulation of anything 'natural.'"[42] Consequently, *The Tin Drum*

. . . belongs not to the realist tradition of the picaresque or pedagogical novel but rather to the satirical enlightenment genre of Swift, Voltaire or Diderot. It corresponds throughout to the tradition of those humorous-satirical novels wherein the narrator, that is, the actual author of the novel, establishes a secret understanding with the reader by pushing aside for a time the frame figure, who supposedly reports the action, as a hindrance in order to turn to the audience himself behind his chronicler's back.[43]

Behind Oskar's capricious, limited, and often primitive clown act of drum-narration the implied author draws a much larger and more sweeping satiric panorama of Germany and Europe.

[40] Gelley, "Art and Reality," p. 123.
[41] Ibid., p. 124.
[42] Mayer, "Felix Krull und Oskar Matzerath," p. 40.
[43] Ibid., p. 44.

104

Hitler himself, the original "drummer,"[44] and the entire "deformed" and "deforming" phenomenon of National Socialism are one of the satirist's targets in the story of the grotesque but beguiling dwarf-clown. The Bebras of the period, the court jesters and artists in influential positions who foresaw the coming horrors but adapted to the times and even resorted to complicity and to an "inner emigration," are another, as are the postwar public disavowals of the past, the great purgation of confessed war guilt and subsequent resolves at reform and reconstruction. And much more: generational conflicts, the abominable wartime treatment of minority groups, the pathetic plight of the victimized children, the rampant corruption and self-interest, the excess of recriminations, the disruptions of all normal life, the phantasmagoria of indiscriminate violence exacting its toll on innocent and guilty alike. Through the narrator Oskar's story the author Grass's book is "drenched with history as a retelling of events from below to lend it a dramatic meaning," notes Ralph Freedman:

Usually it is the personal event and episode that would assume such larger proportions and would supply the "privileged moment" of added dimension: History is viewed through the death of Oskar's mother, through Roswitha's calamity on the Western front, through the father's ludicrous death which fixes him in a state of guilt.[45]

The era and the society under scrutiny are too massive, complex, unyielding, and uncomprehending to be vulnerable to direct attack,[46] and such an attack would only constitute an empty polemic. Just as, in Gottfried Benn's words, "God is a bad stylistic principle," so are humanity and morality bad stylistic princi-

[44] Cunliffe notes (*Grass*, p. 53) that Hitler was once contemptuously described by General von Lossow in 1924 as "der Trommler" ("an epithet which Hitler, in his final speech, turned into a compliment"), and also refers to Bertolt Brecht's poem "Beginn des Krieges" (Start of the War), which calls Hitler the same thing.

[45] Ralph Freedman, "The Poet's Dilemma: The Narrative Worlds of Günter Grass," p. 57.

[46] Gelley, "Art and Reality," p. 119.

ples for confronting an age of inhumanity; a "tyranny of the
drum" is required to usher in an exorcism of the demon-pos-
sessed spirit.[47] Grass's weapons, rather, are "mock-innocence
cloaking a savage thrust, madness and fantasy disguising the bit-
terest of realities."[48] The resultant strutting and posturing of the
fool upon the narrative stage creates a completely unobjective,
"wildly subjective, totally irreverent and frequently cruel" report,[49] but the echo of that report does not fade with the fool's
passing into silence. Tank explains:

Even if one wishes to see in Oskar only a fool, one should still recognize that in foolish times this fool fulfills a function in which preachers
and pedagogues often fail, because they do not encounter and address a
man where he should be addressed: in his subconscious, in his dreams.
What takes place in The Tin Drum . . . is a process. A process of the
imagination, into which each reader, willingly or unwillingly, is drawn.
When some figure created by the writer, a quickening one such as the
drummer Oskar, once gains sway over us, he awakens powers in us with
his own demonic powers: powers of affirmation and defense which accord us self-assertion in a new realm of freedom not devoid of danger
and never unmenaced. With such a figure which, whether designed as
negative hero or fool, both possesses and fashions substance, deeper
layers of the soul are unlocked. With him, what once was is brought to
life; buried, forgotten images, legends, fairy tales and myths emerge
anew in our consciousness. And these older, deeper, ineradicable stores
become the criterion for the new. [Pp. 11–12]

The effectiveness of the implied author's technique is reflected in
such praise as that of author-critic Hans Magnus Enzensberger:

I know no epic portrayal of the Hitler regime which can compare in
precision and accuracy with that which Grass, both incidentally and
without the slightest anti-fascist ado, presents in The Tin Drum. Grass is
no moralist. In almost neutral fashion he slits open those years of

[47] Kurt Lothar Tank, Günter Grass, p. 69.
[48] Gelley, "Art and Reality," p. 119.
[49] Keith Miles, Günter Grass, p. 82.

"world history" from 1933 to 1945 and shows their inner lining in all its shabbiness.[50]

Through the figure of the clown Oskar, Grass conveys a picture that is both painful and penetrating in its truthfulness.

From the foregoing discussions I think it is reasonable to see the figures of Folly, Tristram, Humbert, and Oskar as fitting Welsford's definition of the Fool: ". . . a man who falls below the average human standard, but whose defects have been transformed into a source of delight, a mainspring of comedy."[51] It is readily apparent and has been noted by numerous critics—and often by the respective authors themselves—in each case that delight, laughter, entertainment, or esthetic bliss is of major interest in the presentation of the narrative through a clownish persona. Such was the original function of the clown or fool in antiquity, and such it still is, for example, in the circus arena or the raree show. But just as medieval clowns later combined the court fool's assumed impunity and satiric freedom, the festival king's role as scapegoat and sacrificial victim, and the *sottie* clown's chaotic madness in varying degrees and toward what were often more than merely comic ends, so do the four figures under examination here produce more than mere comic diversion through their antics and natures.

There is much of the sage fool in Folly and Tristram, indeed a highly Christian aspect about them, producing a refined form of clownage which reveals the foolish foibles of humankind but also points toward a loftier and more noble spiritual capacity in human nature. A farcical mood rather than one of contemptuous or bitter satire dominates the clowning. There is much of the same air of farce in the narratives of Humbert and Oskar, but these two figures also possess a darker side. There is something brutal, aberrant, even destructive about them, affecting events and people

---

[50] Hans Magnus Enzensberger, *"Wilhelm Meister* auf Blech getrommelt," p. 224.
[51] Welsford, *The Fool*, p. xi.

107

around them as well as coloring their narratives, something which rises through and above their antics and tinges the laughter. And like the festival scapegoats and the often demonic *sottie* clowns and Harlequins of old, they are cast out, as it were, at the end of their respective performances after indulging their excessive natures to the hilt. Though they entertain us mightily, their antisocial abnormality serves to create in their audience a community of spirit which reinforces the very norms that they themselves imply by breaking them. Consequently, these figures are, so to speak, expelled by the very laughter they produce. And "in this sense laughter is superiority, though always the superiority of a group which follows the mean over the abnormal individual whose excess it constrains."[52] Just as in the cases of Erasmus and Sterne the enjoyment of the fun and the appreciation of the moral uplift are dependent upon the recognition of the congenially clownish character of the narrators, so are this "laughter of superiority" and the simultaneous rejection of the clown personae presented by Nabokov and Grass ultimately dependent upon the recognition of the fundamental amorality or abnormality of their respective fictional narrators. In other words, the full import of the four works is gained through a perception of the unreliable narration at work in them all.

[52] Albert Cook, *The Dark Voyage and the Golden Mean: A Philosophy of Comedy*, p. 139.

CHAPTER 5

The Madman

THE INTRODUCTION to this study opened with a passage from John Fowles's novel *The Collector* in which the narrator, the young ex-clerk Clegg, unwittingly demonstrates his perversity and derangement by painting a romantic and indignantly self-justifying picture of his abduction and detention of the young art student Miranda. Clegg's situation is readily seen at this point—a hundred pages into the novel and several days into the kidnapping— as a patently unreliable one wherein his testimony and opinions can by no means be accepted at face value as representative of the implied author's attitudes toward the events depicted. As noted later in the Introduction, the reader becomes aware of this untrustworthiness of Clegg's narrative much earlier—within the first few pages, in fact, as he reads incredulously but with considerable fascination the careful, "logical" plans that are laid to abduct Miranda and ultimately win her love by holding her "captive in a nice way." Perhaps on one's initial reading, the first inkling of Clegg's madness occurs when the narrator declares that he is not mad for "deciding" on the lovely Miranda; perhaps it comes during the clerk's recitation of his rather unfortunate childhood, as if offering an excuse or displacing responsibility for his present activities; perhaps it comes with Clegg's defensive account of his interest in pornography, or with his frequent comparisons of people to specimens in his butterfly collection; or possibly it comes as Clegg talks of his acquisition of the isolated country house in obvious anticipation of something mysterious—sending people away, cutting off phone service, installing locks, and furnishing the place with an eye toward Miranda's presumed "advanced" taste.

Even if the realization of Clegg's madness does not set in until the clerk actually goes about the business of abducting Miranda, the reader is fully aware within fifteen pages that he is listening to the narrative of a criminally unbalanced mind, and he proceeds to deal with the remaining two-hundred-odd pages of the account on those terms. The novel thus poses no real threat of confusing the reader about Clegg's value as a spokesman—unless one is unduly swayed by Clegg's economic and sociological rationales ("money corrupts," "there was always class between us")—and permits the reader to follow the account by Clegg and Miranda as an engrossing case study in the pathology of criminal insanity and its effects on the victim of that insanity. Although both Clegg and Miranda are finely and successfully drawn as individuals through their complementary narratives and as a consequence of their strictly delimited dramatic situation, the predominant image one retains of the story is that of persecutor and victim, an effect attained largely through the early establishment of Clegg as a criminally mad and thoroughly unreliable narrator.[1]

In several ways Clegg's situation represents a paradigm of numerous literary madmen before him: insignificant, petty, withdrawn, defensive, dreaming, spiteful, perversely logical, self-deluding, ultimately more of a type than a genuine individual, and a speaker who is soon if not immediately perceived as possessing all these traits and therefore of questionable trustworthiness in the presentation of his own account. One need not look very far in seeking examples from works both more widely known and more seminal than *The Collector*.

[1] Many reviews of *The Collector* were in fact typified by the remark in *Time* magazine cited on the cover of the paperback edition of the novel (New York: Dell, 1964): "Evil has seldom found quite so many excuses for itself and has seldom been so sinister."

Nikolai Gogol's "Zapiski sumasšedšego" (literally "Notes of a Madman," but more generally known under the title "Diary of a Madman"), which appeared in the collection *Arabesques* in 1835, indicates from its very title, even before one begins reading, that the story will be told in the words of a neurotic individual and therefore sets up expectations of unreliability in the narrative. There is of course the possibility of authorial irony in the use of "madman" (as in the case of Sterne's use of "gentleman" in the full title of *Tristram Shandy*), but one is far more prepared at the outset to take the text as anything from incoherent ravings to rambling absurdities to clear but twisted logical musings—at any rate, not to accept it as authoritative in any sense. One is pre-disposed, rather, merely to listen to the madman talk, to watch him move, to study him as a case—he is called simply "*a* madman" after all, at least in the English, German and French titles—possibly to laugh at his antics or lament his overall condition. The madman's story actually meets all these expectations and evokes all these reactions.

Like his descendant Clegg, Aksenty Ivanovich Poprishchin is a petty official in the government bureaucracy, older than Clegg at forty-two, but like him an unimportant and expendable drudge with no apparent chance for advancement, and a withdrawn and friendless individual outside the office with little more than his diary and his dreams to occupy him. And also as in Clegg's case, the first few pages reveal a mind which is obviously already far along an aberrant course as a result of the character's general situation: Poprishchin's routine and work have fallen into disarray (he is two hours late in reporting to the office, and his copywork has grown shoddy of late); he is bitter toward co-workers and toward people in general (the "old Jew" of a cashier, the well-dressed merchants, the high Civil Service officials, his gruff department head); he is obviously self-deluding about the worth and security of his position (believing that his immediate superior is jealous of him because he sharpens the Director's quills, and blithely asserting that he would have resigned long ago had it not been for the

111

"snob value" of his office and his position); and he has given himself over to patently unrealizable dreams (winning the love of the Director's daughter Sophie and gaining wealth and status). The unjustified self-delusions and the preoccupation with unattainable goals mark the narrator already as a rather unreliable figure and make, for example, his judgments of the office head and of his co-workers somewhat spurious. But as yet there is nothing to indicate any sort of madness—at most a slight neurotic concern over his life, position, and self-image.

On the third page of the first entry (October 3rd), however, Poprishchin's narrative goes over the edge into the absurd, as he "overhears" two dogs talking, adding quite candidly that he has "begun hearing and seeing things" just recently that he had never noticed before. This motif is later taken up again (in the entry dated November 12th) as Poprishchin steals the "papers" of one of the dogs (Fidèle) in order to examine the "correspondence" between the two and possibly learn something about Sophie's feelings toward him.

These two episodes definitively mark Poprishchin as a madman, confirming the expectations fostered by the title of the story; and since the first of the two instances comes in the initial entry of the diary, virtually the entire log is cast into the shadow of total untrustworthiness. That first instance follows directly upon a sudden disruption by reality in Poprishchin's self-deluding world of dreams, as he unexpectedly encounters Sophie emerging from a carriage:

While I was making this reflection I saw a carriage driving up to the shop which I was passing. I recognized it at once. It was our director's carriage. "But he can have nothing to go to the shop for," I thought; "I suppose it must be his daughter." I flattened myself against the wall. The footman opened the carriage door and she darted out like a bird. How she glanced from right to left, how her eyes and eyebrows gleamed. . . . Good God, I am done for, completely lost! And why does she drive out in such rain! Don't tell me that women have not a passion for these rags. She didn't know me, and, indeed, I tried to muffle myself up all I could, because I had on a very muddy old-fashioned overcoat. Now people wear cloaks with long collars, while I had short collars one above the other, and, indeed, the cloth was not at all rainproof. [October 3][2]

Instead of sweeping Sophie off her feet and eventually winning her hand, as in his dreams, Poprishchin can only hide his poverty and shame; and the consequence of this sudden shattering of his dream seems to be a retreat into the more elaborate fantasy of the talking, letter-writing dogs.

By the time the dog-papers episode rolls around a month later, Poprishchin has suffered a demeaning rebuff by the Director's servants, a second bumbling encounter with Sophie, and a brutal dressing-down by the department head:

"Come, kindly tell me what you are doing?" "How do you mean?" I said. "I am doing nothing." "Come, think what you are about! Why, you are over forty. It's time you had a little sense. What do you imagine yourself to be? Do you suppose I don't know all the tricks you are up to? Why, you are philandering after the director's daughter! Come, look at yourself; just think what you are! Why, you are a nonentity and nothing else! Why, you haven't a penny to bless yourself with. And just look at yourself in the mirror—how could you think of such a thing!" [November 6]

Poprishchin's unconscious defenses seem to handle this direct blow with no trouble by again attributing the outburst to "jealousy" and by reaffirming his own nobility of nature and prospect of success; and a retreat into the world of the satirical theatre (November 8th) seems to soothe him a bit so that he can continue to dream of Sophie.

The dreams now have only voyeurism as their object, however, not actual conquest:

I long to have a look in there, into the part of the house where her Excellency is, that's where I should like to go! Into her boudoir where

[2] Nikolai Gogol, "Diary of a Madman," in *The Collected Tales and Plays of Nikolai Gogol*, trans. Constance Garnett, ed. Leonard J. Kent, pp. 453–73.

there are all sorts of little jars, little bottles, and such flowers that one is frightened even to breathe on them, to see her dresses lying scattered about, more like ethereal gossamer than dresses. I long to glance into her bedroom; there I imagine there must be marvels . . . , a paradise, such as is not to be found in the heavens. To look at the little stool on which she puts her little foot when she gets out of bed and the way she puts a little snow-white stocking on that little foot . . . Aie, aie, aie! never mind . . . silence! [November 9]

In the same voyeuristic vein Poprishchin steals Fidèle's papers from her basket in the corner so as to read of his beloved in the letters from the dog Medji to Fidèle:

Now I shall find out all their doings and ways of thinking, all the hidden springs, and shall get to the bottom of it all. These letters will reveal everything. Dogs are clever creatures, they understand all the diplomatic relations, and so no doubt I shall find there everything about our gentleman: all about his character and behavior. There will be something in them too about her who . . . never mind, silence! [November 12]

What Poprishchin "reads" in Medji's "letters" can seemingly only be interpreted as the range of his own imaginings and fears concerning Sophie, her father the Director, and himself. His inner defenses hold the most crushing blows at bay for a while by focusing on the "jerky style" and the "trashy" nature of much of the letters' contents; but the fears ultimately do come through, revealing Sophie's fondness for a young court chamberlain and indicating her disdain of Poprishchin:

—It seems to me that if she is attracted by that court chamberlain she will soon be attracted by that clerk that sits in Papa's study. Oh, *ma chere*, if you knew what an ugly fellow that is! He looks like a turtle in a bag. . . .
What clerk is this? . . .
—He has a very queer surname. He always sits sharpening the quills. The hair on his head is very much like hay. Papa sometimes sends him out instead of a servant. . . .

114

I do believe the nasty little dog is alluding to me. But my hair isn't like hay!
—Sophie can never help laughing when she sees him.
That's a lie, you damned little dog! What an evil tongue! As though I didn't know whose tricks were at the bottom of that! This is all the doing of the chief of my section. The man has sworn eternal hatred, and here he tries to injure me again and again, at every turn. [November 13]

When, finally, the Director's plans for Sophie's marriage are mentioned, Poprishchin can bear no more and destroys the letters:

Damn it! I can't read any more. . . . It's always a court chamberlain or a general. Everything that's best in the world falls to the court chamberlains or the generals. If you find some poor treasure and think it is almost within your grasp, a court chamberlain or a general will snatch it from you. God damn it! I'd like to become a general myself, not in order to receive her hand and all the rest of it; no, I should like to be a general only to see how they would wriggle and display all their court manners and *équivoques* and then say to them: I spit on you both. Oh, damn it! I tore the stupid dog's letters to bits.

The recognition of his ridiculousness, occasioned through the absurd externalizing device of the dog's letters, crushes Poprishchin's dreamworld of love and material success.

What then follows is an alternative attempt at escaping the miserable reality of his existence, this time into dreams of political power and prominence as the long-lost King of Spain. The degeneration of Poprishchin's mind is by now so far advanced, however, that besides forsaking the government office—his last vestige of contact with actuality—he abandons everyday reality completely: he smashes his food plates, shuts himself in and acts generally "distracted," enters fantastic dates into his diary ("April 43rd, 2000"; "86th Martober, between day and night"), rewrites world history, and makes himself a "royal mantle" in a "completely different" style in anticipation of a "Spanish delegation" to take him to Spain and restore him to the throne. The "delegation" does of course eventually cart him away to "Spain" in a

115

journey of only a half-hour, then shaves his head and throws him into a small room, later beating him and subjecting him to cold-water treatments, all of which he views as an initiation procedure preliminary to his restoration to the crown. Only in his final entry does Poprishchin seem to realize what is actually happening, as he laments his treatment and his fate and prays for a troika to carry him away far above and beyond all his misery. Even here, however, he soon reverts yet again to the ridiculous in a closing sentence about a boil on the nose of the Dey of Algiers.

What we witness in Poprishchin's diary, then, are the final two-to-three months of his complete mental deterioration, a course which runs from the tragicomic ludicrousness of his love aspirations and social ambitions in the early entries, through pathetic delusions of political prominence, to the totally tragic realization of his madness and nothingness in the asylum cell. Since we very soon recognize him as deranged, indeed approach him from the start as a mad narrator, we take nothing from his pen literally, except perhaps the barest outline of the incidents recounted. Rather, we laugh at many of his early actions and at a number of his more fantastic pronouncements (even in the latter portion, as when he asserts that the moon is manufactured out of tarred cord and lamp oil by a lame barrel maker in Hamburg), and we point accusingly at him for his universal spite toward his equals and betters and for his blatant biases and misrepresentations in his account. But our predominant reaction is one of pity—not so much for Poprishchin himself, since he is hardly characterized individually, as for his deplorable situation and the mental and emotional condition to which that situation has seemingly contributed in considerable measure. Poprishchin is scarcely more than a cipher, a nonentity without the means to buy a decent coat or two solid meals in succession and without the opportunities or the self-esteem to have formed any personal relationships and developed a social life. He is only a lowly civil servant, a quill-sharpener and copier, filled with vaguely generalized desires and spites, whose objects (Sophie, the cashier, the throne of Spain, the office head) are purely coincidental to his disposition and can change from instant to instant as circumstance (a meeting on the street, a random newspaper item) and whim dictate. Even his name (from *pryšč*, or "pimple")[3] contributes to his deindividualization at the hands of the implied author.

In short, Poprishchin must be seen as a purely representative figure, a case study in the psychology of the aberrant mind, and one which, I feel, ultimately takes a sympathetic view of the situation represented in Poprishchin's diary and of Poprishchin's "kind." For what we see is the plight of a figure who is firmly relegated to a lowly position, who is continually reminded of his lowliness by the people and events of his daily life, whose fondest ambitions are forever being thwarted and shattered by fate, and whose frustrations have subsequently induced "madness," since all other escapes have proved futile. Granted, Poprishchin may well have possessed the seeds of neurosis from childhood; but we are given no indication whatsoever on this point, and hence the assumption must be that it is primarily the nature of his adult life which has induced his insanity.

Thus, while a certain social critique may be implied, the "Diary" emerges primarily as a psychological study of an individual devoid of any sense of material or spiritual value. Though Poprishchin raves against his superiors, he is in fact no rebel, no critic of the system. On the contrary, his ambitions are quite simply to attain some of the system's benefits and accouterments for himself: a lovely wife, nice clothes, spending money, social activities, a warm house, business and political influence. His criticisms are only the spiteful comments of an envious and ambitious have-not at the seeming (and often genuine) insensitivity of many of the haves. He criticizes only sporadically, randomly, reflexively, out of momentary pique and repeated frustrations, not out of principle. His life of continual degradation and humiliation is so at odds with his dreams and aspirations of respectability, success, and well-being that a pathological split is induced in his psyche which ultimately forces him to turn totally inward

[3] Victor Erlich, *Gogol*, p. 91.

upon ever more fanciful delusions and away from reality altogether. What results is a moving portrait of a downtrodden and abused figure, a portrait which is at least slightly reflected in Poprishchin's own pathetic final outburst: "Mother, save your poor son! Drop a tear on his sick head! See how they torment him! Press your poor orphan to your bosom! There is nowhere in the world for him! He is persecuted! Mother, have pity on your sick child!" But the portrait is also, as noted earlier, again immediately undercut by the reemergence of ridiculous fancy: "And do you know that the Dey of Algiers has a boil just under his nose?"

Gogol's work thus takes on considerably more of a symbolic, almost fablelike quality in its portrayal of a deranged mind from the inside than does Fowles's novel, delineating an only tokenly individualized process of advanced psychic decline and lifting that madness into a more generalized representation of despair, misery, and a fateful turning inward. Where Fowles used highly individualized characters to produce a genuinely dramatic tension as well as a sense of evil versus virtue, the implied author here uses the comic and painful writhings of a mad consciousness primarily to present a serious psychological study of man deprived of all spiritual value and human worth. Although Gogol's satiric wit and caricaturizing detail and his use of a deluded, unreliable speaker produce several highly comic and seriocomic scenes, the "Diary" is ultimately a pathetically moving dissection of total psychic disintegration.

A far more ambitious, complex, and explicitly programmatic work using a neurotic narrator is Dostoevsky's *Zapiski iz podpol'ja* (*Notes from Underground* [1864]). Extrinsic evidence concerning the work's composition is plentiful—in the author's correspondence, in his notebooks, in the echo of the themes and motifs of the *Notes* in the four great novels which followed, in the ideas and attitudes expressed in such writings as the *Winter Notes on Summer Impressions* (1863), and in the commentary of contemporaries. From all these we know that *Notes from Underground* was written in late 1863 and early 1864, a period that

118

brought the slow, painful death of Dostoevsky's first wife and the sudden death of his brother. The time was also one during which Dostoevsky was still evolving from the relative liberalism of his days with the journal *Vremya* (*Time*) to the conservatism of his new journal *Epokha* (*Epoch*,which was to publish the *Notes*), largely as a result of the unfavorable impressions of the West gathered during his travels in the summer of 1862 (which produced the *Winter Notes*). He was subsequently becoming more and more antagonistic toward the "progressive" and Westernizing elements in Russian society and toward their talk of socialist utopias founded upon strictly rationalist principles—ideas most vividly embodied in N. G. Chernyshevsky's novel *What Is To Be Done?* (1863) and in the famous Crystal Palace erected for the London Exposition of 1861.

Notes from Underground is a product of all these factors: there is a darkness and desperation about the work which reflect the tragic personal losses and setbacks that befell Dostoevsky in 1863–64; there is a virulent strain of anti-Westernism and antipathy toward the rational, scientific basis of the developing industrial world of Europe; and there is a scathing polemic in part 1 against the radical socialists of Russia, as embodied in Chernyshevsky and his followers, who implicitly believed man to be innately good and capable of acting rationally and beneficently in his own interest and for the good of all. In part 1 the nameless narrator exposes the simplistic and mechanical character of the radicals' conceptions regarding human nature, asserting that, if taken seriously and carried consequentially to their logical end, these ideas would render all moral action impossible and would eliminate all emotional responses such as anger, revulsion, and willful desire. The narrator sees man as a more complex creature and basically an irrational one who finds himself in constant conflict between will and reason and one who would rebel against any imposition of a totally rational order solely to assert his freedom of will, even though such an assertion might well be detrimental or even destructive, leaving him a victim of his own capriciousness and impulse. In this respect the narrator echoes Dostoevsky's

119

own sentiments—which can be read in, for example, the *Winter Notes* and seen at work in *Crime and Punishment*, *The Possessed*, and *The Brothers Karamazov*—bearing out the factually based claim of many critics and literary historians that the work was originally begun as a polemic against the socialist radicals and was conceived and executed as a cruel and deliberate parody of their ideas.[4] Thus on one level the narrator is a reliable spokesman for the implied author.

To read the *Notes* on this level alone, however, is to underread the work greatly and do Dostoevsky a serious injustice, for it reduces the work to a simple frontal attack that might well have been relegated to obscurity within a few years after its publication or at best remained a historical curiosity in the author's oeuvre. Such a reading also ignores the authorial notes inserted at the beginning and at the conclusion, the extraordinary vacillations in the character of the narrator himself as he presents his arguments in part 1, and the entire import of the narrator's actions and his account of those actions in part 2. It is through these three elements that the narrator is first set off from the implied author, then established as an extensively characterized individual case and woven into the fabric of the work's satiric plan, thus making the *Notes* into not only a more complex and sophisticated sociopolitical satire but a well-executed piece of literary writing as well.

Before the narrator begins the first part of his notes, Dostoevsky inserts the following statement:

The author of the diary and the diary itself are, of course, imaginary. Nevertheless it is clear that such persons as the writer of these notes not only may, but positively must, exist in our society, when we consider the circumstances in the midst of which our society is formed. I have tried to expose to the view of the public more distinctly than is commonly done, one of the characters of the recent past. He is one of the representatives of a generation still living. In this fragment, entitled

---

[4] See, for example, Joseph Frank, "Nihilism and *Notes from Underground*," p. 2; and Ernest J. Simmons, *Dostoevsky: The Making of a Novelist*, p. 125.

"Underground," this person introduces himself and his views, and, as it were, tries to explain the causes owing to which he has made his appearance and was bound to make his appearance in our midst. In the second fragment there are added the actual notes of this person concerning certain events in his life.—AUTHOR'S NOTE.[5]

Thus Dostoevsky clearly establishes a distinction between himself and the fictional narrator and indicates that he is presenting the narrator as a representative figure, "a character of the recent past," an anonymous member of an aging generation, a nameless and faceless entity of whom there are many in present-day Russia. Nothing here unequivocally indicates that Dostoevsky has anything satirical or derogatory in mind in establishing this separation, but the phrase "positively *must* exist in our society" and the setting of a "mousehole" or "underground" retreat certainly raise that possibility, as does the remark that the narrator "*tries* to explain why he has appeared" (stress added).

With the establishment of a certain distance between narrator and implied author, and with the slight wariness toward the author of the "notes" induced by the phrasings just cited, the reader is prepared to encounter the narrator with a somewhat critical eye. The first two sections need such critical detachment, if confusion is to be avoided, for they present a narrator who by turns reviles himself as a sick and spiteful person, then "confesses" his basic sweetness of character, then acknowledges his lies of a moment before, then apologizes for his bewildering babble, then praises his great lucidity, then laments this same lucidity as a grievous affliction for making him conscious of "the good and the beautiful" but also for enabling him to recognize his own depravity, then describes the "pleasure of despair" that this recognition of "heightened consciousness" has brought. Where this

[5] Fyodor Dostoevsky, "Notes from Underground," in *White Nights and Other Stories*, pp. 50–155. Some translations use the name "Fyodor Dostoevsky" instead of the designation "Author's Note" employed here by Constance Garnett; see, for example, Andrew R. McAndrew's translation of the novella in *Notes from Underground, White Nights, The Dream of a Ridiculous Man, and Selections from The House of the Dead* (New York: New American Library, 1961).

elaborate and seemingly endless chain of contradictions will lead is not yet clear, if it is indeed to lead anywhere except back upon itself.

Section 3 sheds light on the dilemma for the reader, as the narrator begins to define himself and his position, contrasting the "'direct' persons and men of action" with "us people who think and consequently do nothing," a "retort-made man," who is cognizant of this antithesis and so subdued by it that "he thinks of himself as a mouse and not a man" and therefore "creeps ignominiously into [his] mousehole," his "nasty, stinking, underground home," where he nurses all the insults and humiliations he has ever suffered, "spitefully teasing and tormenting [him]self . . . for forty years together." Describing in general terms a situation remarkably like his own years-long grievance against an officer who once inadvertently shamed him (as related in part 2), he notes that the mouse may

. . . begin to revenge itself, too, but, as it were, piecemeal, in trivial ways, from behind the stove, incognito, without believing either in its own right to vengeance, or in the success of its revenge, knowing that from all its efforts at revenge it will suffer a hundred times more than he on whom it revenges itself, while he, I daresay, will not even scratch himself.

The result is "an artificially induced hopelessness, . . . a hell of unsatisfied desires turned inward, . . . that fever of oscillation, of resolution determined for ever and repented of again a minute later," all of which produce a "cold, abominable half despair" that only such a lucid and intelligent figure can experience, a "strange enjoyment . . . so subtle, so difficult of analysis, that persons who are a little limited . . . will not understand a single atom of it." Such a nature, the narrator goes on to note in the rest of section 3 and in section 4, will even refuse to recognize a stone wall of scientific law such as $2 + 2 = 4$, deriving pleasure from the very impossibility of ever refuting that law, and will

122

also take delight in a toothache, drawing a certain voluptuous satisfaction from the implacability of his pain, from his "spiteful and vicious" display of moaning, and from his "degradation" and particularly the realization of this degradation. He will derive such spiteful pleasure because of the effect of his education and his contact with European civilization, through which he "has been uprooted from the soil and lost contact with the people."

By this point it will most probably be apparent to the reader of the *Notes* that he is dealing with an articulate but rather slippery entity who vacillates in somewhat schizophrenic fashion from venomous invective to carefully elucidated argument and back again, an individual who is both a rationalist and a solipsistic advocate of irrational desire and who has been relegated to a state of inert neurotic withdrawal as a consequence of these irresolvably conflicting components of his nature. Like his postulated interlocutors and unlike the natural man of action, he is an educated individual thoroughly inculcated in the scientific rationalism and logic imported from the West; but unlike these interlocutors, he also recognizes that he, as a human being, is composed of desires as well as intellect. He knows too that these desires will often lead a man to act against what he rationally sees as his best interest merely in order to assert himself and prove nothing other than that he is human and not "a piano-key." The problem is that the narrator's lucidity leads him to recognize this conflict between reason and will and to discern its consequences but at the same time renders him totally unable to act out of anything other than intellectual spite or sheer boredom, which in turn are perceived for what they are and thus prove again unsatisfying. He acts merely to assert what he believes to be his free will, because "twice two makes five is sometimes a very charming thing too," but of course realizes the futility and gratuitousness of these exercises as well. In short, for the narrator, "consciousness is the greatest misfortune for man," but one that he cannot give up and which therefore leads him in his logical circles unendingly and produces in him the neurosis of total impotence and inertia.

123

The narrator's argument in part 1 thus accomplishes several things: (a) it takes a direct shot at the socialist utopians and their dreams of a Crystal Palace world where men will always act rationally in their own and society's best interest; (b) it counters the socialists' view with an assertion that man will exercise his free will against his best interest merely to prove that he possesses such free will and is not a mechanical servant to logic; (c) it undermines the rationalists' argument from within by recognizing the full implications of the will-versus-reason conflict, by delineating these implications in contortedly logical fashion, and by revealing the willful assertion of desire as the logical outgrowth of prolonged exposure to rationalist existence; and (d) it exposes the hopeless neurotic deadlock to which the conflicting impulses of rationality and the irrational will ultimately lead. As the narrator realizes—naturally, again, since he is so lucid—all this makes him more of a non-hero than a hero, a "harmless, vexatious babbler" who "will talk and talk and talk" but who, for all his intelligence and insight, is "able neither to begin nor to finish anything."

Ultimately the narrator can confirm and advocate only the inertia and inactivity of the mousehole and is even of several minds as to why he has written, how he has written, and what he has written:

Such confessions as I intend to make are never printed nor given to other people to read. Anyway, I am not strong-minded enough for that, and I don't see why I should be. But you see a fancy has occurred to me and I want to realize it at all costs. Let me explain.

Every man has reminiscences which he would not tell to every one, but only to his friends. He has other matters in his mind which he would not reveal even to his friends, but only to himself, and that in secret. But there are other things which a man is afraid to tell even to himself, and every decent man has a number of such things stored away in his mind. The more decent he is, the greater the number of such things in his mind. Anyway, I have only lately determined to remember some of my early adventures. Till now I have always avoided them, even with a certain uneasiness. Now, when I am not only recalling them, but have actually decided to write an account of them, I want to try the experiment whether one can, even with oneself, be perfectly open and not take fright at the whole truth. . . . I write only for myself, and I wish to declare once and for all that if I write as though I were addressing readers, that is simply because it is easier for me to write in that form. It is a form, an empty form—I shall never have readers. I have made this plain already. . . .

I don't wish to be hampered by any restrictions in the compilation of my notes. I shall not attempt any system or method. I will jot things down as I remember them.

But here, perhaps, some one will catch at the word and ask me: if you really don't reckon on readers, why do you make such compacts with yourself—and on paper too? . . . Why are you explaining? Why do you apologize?

Well, there it is, I answer.

There is a whole psychology in all this, though. Perhaps it is simply that I am a coward. . . . If it is not for the benefit of the public why should I not simply recall these incidents in my own mind without putting them on paper?

Quite so; but yet it is more imposing on paper. There is something more impressive in it; I shall be better able to criticize myself and improve my style. Besides, I shall perhaps obtain actual relief from writing. . . .

Besides, I am bored, and I never have anything to do. Writing will be a sort of work. They say work makes man kind-hearted and honest. Well, here is a chance for me, anyway.

The narrator would like to impress the reader and win approval with his carefully reasoned attack on rationalism; yet, in a confusion of cross-purposes, he also invites the reader's vituperation down upon his head through periodic outbursts of spleen and self-denigration in a kind of perpetual motion that is also reflected in his style:

Even after the most resolute affirmations there always remains a loophole: to deny one's words or completely to alter their meaning. "I swear to you, gentlemen, that I do not believe a single, not one single little word of what I have now scribbled down! *That is, I also believe it*, if you like, but at the same time, for some unknown reason, I feel and suspect that I'm lying like a shoemaker." Such is the unending circle through which the sick consciousness is revolved. Indifference toward the hostile world and a shameful dependence upon it—this is a mouse's scurrying about, a *perpetuum mobile*.[6]

He attacks rationalism, that is, yet is himself in its grip; and he posits the assertion of free will as a morally superior alternative to a life based on rational self-interest, yet reveals the exercise of such will to be equally sterile and unpraiseworthy, since it leads only to a self-absorbed withdrawal from life. He longs to replace rational conduct with more romantic emotional responses such as anger, love, and revenge but can only grovel impotently within his subterranean retreat. He has become his own adversary and fought himself into a no-win situation.

This hopeless impasse, which the narrator himself realizes and which is simultaneously the cause and the result of his neurosis, is, the implied author seems to be saying, the dilemma of the nineteenth-century intellectual "divorced from life" and devoid of any means of salvation. The narrator's neurotic deadlock is thus again a representation of a generalized condition which the author wishes to expose and, in this case, attack as well. We know from Dostoevsky's letters that he originally intended for the narrator's—and therefore man's—salvation to lie in an embrace of Christ and in a resurrection through faith. Without that addition, however, which was deleted by censors and never restored by Dostoevsky in subsequent editions, the esthetic design is nonetheless clear as a product of the distinct distancing between narrator and implied author. As the former writhes hopelessly in a tangle of intellect and emotion, the latter watches impassively and condescendingly.

In part 2 this condescension is seen to be negative and even mocking, as the romanticism characteristic of the 1840s intellec-

[6] Konstantin Mochulsky, *Dostoevsky: His Life and Work*, trans. Michael A. Minihan, p. 248.

tual in Russia is pilloried both through allusion—in the ironic use of quotes and motifs from that period's literature—and in the demonstrated moral impotence of such romanticism in confrontation with the real stuff of life. The implied author prefaces this section with a quote from a poem by Nekrasov on the redemption of a prostitute—a common theme both of Chernyshevsky and of social romanticism of the period—and blithely cuts it off with an "etc., etc., etc." (Garnett does not translate this tag, though it is present in the original and in several other translations), thus already indicating a definite disdain for romantic sentiments. Then we watch the narrator as he goes through the motions of indulging in low life in an effort to debase himself and contradict his rational desires, as he spoke of abstractly in part 1. We see him make a spiteful object of himself in the Zverkov episode, as he alternately tries to ingratiate himself with his acquaintances and expresses his scorn for them and their opinions. And lastly, we watch him lecture the prostitute Liza on the evils and destructiveness of her life and hold out to her the possibility of redemption through love, only to prove totally incapable of providing that love himself and finally humiliate himself in the most despicable manner by attempting to prostitute her once again as she seeks to save herself through him.

Ultimately the implied author sees no point in continuing with the narrator's notes and arbitrarily cuts him off: "The notes of this paradoxalist do not end here, however. He could not refrain from going on with them, but it seems to us that we may stop here." So, whereas part 1 excoriated the rationalists and adduced the romantic impulse as an at least slightly preferable though ineffective counter-option to their rationalism, part 2 negates this romanticism through the depiction of its total moral impotence. Through the egocentric—though vacillating—concerns evident in the narrator's conduct in the Zverkov episode, and particularly through his despicable treatment of Liza in building up her hopes of love and salvation with his high-flown lecture and then failing to follow through in returning her newborn love, the full

127

shabbiness, the self-centeredness, and the uselessness of all intellectual ideals in the face of genuine spontaneity and unselfish love are revealed.[7]

Thus through the narrator's words the implied author explicitly rejects the rationalist ideology of the 1860s and implicitly places in serious question the romantic ideology of the 1840s; and through the narrator's report of past actions in part 2, that romanticism is likewise rejected—implicitly, over and above the narrator's account, but unmistakably in his detestable conduct toward Liza. The narrator's argument exposes the fallacies of one position; he himself, by his living example, reveals the emptiness of the other. The result is a total rejection, by the implied author, of an intelligentsia divorced from life and devoid of any genuine emotional capacity, of man psychically split and spiritually turned inward upon himself, of the pathological "dreamer." For Dostoevsky, there was a solution to the dilemma through Christian faith; for the implied author of the *Notes* as the work stands, there is only the negative indictment of the rationalist and the romantic positions, both of which lead nowhere and produce only the "neurosis" of moral turpitude, intellectual chaos, and spiritual emptiness found in his nameless narrator, this "character of the recent past."

Neurosis, then, in the worlds created by Gogol and Dostoevsky in the two works investigated here, is presented as a literary analogue of a sociopolitical malaise afflicting a given society in general and certain segments of that society in particular. The import of this madness, though broad, is delimited at least somewhat in both cases through the largely programmatic and ideological intent which seems to underlie them. The "madness" of a certain social order or ideology, as viewed by the implied author, is transformed into the psychological disorder of a literary protagonist who, through his own words and example, then shows that order or that ideology to be flawed or "mad" in some degree. With

[7] Compare Frank, "Nihilism," p. 27.

Gogol, the "madness" of the social order is its insidious oppression of poor souls such as Poprishchin, whose grotesque psychic deterioration reveals the order's inherent lack of human concern. With Dostoevsky, the narrator himself embodies the ideologies under attack and reveals the moral and spiritual dead end to which those ideologies could lead the educated nineteenth-century Russian.

The effectiveness of this fairly common tack varies considerably, of course, but is generally dependent, on the one hand, upon the extreme but nonetheless convincing lengths to which the oppression-induced madness can be carried, and on the other hand, upon the subtlety with which the implied author lets the narrator either trip himself up in attempting to convey his own ideological viewpoint (as in Dostoevsky) or unwittingly reveal the heartlessness of the social order which has induced his neurosis (as in Gogol). Ken Kesey's *One Flew Over the Cuckoo's Nest* (1963) goes so far as to depict a psychiatric ward as a microcosm of American society in order to make its point against the arbitrary and dehumanizing institutionalization of political power; and black writers such as James Baldwin and Ralph Ellison, in *Go Tell It on the Mountain* and *Invisible Man* respectively, transform the frustrations of blackness into outcries which run the gamut from the primitive to the neurotic to the tragic to the threatening. Philip Roth's *Portnoy's Complaint* presents in wildy and outrageously exaggerated form the libidinously oppressed Jewish boy who has been victimized and made a neurotic mess by overly stern traditional mores (his story is even couched in the form of a monologue delivered to his psychiatrist). And Faulkner's Jason and Quentin Compson reveal in their respective narrative portions of *The Sound and the Fury* the moral vacuum and the existential anguish of a decaying Southern society.

Neurosis can also be used in an even broader sense, however, as a representation of what the implied author views as man's basically irrational or perverse nature. The classic case in point is the prose oeuvre of Edgar Allan Poe—in particular, for purposes of this study, his first-person narratives. The nameless narrator of

"The Tell-Tale Heart" provides a prime example, beginning with the assertion that he is definitely not mad, going on to relate how he painstakingly laid his plans to kill his old wall-eyed master, but then betraying his actual mental imbalance (if it is not already apparent from his strident claims to the contrary) by recounting the frantic nature of the actual murder and his subsequent cracking under the delusion that the anxious pulsing of his own heart during the police investigation is the beating of the old man's heart under the floorboards.

The narrator of "The Black Cat" comes closer to success in concealing his act of murder, which he considers solely the product of a mad horror and terror induced by a hated one-eyed cat. Having assured the investigators that nothing is amiss in his house, the narrator compulsively taps the wall behind which he has sealed his murdered wife's body, whereupon the piercing wail of the cat from inside the wall betrays him to the police. The exposure of the murderer here is thus more plausibly realistic in its attribution to external causes than was the case in "The Tell-Tale Heart," but the narrator's singular insistence on the cat as the precipitator both of the murder and of the revelation of that murder belies a mind which refuses to acknowledge its own criminal derangement and seeks instead to blame the entire sequence of events on outside factors. Possibly the cat was a genuine irritant to the narrator; but the patently frantic and strident quality of the narrator's voice, as well as the strong echoes of "The Tell-Tale Heart," argues in favor of a reading which sees the narrator as so twisted by his hatred, by his deed, and by his present terror at the thought of his impending execution on the gallows that he cannot admit to himself that he alone is responsible for the murder and for his weakness in letting himself be found out. Like the narrator of "The Tell-Tale Heart," he continues to insist that he is sane, to assert his coolness and cleverness under stress, and to defend his moral position. All three points are undermined, however, by the facts and by the frenzied, distorted nature of his narrative.

"William Wilson," "The Cask of Amontillado," "Ligeia," Roderick Usher's secondary narrative within the frame of "The Fall of the House of Usher"—all betray narrative motifs similar to those of the two stories just touched upon. William Wilson's double, never seen except through the narrator Wilson's eyes, must be interpreted as the mere projection of a perverse consciousness, the image of all that this consciousness should have become or desired to become. What is actually self-loathing and self-dissatisfaction is thus given external form, and that external form is then viewed as an impostor and a usurper, thus creating a basis for dispatching the double. Only after the "deed" is irrevocably accomplished does the realization set in—again through an imagined appearance, this time of the "spirit" of the second Wilson in the reflection of a mirror—that Wilson has killed a part of himself.[8] Montresor, in "The Cask of Amontillado," commits the perfect crime in walling up Fortunato deep within an underground vault, thus punishing the latter "with impunity" for some undisclosed offense, of which Fortunato seems unaware. That impunity is voided, however, by the very telling of the tale, which takes the form of a deathbed confessional some fifty years after the fact. Far from giving him lasting satisfaction, Montresor's deed has haunted him all these years, and he cannot rest in peace until he finally admits the murder openly, thereby destroying the impunity which he had desired so as to make his revenge complete. As with the other Poe narrators, his own unrealized sense of guilt denies him any genuine peace of mind and forces his self-incriminating confession.

"Ligeia" presents perhaps the most problematic case and has sparked a controversy similar to that surrounding Henry James's *A Turn of the Screw*, with proponents both of a straightforward, supernatural reading and of an ironic, psychological one. In my own view, the case for the latter is stronger, given the literal reading's failure to explain adequately the mysterious appearance of the red drops that poison the narrator's second wife Rowena and given the narrator's opium addiction and morbid obsession with

---

[8] G. R. Thompson, *Poe's Fiction: Romantic Irony in the Gothic Tales*, p. 169.

the memory of his first wife Ligeia, whom he sees resurrected in the body of the deceased Rowena. Such a reading is also reinforced by the ironic and self-deluding narratives of Poe's other first-person narrators, particularly those already discussed briefly here. In addition, the implied author of "Ligeia" prefaces his story with a spurious quote from Joseph Glanvill which, by its fictitious nature, places the whole idea of resurrection of the dead in a very dubious light and lends support to an ironic reading of the tale.[9]

In short, the strong similarities of style and theme in Poe's first-person gothic tales, with their frenzied self-defensiveness, their excited language, their compulsive confessions, their anxious insistence, their adumbration of supernatural causes and fantastic external factors behind acts committed and events witnessed, betray an almost singular orientation toward the ironic portrayal of psychological perversity. Mystery, criminal activity, and often the supernatural pervade these tales; but in each case the narrative voice is placed within the dramatic context of a confessional and within the implicit but very palpable qualifying frame of an effort at reconstructing the criminal or supernatural events so as to clear itself of guilt. These dramatic frames with their several clues (the red drops and the opium in "Ligeia," the narrator's obvious tension in "The Tell-Tale Heart") suggest the narrators' delusions concerning the experiences narrated and evoke instead a second level of meaning above their self-serving interpretations and conscious understandings of the events related:

In Poe's characteristically intricate, even involuted, patterns of dramatic irony, the apparent narrative voice which pervades the surface atmosphere of the work is also seen within a qualifying frame. . . . Insinuated into [each tale], like clues in a detective story, are details which

---

[9] "And the will therein lieth, which dieth not. Who knoweth the mysteries of the will, with its vigor? For God is but a great will pervading all things by nature of its intentness. Man doth not yield himself to the angels, nor unto death utterly, save only through the weakness of his feeble will." No such passage has even been located in Glanvill's writings.

begin to construct frames around the narrative voice of the work. These dramatic frames suggest the delusiveness of the experience as the first-person narrator renders it. As in the works of Henry James and Joseph Conrad, there is often in a Poe tale a tale within a tale; and the meaning of the whole lies in the relationship of the various implied stories and their frames rather than in the explicit meaning given to the surface story by the dramatically involved narrator.[10]

The resulting portraits are ones of similarly diseased minds, in many cases criminally perverse and in each case self-deludingly myopic concerning the respective narrator's own guilt and aberrant nature.[11]

The recurrence of such unconsciously self-deluding narrators suggests a saner mentality in the implied authorial voice which created them, a mentality which is eminently aware—at least in retrospect[12]—of the human mind's capacity not only for rational and successful grappling with life but also for falling into the self-consuming and ultimately destructive folly of fantasy and mad irrationality.[13] In each of these strikingly similar narrators the mind has fallen victim to the emotions and to mere "fancy," and although all try to reassert their rational faculties, each betrays his failure to do so and reveals himself as hopelessly deluded. "Madness" in Poe is thus a universally potential human condition aris-

[10] Thompson, *Poe's Fiction*, pp. 13–14.

[11] Interestingly, "The Sphinx" features a narrator whose vision is literally in error, as he mistakes a curious moth crawling on a spider's web by a window sash for some monstrous creature on a distant hill outside the window.

[12] The Argentine writer Julio Cortázar, a confessed admirer (and translator) of Poe and an author whose own "fantastic realism" is very much akin to the spirit of Poe's work, once remarked (in a lecture at the University of Oklahoma on November 13, 1975) that there is often a total identification between himself and his narrator during the actual writing of a story such as "The House Taken Over," but that this identification ceases with the conclusion of the story, allowing him to speak quite easily of the limitations of the (frequently unreliable) narrator and of a division between narrator and implied author. He feels that Poe created his works in similar fashion.

[13] Compare James W. Gargano, "The Question of Poe's Narrators"; and Marvin Mengeling and Frances Mengeling, "From Fancy to Failure: A Study of the Narrators in the Tales of E. A. Poe."

ing when the faculties of mind and spirit are out of tune, and his first-person tales present in ironic fashion the destructive nature of that perverse imbalance in the psychological makeup of man.

As many commentators have noted, Poe's interest in his failed narrators was primarily a psychological one and not a moral one, a concentration on the destructive psychic chaos produced by some imbalance in the faculties which leads in turn to some criminal or perverse action, inducing a subconscious guilt which then completes the destruction of the narrator by insidious means. Similarly afflicted narrators continue to appear frequently in modern fiction. Choosing only from among the last few years' production, one might cite, for example, the homicidally deranged narrator of Argentine novelist Abelardo Arias's *The Big Coward*, the oneiric and dissolute narrator of French writer Philippe d'André's *The Mummy*, the grotesquely lunatic dwarf Humberto who narrates Chilean novelist José Donoso's *The Obscene Bird of Night*, the child-narrator of Thomas Tryon's latter-day American gothic novel *The Other* who has murdered his twin brother and merged with him mentally and spiritually, and the three hopelessly insane narrators of German writer Marlene Stenten's *Baby*.

The more modern counterpart of this series of phenomena, however, is an existential despair, a sense of aimlessness and meaninglessness of existence, the absence of a moral or spiritual center, which leads to a similar corruption and deterioration of the individual if no solution is found to fill that void. Roquentin in Sartre's *Nausea* indicates rather vaguely that he is on the verge of discovering such a solution in art—specifically the music of a scratchy jazz record—and Meursault in Camus's *The Stranger*, "washed clean" and "emptied of hope" through "a great rush of anger" in response to the prison chaplain's talk of God's love and salvation, "lays his heart open to the benign indifference of the universe" and is filled with happiness over making a new start on the eve of his execution. Dostoevsky's Stavrogin, in *The Possessed*, reaches such an extreme of ennui and nausea, of moral nihilism and destructiveness, that he can find release only through suicide. Camus's Clamence in *The Fall*, though similarly guilty of moral turpitude and callous indifference to everything, even human life, is incapable of such a confession as that made by Stavrogin and instead cleverly implicates the reader and all humankind in his guilt; he thus alleviates his existential discomfort by assuming the exalted position of satanic judge-advocate in a world that is one large hell devoid of all innocence.[14]

One case in which genuine madness goes hand in hand with this existential despair, however, is a short novel by the Persian author Sadegh Hedayat—himself a longtime resident of Paris and a writer strongly influenced by the existentialist currents there in the 1930s and '40s—*Buf-ē kur*, or *The Blind Owl* (1936). The barest outline of the nameless narrator's story here seems to run as follows: born of the illicit union between the beautiful temple dancer Bugam Desi and one of two identical twin brothers (he does not know which and has not seen any of the three since infancy), the narrator is almost immediately given into the foster care of his father's sister and her old nurse. He is smitten by his aunt's young daughter, his foster sister and childhood playmate, and is later compromised into marriage by this cousin. He is then denied her conjugal favors and forced to submit to her presumed extramarital liaisons with everyone from ragman to nobleman. He falls physically ill and degenerates mentally as well, arousing the pity and contempt of all around him. One day he finally enters his wife's bedroom, begins to take her forcibly, kills her with a knife during an embrace, and completes the union once she is dead. He then dismembers her, stuffs the parts into a suitcase, and buries them in the desert, thereafter returning to his room to drown himself in opium stupors and sleep.

I say the story "seems" to run in this fashion, for the narrative is broken into several nonsequential segments which constantly turn back upon each other and which merge the waking and dreaming states to an almost impenetrable degree, so that one

[14] Sara Toenes, "Public Confession in *La Chute*," p. 314.

can never be quite sure what has actually occurred and when, if anything or ever. In fact, in the short chapters 3 and 5 the narrator is just awaking from a deep sleep and/or drug stupor, and the brief opening chapter is written shortly after the entire "ordeal," presumably just following the awakening referred to in chapter 5. The long chapters 2 and 4 seem to depict one entire, extended dream sequence and an actual chain of events respectively. Since chapter 4 includes the account of the presumed murder and chapter 2 the account of the dismemberment and burial of the victim, the actual chronological order of the chapters' events would appear to be 4–5–2–3–1; and judging from the narrative situations described in chapters 1 and 3, the order of the units' composition is 4–5–1–2–3. But all this says little except to indicate a complexity of construction which closely parallels the ambiguity of the narrative content, a complexity which perhaps mirrors the workings of a tortured mind.

As he describes himself in the opening chapter, Hedayat's narrator bears a number of resemblances to the mad narrators already seen in Fowles, Gogol, Dostoevsky, and Poe. He is a solitary individual, both in a literal and an extended sense: he lives in a small room away from the city and totally isolated from contact with other people, from whom he feels himself irrevocably cut off by an ever-increasing and fearsome "abyss." His mind has slowly eroded from this isolation and from drugs, disease, and spiritual suffering, and he has been forever "branded," "poisoned," and "cauterized" by his "case." He is reduced to communicating solely with his own "shadow" and with the phantoms of his memories and imaginings, which he is incapable of separating and distinguishing from each other. In writing, he seeks some self-knowledge, some communication with others, some release from his torment. His effort is thus at once aimed at purgation, relief, understanding, coming to terms with what he has done and been, "warning" others in some vague fashion from the example of his fate, and possibly justifying himself to himself. The tone of the entire introductory chapter, that is, is one of desperate rationality and control, as a mind recognizes itself teetering on the

brink of insanity and tries through sheer determination to keep
from sliding over the edge of that abyss.

Chapter 2 begins with a certain amount of seemingly concrete
detail: it is precisely two months and four days since the "passing"
of the narrator's beloved; he sits within a small room with a small
door and window and an old bottle of wine on an upper shelf; he
has near him one of the many pen-cases which he decorates—
always with the same scene—to eke out a living and "to kill time"
when he is not under the influence of wine or opium. That one
scene is described minutely:

For some reason unknown to me the subject of all my painting was
from the very beginning one and the same. It consisted always of a
cypress tree at the foot of which was squatting a bent old man like an
Indian fakir. He had a long cloak wrapped about him and wore a turban
on his head. The index finger of his left hand was pressed to his lips in a
gesture of surprise. Before him stood a girl in a long black dress, leaning
towards him and offering him a flower of morning glory. Between them
ran a little stream. Had I seen the subject of this picture at some time in
the past or had it been revealed to me in a dream? I do not know. What I
do know is that whenever I sat down to paint I reproduced the same
design, the same subject. My hand independently of my will always depicted the same scene.[15]

Even such touches of apparent realism soon begin to dissolve,
however, as the narrative drifts into an associative and almost hal-
lucinatory sequence of visions, memories, and imaginings. A gap
appears in the wall, and the narrator catches a glimpse of the girl
depicted on the vases; her eyes hold a strange obsessive enchantment for him; the wizened old fakir with the "coarse, grating
laugh" appears as a mysterious coachman of the dead; the narrator later cannot find the gap and spends "two days and four
nights" searching the wall for traces of it; one day the girl enters
his house, lies down, dies, rises briefly, then subsides into cold
stiffness again; the narrator returns home after the desert burial

[15] Sadegh Hedayat, *The Blind Owl*, trans. D. P. Costello, p. 6.

and loses himself in drug-induced sleep, later awaking with the feeling that a great weight has been removed from his chest and that his world has been restored to harmony. The release seems to be that of oblivion to all that has gone before, to the years of loneliness and suffering, to the murder, to the dismemberment and burial. Prior to that release the narrator's mind is marked by obsessive associations which encompass all that he has experienced and imagined throughout his sufferings. The same small set of images and motifs—the old man, the coarse laugh, the girl's eyes, the morning glory, the bundle in the handkerchief, the wine bottle, the cypress—constantly recur in various manifestations and thereby come to appear to the reader more as fixations within the narrator's mind than as realistic elements of an external world.

This view of the narrative gains support from the fourth chapter, as events and figures in the narrator's personal history are depicted: his mother Bugam Desi, his father and uncle, their trial by cobra, the butcher across the street from his aunt's house, the ragged peddler in the street, the beautiful young cousin. Here the same motifs and images occur as in the dreamlike dismemberment-and-burial sequence of chapter 2 and begin to merge into one fused mass: the eyes of the narrator's dream girl and those of the girl on the bed and on his pen-cases resemble those of Bugam Desi and of his young cousin; the coarse laugh of the old peddler is echoed in the laugh of his deranged uncle following the harrowing cobra trial and recalls the old, wizened ragman of the burial scene and the old fakir on the cases; the butcher's daily slaughter of animals is soon mirrored in the narrator's murder of his cousin/wife and has its earlier parallel in the dismemberment; and the narrator himself, after the murder, finally becomes a conglomerate of his father/uncle and the peddler/ragman/fakir as he stands over his murdered wife, white-haired, holding her eye and laughing a coarse, hollow, grating laugh.

Other, lesser motifs are similarly repeated with almost equal obsessiveness: coughs, nail-biting, tastes and smells, crazed shrieks, snatches of songs, blister flies, the wine jug and the cobra venom, a jar and the handkerchief. The reality of the images and events consequently evaporates, for everything in the narrator's world comes to resemble everything else, leaving only his obsessive, associative, mad mind as the prevailing reality.

In moments that seem to approach cogency the narrator acknowledges the incipient fantasy world to which he is susceptible, the dream world which he cannot control, the frequent ascendancy of his subconscious over his conscious mind and his physical body (as in his psychosomatic illness following his early rejection by his wife), his childlikeness. Just as significantly, however, he also reveals unintentionally a number of traits which have marked other literary madmen: grotesque grimaces and antics which frighten his nurse out of her wits; a frequent sense of superiority over all those who supposedly talk behind his back, even an assertion of godlikeness; and occasionally a groveling and even masochistic subservience which practically invites the heaping of further abuse and maltreatment upon him and makes him the constant dupe and stooge of others, particularly his wife. He shares the isolation and the scorn and abuse suffered by Poprishchin and the Underground Man; his opium habits and his vision of the dream girl's rising from her deathbed and then sinking again into cold death parallel the account given by the narrator of "Ligeia"; his fixation on the eye of the victim recalls the narrator of "The Tell-Tale Heart"; his burial of the victim recalls both "The Tell-Tale Heart" and "The Black Cat"; and his compulsion to narrate his account echoes the burning compulsion of all the aforesaid Poe narrators.

Combined with these traits, however, is an admixture of existential angst and despair seemingly born of the narrator's lengthy sufferings and of his gradual realization of the extent to which he is presumably abused; for it is immediately following the account of this realization that he begins to intone about his feelings of emptiness, despair, self-effacement, world-weariness, coldness to religion, estrangement, and anguish. The series culminates in the assertion of his own godlikeness and superiority and in his eventual retreat into total solitude and the darkness of an imaginary world of shadows shortly preceding the murder of his wife. In such utterances there are often strong echoes of Sartre (nausea, the use of art as a saving grace from despair) and of Camus (particularly in the depths of despair and subsequent heights of release occasionally reached, recalling Meursault's pre-execution euphoria), and lesser ones of Dostoevsky (the arrogant assertions of moral superiority over his imagined or real tormentors). Just as often, however, the narrator's angst blends with his obsessive fixations so completely that it is rendered almost ridiculous, as when his desire to pass into oblivion is tempered by his fear that "the atoms of [his] body should later go to make up the bodies of rabblemen."

The resulting mix of madness and estrangement thus presents a complex situation in regard to the reliability of the narrator. On the one hand, his obvious derangement, the aberrations and fixations and compulsions he shares with a long line of untrustworthy neurotic narrators, plus his pronounced inability to distinguish reality from imagination, mark him as a patently unreliable guide to his past experiences and present circumstances. On the other hand, the relative cogency and sincerity of many of the expressions of estrangement, as well as their parallels with such reasonably reliable speakers as Roquentin and Meursault, lend occasional touches of seeming trustworthiness to the narrative. These touches are then at least somewhat undermined, however, by their frequent combination with facets of the narrator's neuroses. Also—turning for a moment to extrinsic considerations—the existentialist despair and angst closely resemble the moroseness and estrangement frequently voiced by Hedayat himself which ultimately culminated in his suicide in 1951, thus again adding a certain reliability to the narrative voice through compatibility with the known sentiments of the actual author. But other extrinsic considerations such as the strong echoes of Poe, Dostoevsky, and the French existentialists—with all of whom Hedayat was quite familiar—are indicative of the implied author at work behind the narrator's back, adding depth and breadth and extra dimensions to the narrative and thereby both establishing a definite distance between implied author and narrator and, on balance, rendering that narrator almost wholly unreliable.

The narrator's efforts at speaking to his shadow and gaining some understanding of himself and of his ordeal result only in continued confusion and darkness—even blindness in that darkness, if we accept his image of a blind owl, which he indicates he has become in contrast to the comprehending owl of his shadow reading over his shoulder. Hedayat, on the other hand, seems to have had a better grasp on his quandary—albeit one with negative but nonetheless consciously executed consequences—and was able to articulate that dilemma successfully in this complex narrative with its frightening psychological finesse and its finely interwoven literary and philosophical resonances. The fact that the novel does indeed graphically portray those "sores which erode the mind like a canker" but does not bring the narrator the clarity and release he seeks in writing is both evidence and product of the distance between implied author and narrator and of the unreliability consequently established in the narrative voice.

The various mad narrators examined here thus cover a wide range of narrative possibilities: in terms of narrative distance, the range extends from the total and obvious cleft between narrator and implied author in Fowles's *The Collector* and Gogol's "Diary of a Madman," to the close parallels between Hedayat and the narrator of *The Blind Owl*, where only the superior artistic turn of the implied author's ordering mind achieves some coherence out of the narrator's otherwise chaotic and darkened world. Between these poles lie the two other cases examined: the slightly less complete distancing between Dostoevsky and the narrator of the *Notes from Underground*; and Poe's narrators, with their strikingly similar stores of repressed guilt and their compulsions toward confessional self-destruction, together indicative in each instance of a mind itself at least preoccupied—if not obsessed—with the mad and the irrational and possibly skirting dangerously close to the brink of insanity. The narratives range from outright polemic in Dostoevsky, to veiled social critique and psychological studies in Gogol and Fowles, to fictional journeys into the world of irrational fancy in Poe, to a deeply personal foray into existential despair and morbid neurosis in Hedayat. The narrators themselves include intellectuals (the Underground Man) and aristocrats (Montresor and the narrator of "Ligeia"), as well as the dull-witted (Clegg) and the middle-to-lower-class (Clegg, Poprishchin, the narrators of *The Blind Owl*, "The Tell-Tale Heart," and "The Black Cat"); and the accounts by these neurotics variously take the form of the diary, the disputative address, the retrospective investigation, the jail-cell testimony, the deathbed confession, and the soul-searching attempt at self-therapy and self-knowledge.

Despite this great diversity of form, content, milieu, character, and narrative distance, the paradigm of the pathological narrator outlined earlier remains valid. In each case the narrator's situation is one of increasing or even total isolation, often physical as well as spiritual. Alienation, withdrawal, nonconformity, inability to cope with human contact or to handle human relationships, and absorption with personal whims and fancies are mirrored by a physical retreat into a small garret, an isolated house, a shabby room, a jail cell, or a "mousehole." And other people exist only as the exaggerated objects of love, hatred, revenge, persecution, admiration, oppression, or emulation. Reality of the outside world disintegrates (or has already crumbled by the time of narration), and the narrator's world gradually comes to consist of nothing more than the feverish imaginings and distortions of his own psyche.

A vicious circle of cause and effect pushes the narrator into this retreat, as he is scorned and abused by others for his strangeness, only to become even more pathological as a result of such maltreatment. The circle continues until the narrator either goes over the edge of sanity into delirium or commits acts of irrational violence, or both. His narrative then becomes an effort to justify or somehow to explain his actions and simultaneously reveals repressed stores of guilt and shame which force him into largely unwitting confessions. At the time that he narrates the final phase of his degenerative process—and in most cases the time of the entire narration *is* this final phase—he has drifted so far into neurotic solipsism that he can no longer adequately distinguish the real from the imagined in respect to causes, actual events, motivations, and personalities involved.

The madman's narrative is therefore extremely unreliable in rendering an accurate picture of the occurrences and actions which constitute his story and also in the valuative and evaluative interpretations which he places on those elements of his narrative. Corrective interpretations such as Miranda's section in *The Collector* or the author's introductory footnote in *Notes from Underground*, or other overt signs of the implied author's presence such as Gogol's title "Diary of a Madman," establish advance or belated notice of their narratives' unreliability and set up more or less definitive guidelines as to how each narrative is to be approached. But with or without such clear guideposts to their accounts, the narrators in each case very soon evoke doubts in the integrity and trustworthiness of their narration through sundry means: obviously unacceptable value judgments, incongruous reasoning, gross errors or contradictions in fact which they unwittingly expose, stridency of tone and unwarranted defensiveness of posture, blatant absurdities in ideas or supposed facts, and obsessive preoccupations which unconsciously dominate their minds and therefore their narratives. Form and content thus coalesce to present not a picture of the narrator's past and present external reality, but rather one of his present psychological derangement and, in many cases, his criminal culpability. The reader, cued by the overt or surreptitious signals of the narrator's pathological unreliability as his own witness, joins with the implied author and watches the narrator reveal nothing so much as his own variously comic, grotesque, or tragic madness.

CHAPTER 6

The Naïf

UNRELIABLE NARRATION need by no means always function to the greater or lesser detriment of the narrating "I" as it does in the majority of the accounts examined in the preceding chapters of this study, revealing the hypocrisy, amorality, immorality, monomaniacal obsessions, destructive neuroses, distorted self-images, or sheer ineptness of the respective first-person narrators of those works. Take, for example, the following passage from a work which demonstrates a number of picaresque features, Mark Twain's *Huckleberry Finn* (1885):

They went off and I got aboard the raft, feeling bad and low, because I knowed very well I had done wrong, and I see it warn't no use for one to try and learn to do right; a body that don't get *started* right when he's little ain't got no show—when the pinch comes there ain't nothing to back him up and keep him to his work, and so he gets beat. Then I thought a minute, and says to myself, hold on; s'pose you'd a done right and give Jim up, would you felt better than what you do right now? No, says I, I'd feel bad—I'd feel just the same way I do now. Well, then, says I, what's the use you learning to do right when it's troublesome to do right and ain't no trouble to do wrong, and the wages is just the same? I was stuck. I couldn't answer that. So I reckoned I wouldn't bother no more about it, but after this always do whichever come handiest at the time.[1]

[1] Mark Twain, *The Adventures of Huckleberry Finn*, chap. 16.

144

The casuistic distinction drawn here smacks strongly of the improvisitory morality typically indulged in by the *pícaro*, opting as it does for the more pragmatic path without strict regard for accepted ethical standards in deciding on a course of action at a critical juncture. What differentiates the decision here, however, from the true *pícaro*'s usual justifications for pursuing questionable courses of action—for example, Pablos's decision to join with the Toledo toughs in *The Scavenger*—is the fact that what Huck labels the "wrong" path is actually and unequivocally the more praiseworthy moral and human alternative involved in his dilemma. For several miles of river his conscience has been making him terribly uneasy about his (unintentional) complicity in helping Jim reach free territory. It now has brought matters to a head as the raft nears Cairo, the entrance to the Ohio River and to freedom for the runaway slave:

I begun to get it through my head that [Jim] *was* most free—and who was to blame for it? Why, me. I couldn't get that out of my conscience, no how nor no way. . . . I got to feeling so mean and so miserable I most wished I was dead. I fidgeted up and down the raft, abusing myself to myself, and Jim was fidgeting up and down past me. We neither of us could keep still. Every time he danced around and says "Dah's Cairo!" it went through me like a shot, and I thought if it *was* Cairo I reckoned I would die of miserableness.

Jim's euphoric talk of later working to buy the freedom of his wife and two children then caps Huck's agony:

Thinks I, this is what comes of my not thinking. Here was this nigger, which I had as good as helped to run away, coming right out flatfooted and saying he would steal his children—children that belonged to a man I didn't even know; a man that hadn't ever done me no harm. I was sorry to hear Jim say that, it was such a lowering of him. My conscience got to stirring me up hotter than ever, until at last I says to it, "Let up on me—it ain't too late yet—I'll paddle ashore at the first light and tell." All my troubles were gone.

145

Paddling ashore at the next opportunity and "all in a sweat to tell on him," Huck finds, however, that he cannot bring himself to report Jim's presence to two gun-toting bounty hunters in a skiff, the first folks he meets:

I didn't answer up prompt. I tried to, but the words wouldn't come. I tried for a second or two to brace up and out with it, but I warn't man enough—hadn't the spunk of a rabbit. I see I was weakening; so I just give up trying, and up and says: "He's white."

Not man enough, no spunk, weakening, giving up—all clearly indicate Huck's acceptance, on the conscious level, of an antebellum ethical code which views the black man as chattel and not as human, as do his earlier incredulous remarks on Jim's audacity in asserting ownership of his own children.

At odds with this conscience is Huck's natural feeling for Jim as an individual and, more importantly, as a friend—a friendship born initially of their common lot as runaways thrown together by fate and then gradually cemented by their interdependence and their discoveries of genuine warmth and human kindness in each other. Together these discoveries bring Jim to love the adopted child of his owner's sister and bring Huck—the offspring of an ignorant bigot and the ward of a slaveholding family—to humble himself more than once to a simple "nigger."[2] It was this feeling which had made the dilemma such a struggle for Huck in the passages cited above, and it is this feeling which is called to mind for Huck once more in Jim's parting words as Huck sets out for shore, ostensibly to determine whether they have reached Cairo:

"Pooty soon I'll be a-shoutin' for joy, en I'll say, it's all on accounts o' Huck; I's a free man, en I couldn't ever ben free ef it hadn' ben for Huck; Huck done it. Jim won't ever forgit you, Huck; you's de bes' fren' Jim's ever had; en you's de *only* fren' ol' Jim's got now." . . . When he

---

[2] Most notably in the rattlesnake sequence and in the oft-cited passage where Huck apologizes for having tricked Jim following their separation in the river fog, only to be lectured by Jim for treating him like "trash."

says this, it seemed to kind of take the tuck all out of me. I went along slow then, and I warn't right down certain whether I was glad I started or whether I warn't. When I was fifty yards off, Jim says: "Dah you goes, de ole true Huck; de on'y white genlman dat ever kep' his promis to ole Jim." Well I just felt sick.

Thus, when Huck tells the two hunters that his companion back on the raft is white and when he adds that the person is his father and "confesses" that the latter has smallpox, he has, technically, committed a "wrong" in a legal sense by going against the prevailing social and statutory order, whereby Jim and his race are considered only as the rightful property of their owners. But at the same time Huck has made a decision which affirms Jim's personal identity and his race's right to individual liberty and human dignity—a decision which most readers will certainly consider a "right" in a higher sense and which they will feel to be shared by the author. Huck's narration, that is, is felt to be patently unreliable here and in many such instances, but in a fashion which renders him a far more positive and admirable figure than he considers himself to be.

Twain has, of course, made part of this question—namely, the authorial attitude—academic through his oft-cited remark that *Huckleberry Finn* depicts the triumph of a "sound heart" over a "deformed conscience";[3] and his long and assiduous cultivation of an "artful artlessness" in stage manner and writing style (most prominent in *Innocents Abroad*), indeed the whole persona of "Mark Twain," argues strongly in favor of an ironic reading of Huck's narrative pronouncements.[4] But even without these extrinsic data as guides, it is apparent that Huck's narrative strews

[3] Henry Nash Smith, *Mark Twain*, p. 203, n. 140.24. Smith cites Notebook 28a(I) of the *Mark Twain Papers* (1895), p. 35, as his source.

[4] Compare Tony Tanner, *The Reign of Wonder*, p. 129: "Clemens's appearances as Mark Twain—on stage, in books—reveal the most artful artlessness: it is more than art concealing art, it is rather art *destroying* art. He does not wish to appear easily sure of himself, but instead rather confused—more bewildered than insouciant, more naïve than masterful. The planned artlessness of Mark Twain's stage talk is the essential step in Clemens's art toward Huck's own speech in which naïve artlessness ('I don't know the words') reaches, perhaps for the only time in Clemens's work, the level of great art."

147

dozens of clues about which betray the wry frontier moralist behind the mask of artlessness and intellectual naïveté.

To begin with, Huck is still a mere youth at the time of the writing of the story: he himself indicates in his closing paragraph both that he has actually *written* the tale (which seems to have taken quite a bit of effort and trouble on his part) and that the writing has taken place not too long after the Evasion, for Tom Sawyer has now just about recovered from the gunshot wound suffered in that escapade. He is therefore practically the same twelve-year-old at the time of narration as he was during the course of his journey down the Mississippi, scarcely old enough to be able to provide mature, reliable reflection on what he narrates or to offer more than a straightforward record of facts and observations almost completely unglossed by deeper understanding and interpretation. His descriptions of the river in all its idyllic tranquility, its latent danger, its teeming life both in the water and ashore, and its enchanted nights and glorious sunrises are rendered with a naturalness that is vividly direct and evocative without resorting to elaborate romantic conceits or to the overly contrived abstraction and metaphoric style to which Twain falls prey in, for example, *Roughing It*. What little subjectivity intrudes into Huck's descriptions, such as that of the sunrise given in chapter 19, remains simple, sense-oriented, and restricted to comparisons with his own previous experience with nature rather than delving into metaphysical reflection. It is indicative of a rustically naïve oneness with nature instead of the self-conscious empathy with nature seen in, say, Wordsworth.[5]

We slid into the river and had a swim, so as to freshen up and cool off; then we set down on the sandy bottom where the water was about knee deep, and watched the daylight come. Not a sound anywheres—perfectly still—just like the whole world was asleep, only sometimes the

[5] Compare ibid., p. 14, where Tanner speaks of Huck's "innocent eye," vernacular style, and "devotion to the immediate present" as "all part of the attempt to establish contact with the real, living, flowing world," an attempt he considers successful on Twain's part.

bullfrogs a-cluttering, maybe. The thing to see, looking away over the water, was a kind of dull line—that was the woods on t'other side; you couldn't make nothing else out; then a pale place in the sky; then more paleness spreading around; then the river softened up away off, and warn't black any more, but gray; you could see little dark spots drifting along ever so far away—trading scows, and such things; and long black streaks—rafts; sometimes you could hear a sweep screaking, or jumbled up voices, it was so still, and sound come so far; and by and by you could see a streak on the water which you know by the look of the streak that there's a snag there in a swift current which breaks on it and makes that streak look that way; and you see the mist curl off of the water, and the east reddens up, and the river, and you make out a log-cabin in the edge of the woods, away on the bank t'other side of the river, being a woodyard, likely, and piled by them cheats so you can throw a dog through it anywheres; then the nice breeze springs up, and comes sweet to smell on account of the woods and flowers; but sometimes not that way, because they've left dead fish laying around, gars and such, and they do get pretty rank; and next you've got the full day, and everything smiling in the sun, and the song-birds just going it! [Chap. 19]

For the most part, Huck is similarly unreflective regarding the events and characters about which he narrates, limiting himself usually to laconic reactions of a purely personal nature based on private or mundane experiences when he does permit himself to depart from pure description, as in the homely references above to dogs and dead fish and river snags. Actual opinions are even rarer and are often clichéd and aphoristic: the Duke and King's impersonation of long-lost relatives of the Wilks family makes Huck "ashamed of the human race"; his inability to pray for divine guidance in his quandary over Jim is attributed to the fact that his heart "warn't right," for "you can't pray a lie"; and his pangs of guilt about his role in the frauds' humiliation prove to him that "it don't make no difference whether you do right or wrong, a person's conscience ain't got no sense, and just goes for him *anyway*." Miss Watson's Bible-thumping piety, Pap's swinish behavior and self-serving abuse of Huck, the long-standing feud between the Grangerfords and the Sheperdsons, Colonel Sher-

149

burn's cold-blooded shooting of Boggs and subsequent defiance of a lynch mob, and the whole adventure of the Evasion, on the other hand, are all allowed to pass without such generalizing sentiments, however brief. In these portions of the narrative and for most of the account involving the Duke and King—the Wilks Farm episode, the escapades of the Royal Nonesuch—in short, for almost all the events which take place ashore, Huck's role becomes that of a secondary participant reporting the action while not being central to that action throughout. In the Sherburn-Boggs episode he virtually fades away, becoming a pure witness—standing in the street to see the shooting, following to the drugstore to view the body, and tagging along with the mob as it heads to Sherburn's house—with no role in the action itself but to narrate it.

These two aspects of Huck's narrative role—that is, his function as merely a witness-narrator instead of as a genuine protagonist-narrator for much of the novel, and his paucity of generalizing reflections on what he narrates, both ashore and on the river—make this role one of largely straight reportage rather than subjective and interpretive narration. In conjunction with Huck's youth and undeveloped eye for the import—both serious and comic—of what he witnesses and reports, this straightforward style affords an excellent opportunity for irony or indirect satire on the part of the implied author; for if genuine humor, social satire, and serious indictment of certain types and institutions emerge, and if Huck is both largely incapable of seeing or articulating well enough to convey such effects and generally not inclined to do so even if he were capable, the surreptitious commentary must be that of the implied author Twain.

And such features do emerge. Huck's naïve eye does not see the sham and complacent pretentiousness of the Grangerford household with its crockery animals, showy books, ostentatious paintings, and imitation fruit "which was much redder and yellower and prettier than real ones." His ear does not catch the hilarious wretchedness of Emmaline Grangerford's graveyard doggerel ("I Shall Never Hear Thy Sweet Chirrup More Alas"),

150

which he even tries to imitate at one point. He sees but does not note the contradiction of the local preacher's delivering a sermon on brotherly love to a church filled with arms-bearing feuders. He recognizes the Duke and King for frauds immediately, yet has uncomprehending admiration for the impressive bombast of their fractured Shakespearean oratory and has even memorized the Duke's "To be or not to be; that is the bare bodkin" soliloquy. The Sherburn episode provokes no evaluation of any kind from Huck to show that he has in the least comprehended or even been very favorably or unfavorably impressed by Sherburn's bravado.[6] And Huck proceeds straight from the lynch-mob scene to the circus, where he is thoroughly taken in by the "drunken" bareback rider.

On a slightly higher level, Huck seems totally unaware of some of the interconnections within his narrative: how his half-serious preference for "the other place" in view of the dullness and severity of Miss Watson's heaven foreshadows his later decision to "go to Hell" by not turning Jim in; how his readings in European history and his comments on the subject to Jim prepare for the comic entry of the Duke and King; how the Royal Nonesuch's *Romeo and Juliet* excerpts provide a comic parallel to the love affair between Sophia Grangerford and Harney Shepherdson; and how his own elaborate escape from Pap is later parodied (along with all romantic escape literature, according to most critics) by the Evasion. Similarly, Huck fails either to see or to note some of the larger discrepancies and implications of his narrative: the fact that, once he hits the river, every foray ashore involves his witting or forced assumption of a false identity (as the King's lackey, "Sarah Williams," the Duke's "valley," "George Jaxon," and finally, "Tom Sawyer"), the majority of which he does not play particularly well; the fact that despite his opening remarks on the subject of lying, he is a rather unconvincing liar, except when his actual safety or Jim's identity or some noble

[6] Compare Jonathan Raban, *Mark Twain: "Huckleberry Finn"*, who feels that the story weakens in this episode by too clearly revealing the voice of Twain in what amounts virtually to a fable.

cause (the Wilks girls' stolen money, the thieves aboard the wrecked *Sir Walter Scott*) is at stake, whereupon he shines with inventiveness and ingenuity;[7] and that all the episodes ashore end on a negative note (the deaths of Buck and Joe Grangerford, the just yet saddening sight of the tarring and feathering of the Duke and King, the distasteful scene between Sherburn and the mob), save for the concluding and highly problematical Evasion sequence, while the briefer river incidents have more positive endings (the imminent rescue of the thieves and the hostage on the *Scott*, the safe passages through rapids and narrows, the drifting house which yields considerable supplies, the escapes from various criminals and bounty hunters, the repeated avoidance of discovery).

In short, Huck is an easily fooled and occasionally uncomprehending narrator, by nature given to recounting events and experiences in a straight-faced style devoid of humor, reflection, lengthy moralization, or verbal adornment. Much humor results for the reader from Emmaline's verses, from the jumble of French history imparted by Huck to Jim, from the bowdlerizations of Shakespeare, from the incredibly elaborate Evasion, and from numerous other passages; and sharp social critique is evident in the Grangerford-Shepherdson feud, in Miss Watson's pious attempts at bringing Huck into the Christian fold, in the con men's mentality, in Pap Finn's bigotry and ignorance, in the small Southern town's hollow morality in the face of Sherburn's challenge to their sense of justice, and in the entire social attitude concerning the slave question as evidenced by people as widely divergent in nature as the Phelpses and the bounty hunters. But

[7] In chapter 29 the Wilkses' shrewd lawyer friend Levi Bell tells Huck, "I reckon you ain't used to lying, it don't seem to come handy; what you want is practice. You do it pretty awkward." And A. E. Dyson, in his "Huckleberry Finn and the Whole Truth," p. 36, says that despite Huck's opening comment that everybody lies at one time or another, "his own lies are always related to a deeper honesty; fidelity to fact and to good sense as he sees them. His lies are, in fact, worked out in the face of much he is asked to believe, evasive action taken not because he is willful or stupid, but because he is generous and alive. They are a technique for surviving in a largely immoral world with as little unpleasantness for himself and for everyone as possible."

that humor and that critique, as well as the irony of the various interconnected features of the narrative as outlined above, are all attributable not to Huck but, again, to Twain.

Huck himself offers personal opinions on others mostly in mere cursory fashion (Buck Harkness looks "tolerable cheap" fleeing Sherburn, and Colonel Grangerford is "a gentleman all over") and only rarely in straightforward declarations such as his admitted disgust and shame at the Duke and King's impersonation of long-lost relatives to the bereaved Wilkses and his expressed admiration of Mary Jane Wilks's strong, benevolent character. In these instances he reflects fairly closely the moral and ethical stance conveyed in the entire Wilks Farm sequence by condemning the obvious villains and praising the one person who possesses some nobility of spirit; and here, then, he represents what one must assume to be the implied author's attitudes. Hence unreliability is not a totally consistent feature of Huck's narrative, only a largely constant one wherein Twain employs a naïve, deadpan, unlettered and unreflective voice to convey from behind that voice the truths which he himself perceives regarding the society represented by the figures and events in his novel.[8]

In conjunction with the naïve and almost exclusively straightforward nature of the narrative, Huck's style is a naïve vernacular perfectly in keeping with his rural, border-state background and his minimally educated, unreflective, nature-oriented, personable, unpretentious, practical, and direct character. He cannot embellish or stylize his speech (his initial efforts to emulate Emmaline's maudlin sentimentality prove futile), nor can he successfully disguise its unlettered and folksy quality for any length of time, as he tries to do when forced into the role of a British "valley" during the Wilks episode or when he attempts to pose as a town-reared girl and visit Mrs. Loftus. His nature descriptions, as noted, put the stylized romanticists and literary realists to

[8] Several critics cite the inconsistency in Huck's perception as a serious flaw in the novel's construction, creating needless ambiguity in terms of the work's morality and narrative viewpoint. See Raban, *Mark Twain*; Smith, *Mark Twain*; and John Fraser, "In Defense of Culture: *Huckleberry Finn*," p. 7.

shame in terms of economy, personal involvement with nature, and simplicity of evocative power when they stand in isolation, as in the sunrise passage cited above; and lyrical sequences often merge effortlessly into his narrative, revealing a strong link between Huck and the natural world:

> When I woke up I didn't know where I was for a minute. I set up and looked around, a little scared. Then I remembered. The river looked miles and miles across. The moon was so bright I coulda counted the drift logs that went a-slipping along, black and still, hundreds of yards out from shore. Everything was dead quiet, and it looked late, and *smelt* late. . . . I took a good gap and a stretch . . . . [Chap. 7]

Huck is occasionally repetitive in the folk-epic manner, particularly in his accounts of the stillness of the river nights, the gray streaks and breezes of dawn, and the steady power of the river as it carries the raft downstream. Words sometimes fail him in his simplicity and in his desire to convey what he has seen and experienced ("You know what I mean—I don't know the words to put in"); and he has the folk narrator's ear and penchant for recording much of his tale in dialogue fashion, even many of his debates with his own conscience ("I says to myself, *this* is a girl that I'm letting that old reptile rob of her money"), thereby often removing himself from any direct narrative participation for long stretches of the novel.

There is of course no inherent virtue in the vernacular itself. As Henry Nash Smith notes, the King is every bit as much a vernacular character as is Huck, yet any narrative by the King would sooner or later be highly suspect, given his constant role of lying rogue. And too, a low vernacular is common to such unlettered picaresque narrators as Pablos and Moll. Huck, however, through his directness of language, his depicted frequent inability to lie convincingly, his dramatized goodness of heart, his obvious naïveté, and his demonstrated naturalness of feeling, conveys a certain "linguistic sincerity which convinces the reader of his complete truth" regarding the factual nature of what he relates and his own attitudes toward those events. "He can lie and steal . . . but he seems quite without the inner equipment which can construct emotional untruths" of the type which cast aspersions on his ethical nature and moral character.[9] He cannot be charged with hypocrisy and self-serving motives, for he readily assumes guilt (for Buck and Joe's deaths and for the near-bilking of the Wilks girls) and just as readily reproaches himself for his occasional carelessness and thoughtlessness (Jim's snakebite, the loss of the raft). He cannot be accused of blind amorality, for he has a strong conscience and marked loyalties regarding human ties and social obligations. He cannot be charged with viciousness, for he censures only in the most blatant circumstances (the defrauding of the bereaved Wilkses) and otherwise allows himself only an infrequent lament on the state of mankind (the tarring and feathering). And he cannot even be correctly termed a likable and harmless but ultimately self-indulgent rogue, for he has too much genuine concern for others (Jim, Sarah Wilks, Buck Grangerford, the hostage on the *Scott*) and is too little addicted to roguery for its own sake. Mere survival necessitates the occasional theft of a chicken and some looting of abandoned houses and boats; the other roles and frauds are forced upon Huck by the Duke and King or by the need to conceal his identity for Jim's sake.

By near-universal critical assessment, Huck is a positive figure through and through,[10] and the epithets describing his character and nature are myriad in variety: generous impulse, fidelity to the uncoerced self, childlike innocence, innocent honesty, unselective wonder, natural human feeling, unconscious goodness, natural acceptance of reality and devotion to the present, instinctive moral soundness, excess of compassion, lack of self-interest, adolescent imaginativeness, and a sound heart. Possessed of such a character, the only ways in which Huck could have pinioned

[9] Smith, *Mark Twain*, p. 121.
[10] Some dissenters are Raban, *Mark Twain*; Jane Johnson Benardette, "Huck Finn and the Nature of Fiction"; and Michael J. Hoffman, "Huck's Ironic Circle."

155

himself through his narrative would have been by the adoption of an overly false modesty entirely out of keeping with his direct nature or by attempting an artificially "literary" style (such as Emmaline's, which he "couldn't seem to make go somehow") equally alien to his own naturalness.

He took neither path, however, and the only vulnerable aspect of his narrative in terms of its reliability is that same naïve, innocent, natural soundness of heart for which it is so universally praised. Not only does Huck, in his naïveté, fail to perceive the humor, the social satire, the many literary allusions, the interconnections, and the serious moral dilemmas contained in his narrative, as already noted; he also fails to view his own crisis of conscience correctly. He thus has serious misgivings about himself, in the passage examined at the outset of this chapter, for not heeding his conscience and social dictates, both of which demand that he turn Jim over; and in the climactic passage of the work (Chap. 31), as Huck again seriously considers betraying Jim (this time even writing, but never sending, a letter to Miss Watson), he makes his famous decision not to do so, with the equally famous resolution, "All right, then, I'll *go* to Hell," fully believing that in following the leanings of his heart over those of his conscience he is indeed choosing the path of eternal damnation. That he was *not* is evident in the text's consistent portrayal of him as a positive character and in its depiction of the relationship between Huck and Jim as an important—if not the most important—feature of Huck's goodness. That he was *not*, for Twain, is evident in the latter's cited remark about the victory of Huck's sound heart over his deformed conscience and in the author's dictum that children and fools always tell the truth. That he was *not*, for critics and readers, is evident in the near-unanimous praise of Huck's human decency.

Huck is dead wrong in his self-condemnation and in his agony over his inability to pay his conscience—and, by extension, the ethical system which formed it—its due. His heart instinctively feels the opposite of that conscience's dictates to be truer and more just, as do Twain and the overwhelming majority of read-

156

ers; but on a conscious level Huck cannot recognize or articulate that sentiment. Narrative unreliability therefore results, both in the crucial junctures cited and throughout the work. The consequences of this unreliability are threefold: (1) the creation of a union between implied author and reader in admiration of Huck's victorious ethical and human struggle and of his strength of character;[11] (2) a concomitant reinforcement or even augmentation of the positive nature of that character;[12] and (3) a second union of implied author and reader in rejecting the tenets of antebellum Southern society.[13] As Dyson concludes concerning the narrative's effect:

> Mark Twain's irony . . . is a direct communication between writer and reader. No-one at all in the novel, including Huck, knows that the raft is a place of virtue; it is the secret communication of the irony. . . . The reader is challenged wholly at the level of moral response; failure to perceive the direction of the irony is indistinguishable from failure to perceive Huck's virtue. The irony is, indeed, a forcing into the consciousness of readers more educated than Huck himself the reality, as he embodies them, of their own ideals.[14]

Among the most important works of literature in the Western world, there are to my knowledge very few which match *Huckleberry Finn*'s exhaustive exploration of the possibilities of the naïve narrator. That is, few of these works use a child or adolescent or child-man or unconsciously good individual as a narrator to begin with, and fewer still use such a narrator as much more

[11] Compare Richard P. Adams, "The Unity and Coherence of *Huckleberry Finn*," p. 93, where he notes that the paradox of Huck's doing right by doing what he thoroughly believes to be wrong makes Twain's satire the brilliant piece of work that it is.

[12] Compare Dyson, "The Whole Truth," p. 38: "The final victory when [Huck] says, 'All right, then, I'll *go* to Hell' is all the more powerful for being unrecognized by Huck himself as savouring of either paradox or irony. . . . Huck really thinks he *is* being wicked, and the irony here cuts straight from writer to reader, bypassing Huck himself, though naturally enhancing his stature."

[13] Adams, "Unity and Coherence," p. 93, sees Huck's repudiation of his conscience as an innocent and unconscious repudiation of Southern society; but "the innocence is of Huck, not Clemens."

[14] Dyson, "The Whole Truth," pp. 39–40.

than a persona or a vehicle for satire, with only minimal characterization of the narrator himself. Many of the more famous works employing a naïve perspective do not even use first-person narration but are told instead through a third-person voice limited to the perspective of the naïve protagonist: one thinks of Voltaire's *Candide*, Carroll's *Alice in Wonderland*, St. Exupéry's *The Little Prince*, and Stevenson's *Treasure Island*. The first-person narrative of the retarded Benjy Compson in the opening section of *The Sound and the Fury* is not "pure": Benjy does not actually write or speak his "narrative," for his consciousness is incapable of such activity and can only be rendered through the author's transcriptions of that childlike mind's shifting impressions and memories. And books such as Tolstoy's *Childhood, Boyhood, Youth*, Maxim Gorky's *My Childhood*, Dostoevsky's *Netochka Nezvanovna*, Jerzy Kosinski's *The Painted Bird*, and Harper Lee's *To Kill a Mockingbird*, while focusing on events through a child's eyes, are narrated by the protagonists at a considerable temporal remove from the respective childhoods depicted; as David Copperfield notes regarding the early portion of his own history, later knowledge and insight come to their aid, contrasting the naïveté of the child with the gently ironic retrospective glance of the mature narrator.

Much irony and outright satire of social practices, norms, institutions, philosophies, and character types result in each of these works, of course; but with the possible exception of Benjy's narrative, none reveals the positive nature of the naïve protagonist solely through his own narration and without his conscious awareness, as is the case with Huck and his account. David Copperfield, Netochka Nezvanovna, and Esther Sommerson in Dickens's *Bleak House* are positive individuals but cannot really be termed naïve. They realize some of their shortcomings and are too modest to admit their goodness, but they do not confuse the two, as does Huck.

Several other works of recent vintage are a bit stickier. Hans Schnier, the title figure of Heinrich Böll's *The Clown*, is revealed through his shifting and complex interior monologue as a naïve, middle-aged, down-at-the-heels professional clown; and like his stage persona, he is by turns lovable and pitiful. But he is also seen to possess a child's pettiness, self-centeredness, and spitefulness as well in his random and sometimes unprovoked lashes at individuals and institutions such as Catholicism. And two recent British works, Anthony Burgess's *A Clockwork Orange* and Alan Sillitoe's short story "The Loneliness of the Long-Distance Runner," offer jargonized, vernacular narratives by relatively naïve adolescents who in this respect somewhat resemble Huck. Their narratives, however, like Schnier's, reveal their characters as at best problematical, presenting on the one hand a violence-loving street tough with a counterbalancing love for the music of "good old Ludwig Van," and on the other hand a hostile young juvenile offender from the lower-class district of Nottingham with a surprising sensitivity toward nature along with his antisocial tendencies.

Perhaps the only work which really comes close to *Huckleberry Finn* in the sense adduced here is another American novel, J. D. Salinger's *The Catcher in the Rye* (1951). Like Huck, Holden Caulfield is an adolescent (seventeen years old at the time of narration) and runaway (from a prep school) who tells his story in the current vernacular from a point in time not far removed from the actual narrated events (the time of narration is less than a year following those events). At the time of narration Holden is a patient in a California sanatorium, where he has been sent for professional help in sorting out his emotional problems. Like Huck, he is in a lull, poised between the adventures recounted and the promise of a new world of experience to come (Huck's lighting out for the frontier; Holden's release from the clinic and return to the outside world). Holden has already told his story twice (once to the clinic psychiatrist and once to his brother D. B., a Hollywood writer) and is now transcribing it for an imagined reader in what amounts to an effort at communicating and at unburdening himself in a kind of talk-therapy fashion, just as he constantly seeks someone to talk with (through phone calls, bar chatter, visits) during that December weekend in New York City which forms the subject of his narrative. And as in Huck's case, the act of narration proves rather exhausting and not particularly satisfying for Holden, who finds himself at the narrative's conclusion no clearer about himself and his experiences than when he started, even a trifle regretful of the fact that he has gone to all the trouble.

Holden is, however, very different from Huck in a number of more basic respects, and his narrative points up some interesting differences in the use of the naïve narrator. First, he is slightly older and more educated than Huck, though not necessarily more intelligent or industrious—he does not really care for school and is flunking everything except English literature. He is therefore a more self-conscious artist of sorts in narrating his story, at least to the extent that he chooses not to recount his "whole goddam autobiography" and include his childhood experiences and "all that David Copperfield kind of crap," focusing instead on that "madman stuff" of one weekend some six months earlier. He is competent enough in writing to ghost term papers for others, as he does to no avail for his prep-school roommate Stradlater; he sees through the sham of the sentimental film at Radio City; he is conversant with the names of public figures and movie stars; he enjoys listening to good intellectual talk from persons such as his older friend Carl Luce and his former English teacher Mr. Antolini; he is familiar with writers from Shakespeare to Hardy to Isak Dinesen; and he has done at least some thinking on his own and possesses some appreciation of subjects such as ancient history—in fact, the historical museum is one of his favorite haunts.

Second, Holden is a city youth, not a frontier child like Huck, and hence has never enjoyed and does not display an intimate contact with nature. Within limits, however, he demonstrates a certain sensitivity toward the natural world—his love of Central Park, his concern for the ducks there in winter, his disapproving comment on the workmen who refer to a large, unwieldy Christmas tree as a "sonuvabitch"—and talks on occasion of an eventual idyllic retreat to a cabin in the New England woods where everything and everyone would be required to be "natural" at all times. And third and most important, he is far more subjective than was Huck, given to reflection on and personal reaction to virtually everything that he sees, hears, and experiences.

This third aspect in particular makes Holden radically different from Huck in regard to narrative style, a fourth point of distinction between the two. Where Huck was basically a chronicler of the events and characters in his story, rendering whole episodes such as the Shepherdson-Grangerford feud and the Evasion virtually devoid of narrative asides, Holden cannot report even the briefest incident or conversation without adding his own commentary or reaction. Huck gives us Emmaline's poetry and the King's "To be or not to be" soliloquy with only grace notes of approval at the ends of the respective passages; but Holden interlaces his accounts of the Radio City movie and the Lunts' stage performance with a running barrage of largely disapproving criticism. Huck reports his encounter with Mrs. Loftus in straight dialogue style with only enough narrative filler to let us know his uneasiness as the conversation proceeds; Holden's account of his train conversation with the mother of a fellow student is interrupted every several lines with opinionated remarks on luggage, the woman's readiness to believe anything good about her son, the son's utter loathsomeness, and the negative features of Pencey Prep. And where Huck can narrate with nearly complete self-effacement those events and conversations in which he is not directly involved (the Sherburn-Boggs episode, Tom's explanation of the elaborate escape plans to Jim), Holden punctuates description with personal reaction, speaking, for example, of the "perverts" whom he watches through his hotel window and of the "phony" conversations at neighboring tables in a bar. In brief, where Huck rarely sees or reports anything beyond the surface facts of his experience, Holden's narrative consists at least as much in his commentary on the events and people of his experiences as in the actual narration of those experiences; and where

Huck's narrative unreliability was a product of his largely literal, conscious acceptance of reality as he had experienced it, the source of Holden's unreliability must be sought elsewhere.

The very language used by Holden is perhaps the first indicator of a certain unreliability in his narrative. Whereas Huck's vernacular was both indigenous to his native region and a consequence of his only minimal literacy, Holden's slangy speech is an acquired argot typical only of a certain age group in a particular era and indicative more of an assimilated attitude than of a natural heritage. This jargon is also imprecise in many respects, so that a number of its stock phrases become so clichéd and/or vague as to be rendered almost meaningless.[15] When Holden says that something "kills" him, he sometimes means that the person or thing impresses him greatly (his sister Phoebe's precocious quirks and comments) and at other times is saying that he finds the subject negative in some sense (his mocking disapproval of the behavior of the three Seattle girls he meets in a bar). His profanity can likewise be used pejoratively ("the goddam fencing foils"), for emphasis in a positive sense ("I wouldn't let you [Ackley] in my goddam family"), or simply as an expletive devoid of any real connotation of value ("I took a last look down the goddam corridor"). "Crap" can mean foolishness or actual excrement, and "crazy" can be used to indicate both violent dislike ("that drives me crazy") or its opposite ("I'm crazy about . . ."). Holden constantly appends verbal tags devoid of any specific meaning to his sentences, usually the phrases "and all" and "or anything" ("he's my brother and all," "it was December and all," "no gloves or anything"), and he seems to feel compelled to reinforce his sincerity with frequent use of the phrases "it really is," "it really did," and "I really mean it." He repeatedly resorts to a limited battery of adjectives and adverbs such as "lousy," "pretty," "crumby," "terrific," "old," and "stupid," all with little or no specificity of meaning. His similes are no better, usually consisting

[15] Many of the examples which follow are taken from Donald P. Costello, "The Language of *The Catcher in the Rye*."

of "as hell" or "like a madman" to describe the most disparate activities; and he is constantly dredging up such trite figures of speech as "sharp as a tack" or "laughed like a hyena." Holden's language is, then, for the most part typical teenage slang, "versatile yet narrow, expressive yet unimaginative, imprecise, often crude, and always trite,"[16] and therefore indicative of a mind which is not yet sufficiently perceptive or discriminating to render a reliable account of its experiences.

Second, while Holden does realize that he possesses a "lousy vocabulary," he fails to see a number of other shortcomings in his own character. Some are verbal, such as his disdain of inarticulate people who try to sound intelligent by saying things like "that's between him and I," when he himself makes that selfsame grammatical error on numerous occasions. Others are a bit more serious and reveal a discrepancy between attitude and action on his part: he complains that Ackley always seems to stand right in a person's light, then does the same thing himself to Stradlater; he abhors the pedantic snobbery of people like old Professor Spencer and the pseudo-literati at the theatre, yet himself entertains pretensions of intellectuality when trying to converse with Luce and comments condescendingly on the low intellect of the girls from Seattle; he decries the phoniness of such role-playing types as Stradlater and one of his brother's old girl friends, yet tries to assume the air of an experienced man-about-town in the bars he visits; and he finds fault with the excessive attention paid to style and appearance by many in the city nightclub crowd and by show-business types, yet picks his roommates on the quality of their luggage. His perceptiveness regarding the nature of his own character is thus still quite undeveloped and again most untrustworthy.

Third, Holden is admittedly inexperienced in many of the areas in which his adolescent personality is undergoing some form of conflict. The most obvious of these, of course, is sex, in which he confesses his basic ignorance—that is, his virginity—and his lack of understanding. This bit of information, if not

[16] Ibid., p. 176.

already apparent during Holden's desperate defense of Jane Gallagher's supposed virtue from the imagined onslaught of Stradlater's unscrupled charms, affords the older reader an added dimension of insight and enjoyment not only in the reading of the fight scene but also of later incidents such as the cavortings of the "perverts" at the Edmont Hotel, the encounter with the young prostitute Sunny, and the close of the scene in Antolini's apartment when the teacher puts a reassuring hand on the boy's leg. Because of Holden's inexperience in such matters, his declamatory judgments are at least open to question, particularly regarding the nature of Antolini's actions.

Similarly, Holden's charges of phoniness are applied in such profligate, undiscerning, and unmoderated fashion as to be rendered again at least somewhat suspect: old folks and academics, people who work in Hollywood, people who frequent certain nightclubs, people who go to Radio City, people who cater to an audience's whims, people who don't care about the ducks in Central Park—all are condemned without exception or qualification. The very absoluteness and generalized inclusiveness of the judgments render them not wholly acceptable. Their wanton use deflates their efficacy to such an extent that Holden often appears a total misanthrope, fully open to Phoebe's charge that he doesn't like "*anything* that's happening" and to Antolini's prognosis that he is "riding for some kind of terrible, terrible fall" and is fast approaching the point where he will hate everything and everybody.

That Holden is *not* misanthropic, however, despite the abundance of negative personality features elucidated by his narrative, is indicated in the youth's reactions to these two charges and borne out by that same narrative. Phoebe's demand that Holden name one thing he likes sets off an extended but confused memory sequence in Holden's mind, touching first on the two nuns in the city to whom Holden had given ten dollars when he himself was getting very low on cash, then recounting at length the suicide of a quiet fellow student named James Castle. Both incidents convey a strong compassionate streak in Holden and mark him as possessing charity and sensitivity to a degree far in excess of those

164

around him. Significantly, however, he cannot articulate these two incidents to Phoebe and instead brings up his deceased younger brother Allie as one thing he likes, only to see his choice refuted by Phoebe's correct and unsparing remark that Allie is dead and so "that is nothing really."

Holden's choice of what he would like to be, again in response to the precocious Phoebe's questioning, is just as "unreal" and as romantic as his evocation of Allie: instead of finding satisfaction with any conceivably real activity, Holden longs only to play "the catcher in the rye," eternally saving children from falling over "some crazy cliff." Holden's vision is not only again "nothing really" in its ephemerality and otherworldliness; it is also, significantly, based on a misconception—namely, his oft-cited mistake (Phoebe notes it in the text) of thinking that Burns's poem runs "if a body catch a body, comin' through the rye," when in fact the verb is "meet" and the context one of a lovers' meeting, not children's games.[17] The vision is of course an inspired one, again indicative of a beautifully sensitive and compassionate strain in Holden's nature, but it is one which has yet to come to terms with the actual business of living. It is again a mark of Holden's immaturity, a kind of groping for some base which will conform to his adolescent idealism and counter the encroaching realizations born of maturity. It represents a retreat from the disappointing "phoniness" of the world he is in the process of discovering and back to the idyll of childhood and innocence where people like Allie were "about a thousand times nicer than the people you know that're *alive* and all."

To Antolini's prediction that Holden will eventually find himself hating all human types, Holden manages a slightly more articulate reply:

You're wrong about that hating business. I mean about hating football players and all. You really are. I don't hate too many guys. What I may

[17] The title of the novel, by focusing on this misconception, emphasizes the false premises of Holden's idealized world, thus undermining both Holden's emotional makeup and his reliability as a narrator.

do, I may hate them for a *little* while, like this guy Stradlater I knew at Pencey, and this other boy, Robert Ackley. I hated *them* once in a while—I admit it—but it doesn't last too long, is what I mean. After a while, if I didn't see them, if they didn't come in the room, or if I didn't see them in the dining room for a couple of meals, I sort of missed them. I mean I sort of missed them.[18]

The remark has much truth in it, for even when Holden had been most disgusted by Ackley's hygiene or outraged by Stradlater's *macho* insensitivity, he found himself often feeling sorry for the former and respecting some of the latter's better qualities such as his generosity. Similarly, his improvised falsehoods regarding his classmate Ernest Morrow to the boy's mother on the train to New York, his impassioned championing of Jane Gallagher's virtue against the stronger Stradlater, his harmless kidding of the three girls from Seattle, his "feeling sorry" for D. B.'s old girl friend despite his dislike of her phoniness, his spontaneous charity to the nuns, his compassion for the young prostitute Sunny, his regret about criticizing Sally Hayes's lack of imagination, his love for Phoebe, and his disgust at the obscenities scrawled on the toilet walls at the museum and at Phoebe's school all demonstrate a good heart essentially like Huck's in its basic self-heedlessness and naturally positive moral instinct.[19]

At times Holden seems to empathize so fully with others as to shoulder their burdens and their guilt for them, as in the cases of Jane and Sunny; and this same Christlike tendency is at least somewhat evident, though in distorted form, in his vision of playing "the catcher in the rye." Holden's profanity and offhandedness of manner and speech would seem to indicate a combination of extreme belligerence and utter indifference toward others. Yet he actually fights only to defend Jane's honor, not in cases where he himself is victimized (as when the pimp Maurice pummels an extra five dollars out of him), and otherwise feels consid-

[18] J. D. Salinger, *The Catcher in the Rye*, chap. 24.
[19] Compare Arvin R. Wells, "Huck Finn and Holden Caulfield: The Situation of the Hero," p. 32.

erable emotional involvement with the problems of people encountered and recalled along his weekend odyssey. And despite the harsh jargon, the studied disinterest, and the grudging reluctance to tell of more than the one weekend, all three of which traits mark the beginning of his account, Holden is moved by the mere recollection of his experiences:

D. B. asked me what I thought about all this stuff I just finished telling you about. I didn't know what the hell to say. If you want to know the truth, I don't *know* what I think about it. I'm sorry I told so many people about it. About all I know is, I sort of *miss* everybody I told about. Even old Stradlater and Ackley, for instance. I think I even miss that goddam Maurice. It's funny. Don't ever tell anybody anything. If you do, you start missing everybody. [Chap. 26]

Missing everybody, even Maurice—hardly the mark of a cold heart or a negative personality. Rather, the portrait that results is one of a compassionate spirit undergoing the painful and disorienting process of physical and emotional maturation, of the development of self-consciousness with all the attendant confusions, agonies, and extremes of mood and perception.

Hence Holden's wild fluctuations of tone between swaggering belligerence—the profanity, the refusal to talk about certain topics and experiences, the roundhouse criticisms of phoniness—and genuine intimacy with his reader: "God I wish you were there," "you shoulda seen her," "it would've knocked you out," and so forth. Unless scores of readers and critics are guilty of misreading Holden's narrative, the youth is to be taken in a positive light.[20] He is culpable only in his bitter disillusionment and in his overly harsh reaction to that disillusionment as he begins to pass from childish innocence and to realize some of the harsh facts about adult life. Not yet mature enough to be able to face this disillusionment with anything approaching full perspective, un-

[20] Several critics take Holden to task for his many failings, as I have done here; but only Maxwell Geismar, in "J. D. Salinger: The Wise Child and the *New Yorker* School of Fiction," takes a totally negative view of him and of Salinger.

167

able to run away from his dilemma for fear of dragging Phoebe down with him, and unable to contemplate suicide seriously, all he can do is lash out verbally at all the phoniness he both sees and believes to see and simultaneously seek to withdraw into the static world of childhood—to play "the catcher in the rye."

The sweeping criticisms Holden utters are, however, as seen, more than offset by his basic sincerity and his respect for simple decency and human dignity. And it is also a positive sign that, despite his wish to protect all children from a similar disillusionment—saving them from the "crazy cliff," erasing the profane graffiti—he decides not to try to protect Phoebe and the other children from falling in reaching for the gold ring on a carousel:

All the kids kept trying to grab for the gold ring, and so was old Phoebe, and I was sort of afraid she'd fall off the goddam horse, but I didn't say anything or do anything. The thing with kids is, if they want to grab for the gold ring, you have to let them do it, and not say anything. If they fall off, they fall off, but it's bad if you say anything to them. [Chap. 25]

Besides having revealed his basic goodness through his narrative, Holden here shows signs of ultimately surviving his adolescent crisis and growing up. His story, like Huck's, harbors distinct and often damning criticism of the society through which he moves; but he himself emerges as a sort of moral yardstick against which that society is measured and found considerably wanting. If he is not as exact a yardstick as is Huck, the reason lies in the fact that he is slightly older and consequently closer to the adult world against which he reacts so strongly. Edgar Branch summarizes the comparison well:

Each book is a devastating criticism of American society and voices a morality of love and humanity. In many important matters . . . Huck and Holden—not to speak of others like Jim and Phoebe—affirm goodness, honesty and loyalty. Huck does so almost unconsciously, backhandedly, often against his conventional conscience, and Holden does so with agonizing self-consciousness and a bitter spirit. In each the perception of innocence is radical: from their mouths come pessimistic judgments damning the social forms that help make men less than fully human.[21]

The naïf's narrative thus resembles that of both the *pícaro* and the madman in one respect: namely, in that the unreliable nature of the narrative is used to convey the implied author's vilification or at least his serious critique of given social norms and practices. Like the *pícaro* and the madman, the naïve narrator himself frequently gives voice to a portion of this critique in his narrative asides and in his direct commentary to the reader at various junctures in the course of his account. And like the commentary of both the *pícaro* and the madman, the sound heart's social criticism also points out in many instances only the most blatant ills of the society in question, leaving unsaid the most damning strictures to be inferred by the reader from the narrative proper. But unlike the picaresque narrative, where extensive worldly experience has produced a glibly amoral creature with a certain pragmatic and self-serving perceptiveness regarding people and social intercourse and hence a rather untrustworthy spokesman in moral and ethical matters, the narrative of the naïf presents a figure who by definition lacks experience with people and society and is thus unequipped to deal in any far-reaching manner with the moral, ethical, emotional, and intellectual questions which arise from his first ventures into the world and from his account of those ventures. Where the former presents its critical view of a rotten society through the warped perspective of a figure who has been fashioned by that society and has mastered its ways sufficiently well to survive and even exploit it with varying degrees of success, the latter delivers its critique through one who has not yet entered the social world and who is largely unfamiliar with it on any direct experiential level. And unlike the madman's narrative, where the narrator's derangement not only indicts but also

[21] Edgar Branch, "Mark Twain and J. D. Salinger: A Study in Literary Continuity," p. 152.

often reflects the social, political, and/or spiritual malaise of the society and era which spawn him, the naïve narrator embodies in his actions, words, and character a positive opposing spirit to the malaise, though he may demonstrate some of its superficial symptoms.

The condemnation of social, political, or spiritual phenomena in the narrative of the *pícaro*, the madman, and in some cases the clown redounds onto the narrator himself, showing him to be in many instances at least as despicable or as lamentable as the society which he depicts. It is a portrait only partly softened by sociological considerations. The naïf, on the other hand, does not carry the stigma of the society which his account calls into question, for he views and encounters that society essentially unmarked by its taints, bringing with him only the "wonder" of adolescence or the incomprehension of simple naïveté. His critique, whether consciously uttered or whether conveyed over his head from implied author to reader, thus does not work to his discredit but rather the opposite, despite his frequent confusion and error as he attempts to describe and come to terms with a world still beyond his ken. Though incapable of fully reliable articulation, he nonetheless reveals himself through his narrative as a positive figure.

CHAPTER 7

Conclusion

IN BOOK 13 of *The Odyssey* Odysseus returns at long last to Ithaka, where the first individual he encounters is the goddess Athena, disguised as a young shepherd. After she has told him the name of the country he has reached and has described it to him, he launches into yet another of his ready store of contrived autobiographies:

> . . . not that he told the truth,
> but, just as she did, held back what he knew,
> weighing within himself at every step
> what he made up to serve his turn.[1]

His story obviously delights Athena, for she smiles, caresses him, changes her form to that of a beautiful woman, and replies to him:

> "Whoever gets around you must be sharp
> and guileful as a snake; even a god
> might bow to you in ways of dissimulation.
> You! You chameleon!
> Bottomless bag of tricks! Here in your own country
> would you not give your stratagems a rest
> or stop spellbinding for an instant?

[1] Homer, *The Odyssey*, trans. Robert Fitzgerald.

You play a part as if it were your own tough skin.

No more of this, though. Two of a kind, we are,
contrivers both. Of all men now alive
You are the best in plots and story telling.
My own fame is for wisdom among the gods—
deceptions, too."

Narrative artifice is thus portrayed as a most useful tool, employed with relish even by Athena herself, and one which brings
both divine favor and earthly success.[2]
    Nearly three millennia later, in a decidedly less lofty and semi-
nal work, Dame Agatha Christie's *The Murder of Roger Ackroyd*,
the Belgian detective Hercule Poirot confronts the tale's first-
person narrator, Dr. Sheppard, with the fact that the latter's very
manuscript proves him to be the murderer of Ackroyd. "A very
meticulous and accurate account," Poirot tells Sheppard. "You
have recorded all the facts faithfully and exactly—though you
have shown yourself becoming reticent as to your own share in
them."[3] The detective goes on to point out several minor discrepancies in time, a few glosses and omissions, and a crucial, uncor-
roborated report of a phone conversation, all of which together
serve to pin the guilt on Sheppard. "You see now why I drew attention to the reticence of your manuscript," Poirot concludes.
"It was strictly faithful as far as it went—but it did not go very far,
eh, my friend?" The hoary detective-story device of withheld evidence is thus used here by the first-person narrator to cover his
own guilt and throw suspicion elsewhere, resulting in an account
that is correct in virtually all particulars but which is ultimately
exposed as unreliable and self-incriminating when subjected to
precise scrutiny. The result here is not so much delight or wisdom as it is a combination of setting things aright and attaining a
certain satisfaction in the intellectual challenge of solving a puzzle
and winning a demanding game.

    [2] Compare Gregory Rabassa, "Lying to Athena: Cortázar and the Art of Fiction,"
p. 542.
    [3] Agatha Christie, *The Murder of Roger Ackroyd*, chap. 23.

I cite these two extremely different works because they illustrate in clear and expressly stated terms the two principal components of the unreliable first-person narrator's nature as narrator:
dissimulation and reticence. Whereas Odysseus uses invented
stories and assumed identities to avoid detection and thereby
achieve success in his various stratagems, whether escaping the
clutches of Polyphemos or ridding his house of the parasitic suitors, Dr. Sheppard omits or ever so slightly glosses a few points
concerning time, incidental details, and certain conversations so
as to appear merely an interested, informed bystander rather than
the murderer he actually is. In each case it takes a kindred or
even superior spirit to expose—and, not coincidentally, to appre-
ciate—the deception; and due to the presence of such a spirit in
each work, there is no problem for the reader in discerning that
deception. Athena and Poirot do the work for him. Similar though
somewhat less authoritative agents were described in the Introduction to this study as operating in *The Collector, The Alexandria Quartet,* and *Kater Murr* to reveal in more or less explicit
fashion the unreliability of those works' respective first-person
narrators.

In the works examined in Chapters 3–6, however, there is no
counterpart to Athena/Poirot/Miranda/Pursewarden/Kreisler, at
best the brief notes of a fictitious editor (*Moll Flanders*) or of the
author himself (*Notes from Underground*), themselves often of
a dangerously two-edged nature. Instead it is the reader who is
faced with the task of divining or deducing the unreliability at
work in each case, drawing on the sum total of the narrator's presentation or spotting certain minute flaws in the narrative fabric.
The task is not always easy and the results not always so clear-cut
and unequivocal as in the cases of Odysseus and Dr. Sheppard.
Yet even where only a relative degree of unreliability is ascer-
tained, the byproducts of wisdom and/or delight are attained as
well in corresponding measure.

The *pícaros,* by virtue of their mobility, their astuteness, their
adventurous lives, are of course much closer in spirit to Odysseus
than to Dr. Sheppard. Several of the picaresque works even offer

definite echoes of *The Odyssey* in their calamitous sea voyages, their sojourns among exotic peoples, and the arrival of the rogue at some Ithaka, some "safe haven" (Lazarillo) or "port and haven of rest and mercy" (Lucius). It is therefore hardly surprising that the *pícaros'* accounts are most strongly colored by Odyssean narrative features: highly episodic, often witty or even ribald, occasionally world-weary, and nearly always mindful of some latter-day version of Athena, whether it be called Fate, Providence, or the will of God. And like the Ithakan "bottomless bag of tricks," the *pícaros* are nearly all confidence artists in word as well as in deed. Their very survival often depends on such verbal adroitness and guile—we might recall many explicit instances where this talent rescued or furthered the careers of Lazarillo, Moll, Augie, and Felix in particular—and their written accounts usually show not only the Odyssean tendency toward lengthy and fluid expostulation but also a facile inventiveness which leads ever so easily into embellishment upon their histories and often into downright distortion or "improvement" upon the truth. Hence the glorifying accounts of the successful gullings which the narrators perpetrated, the exaggerated blackenings of antipathetic characters from their pasts, the frequent shows of winning intimacy toward the reader, the ardent invocations of expediency and necessity, the roundhouse castigations of contemporary society and morality, the hyperbolic praises of any final successes achieved. Where Odysseus used his wits and verbal gifts as much in literal self-defense as in the sheer pleasure of storytelling, the *pícaros* as narrators of their own accounts most often turn those gifts to the spurious task of defending their careers and placing their respective character traits in the best possible light.

There is, to be sure, a certain amount of reticence in the *pícaros'* accounts, in the sense that certain incidents from the past and present may be passed over lightly or omitted when they might work to the individual narrator's disfavor—the exact nature of Lazarillo's marital arrangement, of Pablos's fate in the New World, of Krull's later life—but not in the sense that the narrators efface themselves to any great extent after the fashion of Dr.

Sheppard. Apuleius is a possible exception here, taking something of a secondary chronicler's role for much of his account and relating a number of incidents from the point of view of an ass. Otherwise the accounts are markedly self-centered and self-indulgent, a feature aptly described by Oskar Seidlin's previously cited remark (see Chap. 3) that, in the first-person narrative, and particularly in the picaresque tale or novel, "the world has been swallowed up, . . . the 'I' has become the center of all things." Being such a self-contained center, as well as a rogue and most often a moral or religious convert or a failure to boot, the *pícaro* seems naturally inclined toward dissimulation with the twin aims of boisterous entertainment and self-praise. The frequent leaven of overt religious or moral admonition mixes oddly in such circumstances and in fact often (as seen most readily in the cases of Moll and Augie) is such a spurious additive that it casts the entire narrative in doubt and clues the reader to further dissimulation throughout the account. The consequence of this recognition is a blend of delight at the rogue's spirited narrative efforts and a sobering insight into the hard realities of the world both depicted and embodied by the narrating "I."

The clown, as befits his origin among parasites and idiots and his historical development via court buffoons and stage fools, is likewise given more to dissimulation than to reticence, more to the liberal recasting and reshaping of character and incident than to the withholding of information, more to self-indulgence than to self-effacement. Grotesque distortion, farcical exaggeration, satirical reversal, and imaginative chaotic play are his tools in trade, reducing the world to stock situations and skewering the rich and the poor, the great and the small, the wise and the foolish with equal impunity. Crude house buffoons regaled banquet guests with lewd attacks on the morals and physical attributes of other guests; medieval fools offered a parade of imbecilic scholars, cowardly knights, and corrupt clerics; and the more sophisticated later clowns turned supposedly stable social and cosmic orders upside down in a comic frenzy of mad disorder.

As the first major literary descendant of this tradition, *The*

Praise of Folly presents Stultitia herself as the speaker and admitted mask of the author Erasmus. The praise of foolishness in itself cannot be taken seriously, and the overt dissimulative device of using Folly to voice that encomium compounds the enterprise, in effect mocking the mock nature of the speech. The doubling of the irony not only prevents a literal acceptance of the speaker's praise of foolish behavior, but also attenuates a reading of the work as a simple reversal of values debunking, for example, rashness and exalting prudence. Rather, the work aims at a more complex effect, qualifying both readings, achieving a transvaluation of stated negative values and implied positive ones and attaining composite new values through the sympathetic understanding of human frailty and experience. The usual straightforward and gleefully destructive satire of the stage clown and the *sottie* fool is thus refined by Erasmus into a tool for use toward positive and constructive ends. Assumed folly is thus shown to be most adaptable to the service of wisdom as well as to that of entertainment and diversion.

Later literary clowns retain perhaps more of the entertainment aspect of the earlier buffoons and fools than does Stultitia. Tristram Shandy's long cock-and-bull story and Humbert Humbert's pun-filled American tragicomedy would be worth the reading for the sheer fun they offer, if nothing else, and Oskar Matzerath's long drum solo is only a few steps below these two in comic effects. All three narrators are self-conscious artists casting themselves in some type of buffoonish role: Tristram as the becapped and begowned inkslinger racing pellmell in several directions at once to get his story told and to catch up with time; Humbert as a combination of urbane satirist, brutish satyr, and sadly gleeful Harlequin; and Oskar as the freakish but gifted musician, actor, and storyteller. All are onstage, so to speak, in their narratives, calling attention to this or that turn, pointing out artifices and comic effects, creating little games for their readers and playing other games *with* them, ever conscious of style and language and of reader reaction and expectation. Tristram's account, in fact, turns out to be an extensive joke, and Humbert's tale becomes in

176

the course of its composition a self-contained esthetic enterprise of wit and sentiment; only Oskar seems ultimately to lose control of his narrative, and its jokes finally turn to fear, uncertainty, and silence.

Tristram's antic efforts also contain a dollop of moral uplift and sympathetically expose a goodly amount of human comedy in himself and his characters alike. All of this is presented in a straightforward manner, however—if such a word can be applied to Tristram's "progressively digressive" technique—and there is virtually no reticence in the sense of concealed information which alters our perception of either narrator or story. Such reticence does color the other two narratives, however, adding a certain dark tint to the psychology of Humbert and a certain tragic hue to his story, and blackening Oskar and his account even more deeply. Humbert has, after all, left several recesses of his mind unexplored and has admittedly fashioned a poetic construct which does not necessarily conform on all points to the realities of character and incident as they supposedly occurred. He thus leaves himself open to possible charges of concealment and self-serving distortion; the charges become largely academic, however, in view of the narrative frame's shift in midcourse from an intent of self-defense to one of a panegyric to love and the beloved, a paean not meant for perusal during the lifetime of the narrator. Oskar's account, playing fast and loose with actual history in microcosm and re-creating that history in highly idiosyncratic and often grotesquely fantastic fashion, lays itself more open to charges of concealment and distortion than does Humbert's. The accumulation of misdeeds, horrors, and tragedies stands in marked contrast to the narrator's blithe verbal acrobatics and moral insouciance, creating strong suspicions of guilt and self-serving narrative gloss. The clown act thus turns sour here, revealing the dwarf Oskar as unsavory and unreliable and thereby implying larger, more resonant and more serious concerns than those voiced by the self-indulgent narrator himself.

With the madman's narrative we move into murkier regions, for by definition he is not fully in command of his faculties and

177

views the world in distorted fashion. His account is therefore in most cases not a responsible, controlled one relating events and portraying characters with any degree of reliability or authenticity, but rather a reflection of his own twisted impressions, confused thought patterns, or neurotic obsessions. Hence the frequent format of rambling notes, diaries, brief sketches, and vague, fused memories instead of sequential narratives as such. The actual world seems swallowed up, lost within the solipsism and delusions brought on by the narrator's mental imbalance. How can one separate, for example, the inner and outer worlds presented by Poprishchin and by Hedayat's nameless narrator? Letters written by dogs are recalled in the same manner as are encounters with office superiors in the one, while people and events both past and present and from both dreams and life become indissolubly fused in the other. And where sequential narratives with some degree of normalcy do occur, the madman's gross imperceptions, stridency of tone, and often absurd logic undermine the reliability of his position as narrator and of his character as a person. Poe's narrators frequently condemn themselves in a literal sense in their desperate confessionals; the Underground Man reveals himself not as a superior creature but as the Dostoevskian dreamer, the man turned inward, morally impoverished and spiritually bankrupt; and Clegg's account serves only to portray him as the embodiment of a horrible pathological sickness, not as a kind and considerate lover of beauty.

Both reticence and dissimulation figure in the madman's narrative, but in most cases these are not the conscious devices seen operating in the accounts of the *pícaro* and the clown. Only the Underground Man seems in sufficient control of his account to use such art in delivering his credo and relating his story. In fact, perspicacity and lucidity are his problems, creating the intellectual and spiritual impasses which characterize his nature and his neurosis; he virtually glories in the distorted, unflattering portrait he paints of his misery. With the other madmen studied here, however, the extent of the madness virtually precludes such conscious artifice. It is the madness itself which occasions the shrill and obsessive focus on a certain incident or series of incidents to the exclusion of more mimetic completeness in recounting past events: an old man's wall-eyed stare, a black cat's cry, a ragman's cough, a pretty girl's walk, a lost coat button, a chance encounter on the street, a newspaper item, a slighting or insulting remark, a pounding heart. And it is the madness which creates the distorted representation, the fanciful interpretation, the poses of inno-cence, righteousness, outraged dignity, or superiority. Whether induced by oppressive fear, gnawing guilt, an agonizing spiritual or intellectual crisis, or sheer pathology, it is the narrator's mental aberrance and not the conscious calculation of an Odysseus or a Dr. Sheppard which is the primary source of the narrative decep-tions, omissions, distortions, and unreliability.

The naïf, and in particular the child or adolescent, is more closely akin to the madman than to the rogue and the clown as narrator, for by virtue of his inexperience and naïveté he is not shrewdly self-conscious in telling his story nor fully aware of many of the implications in his narrative. His account is direct and simple in style, ingenuous in language and phrasing, and neither broad nor deep in perception and interpretation. Events are related sequentially; commentary, where present at all, is offered in seemingly spontaneous fashion; and characters are painted for the most part in stark outlines, often in strict black-and-white terms. Though he may have demonstrated an ability for dissimulation in certain critical situations in his life, in his account the naïf reveals virtually no self-serving deceptiveness or calculating concealment. His only major shortcoming as a narra-tor is the fact that he actually sees less than he tells.

Huck Finn's tale is, on the surface, a boy's story of adventure, with its trip down the big river, the drama of several dangerous episodes, the comedy of various escapades ashore, the tragedy and near-tragedy of other incidents, the dark farce of the Duke and King, the spectacle of the bigger-than-life Sherburn-Boggs duel, and the adolescent fun of the Evasion. Holden Caulfield's account too is that of a youth's adventures, this time a three-day sojourn through New York City, with a number of comic and se-

179

riocomic encounters. Both narratives proceed chronologically, both feature an unsophisticated vocabulary and style, and both display an innocent wonder at the world of nature and a simplistic but budding insight into certain facets of human character and relationships. Huck is content to narrate much of his story with little or no commentary, whereas the older Holden can let virtually nothing pass without offering some opinion concerning the character or incident involved. Huck seems to conceal little, and Holden, while begrudging us more of his past than the weekend's adventures, likewise appears to offer a complete and unreserved account of that brief period. Both boys give voice to some opinions and judgments regarding their own character, and in each case the assessment is somewhat negative—Huck seeing himself as basically bad in nature, and Holden viewing his young life as a failure.

There is, then, little artifice and little self-serving reticence in the narratives of the two adolescents. The directness of style, ingenuousness of tone, and simplicity of judgment all but preclude the employment of such devices. Yet for the mature reader, the two accounts offer more than adventures and simple stock opinions on life and society, presenting richly textured portrayals of the evils of the two societies in question and implicitly condemning them by conveying those portrayals through the medium of basically decent, naïve youths. To the extent that the reader perceives and accepts these social and moral critiques and the concomitant view of the narrators as possessing "sound hearts" which triumph over their "deformed consciences" and flawed worlds, there *is* narrative dissimulation in each account, and hence narrative unreliability. The dissimulation is unconscious in both Huck and Holden, however, a product of their worldly inexperience, immaturity, and naïveté. It therefore does not work to their detriment, but rather enhances the positive image of them which the reader takes from the perusal of their accounts.

Dissimulation, then, whether conscious or unconscious, suffuses each of the narratives studied in the foregoing chapters and

180

is frequently accompanied by a degree of reticence or concealment on the part of the narrating "I." Conscious dissimulation is
in fact the primary feature of the clown's account, as the narrator
adopts the pose of a performing artist and gives free rein to his
comic inventiveness in the telling of his story, and it is an important element of the *pícaro's* narrative, being an ingrained facet of
the rogue's very nature as con artist and master of disguise. Unconscious dissimulation, on the other hand, is the all but inevita-
ble characteristic of the madman's narrative and the naïf's account, the product of the former's obsessions and neuroses and of
the latter's inexperience and immaturity respectively. Reticence
and concealment, where present, may likewise be either conscious or unconscious and are again the products of the particular
narrator's pose, character, and cast or limitation of mind.

Just as Odysseus's ready dissimulative faculties won him the
favor of Athena, so does the narrative dissimulation of the rogues,
clowns, madmen, and naïfs encountered here produce a favorable disposition toward most of these narrators as its first effect.
The combination of narrative energy, inventiveness, and seeming intimacy is a seductive one, eliciting pleasure in the reading
and fostering initially a considerable amount of goodwill, toler-
ance, and sympathy toward the figure who has taken us into his
confidence, even if his artifice is readily apparent. The recognition of unreliability in the narrative, whether early or late, aug-
ments the reader's favorable appraisal of Huck, Holden, and Tristram, detracts but little from his positive attitude toward figures
such as Felix, Lucius, and Folly, and introduces a pity-tinged
sympathy for the likes of Poprishchin and the narrator of *The
Blind Owl.* These narrators have little or nothing of significance
to conceal that could alter one's initial disposition toward them;
or, as in the last two instances, they are so lamentably deranged
that they can hardly be held accountable for the distortions and
glaring discrepancies in their narratives. When the dissimulation
and concealment distort, gloss, or cover lives of spurious morality
(Moll, Lazarillo, Guzmán, Simplicius, the Underground Man,
Augie, Oskar) or outright criminality (Pablos, Humbert, Clegg,

181

the Poe murderer-narrators), however, the result is a marked change for the worse in one's estimation of the narrating "I," as in Poirot's reaction to Dr. Sheppard's chronicle. The recognition here leads to a mix of attraction and distaste, to a largely complete loss of sympathy, to stern disapprobation, or to outright loathing, depending on the nature of the actions concealed or glossed.

Whatever the effect of discovered narrative unreliability in terms of our attitude toward the respective narrators, a perhaps more significant consequence is that the discovery forces us into a confrontation with the slippery nature of truth. In the works investigated here, words often lie; that which goes unsaid is frequently seen to be as significant as that which is said; and truth is seen as not being the exclusive property of a direct, sincere, seemingly omniscient voice, for it may just as well issue from Folly herself or one of her kin. Rogues and innocents alike offer biting portraits of social and moral malaises, but the former are ultimately no better than that which they ridicule, while the latter offer by silent example a positive antidote to the infection. The clowns reflect a world gone topsy-turvy—in actual fact or in the abstract—yet two of them contribute to the chaos and destruction, while the seemingly most inept artist of them all is the one whose laughter is the most benign and who holds out the promise of restored harmony. And the madmen reveal a world that has lost its spiritual compass, not so much through their often absurd accounts of that world as through the incoherent solipsism of their ravings, embodying that loss more than depicting it.

If the goddess of wisdom can champion a liar and even on occasion lie to her own fellow Olympians, then surely the implied authors present behind the unreliable rogues, clowns, madmen, and naïve adolescents investigated here may be permitted the use of such artifice for the sheer delight of imaginative storytelling or for the imparting of certain truths concerning human nature, society, morality, and spiritual values. To share in that delight or wisdom requires that one approach these works in the spirit in which they were written, much in the manner of Athena and Poirot, both appreciating the prevarication and looking beyond it. Only thus do we become proper readers of these texts, and only thus do we participate in the dissimulative process which brings the goddess's fond caress.

Selected Bibliography

Section 1 lists all primary texts discussed in the foregoing study. Section 2, dealing with the nature of fiction in general and with the subjects of narrative theory, first-person narration, and narrative unreliability in particular, includes all items available and consulted in researching those topics for this study and especially for Chapters 1 and 2. Section 3 contains a selective list of the secondary literature consulted in the examination of the primary works discussed in Chapters 3–6 and includes only those items found to be most pertinent to the present study.

1. PRIMARY TEXTS

Alemán, Mateo. *Guzmán de Alfarache.* Mexico City: Porrúa, 1971.
———. *The Rogue, or The Life of Guzman de Alfarache,* trans. James Mabe. London: Constable, 1924 (original, 1623).
Apuleius, Lucius. *The Golden Ass: Being the Metamorphoses of Lucius Apuleius,* trans. W[illiam] Adlington, rev. S. Gaselle. Cambridge, Mass.: Harvard Univ. Press, 1915. (Bilingual edition.)
Bellow, Saul. *The Adventures of Augie March.* New York: Viking, 1953.
Christie, Agatha. *The Murder of Roger Ackroyd.* London: Dodd, Mead, 1926.
Cortázar, Julio. "El perseguidor," in *Los relatos.* Barcelona: Círculo de Lectores, 1974, pp. 545–92.
———. "The Pursuer," in *Blow-Up and Other Stories,* trans. Paul Blackburn. New York: Collier, 1968, pp. 161–220.

Defoe, Daniel. *Moll Flanders*. New York: Modern Library, 1926.

Dostoevskij, Fëdor Mixajlovič. *Zapiski iz podpol'ja*. Chicago: Russian Language Specialists, 1960.

Dostoevsky, Fyodor M. "Notes from Underground," in *White Nights and Other Stories*, trans. Constance Garnett. New York: Macmillan, 1923, pp. 50–155.

Durrell, Lawrence. *The Alexandria Quartet*. New York: Dutton, 1960. (The four novels are *Justine, Balthazar, Mountolive*, and *Clea*.)

Erasmus, Desiderius. *Morias Enkomion, Id est: Stultitiae laus*, in *Desiderii Erasmi opera*, vol. 4. Hildesheim: Ohms, 1962, pp. 405–504. (Unaltered reproduction of the 1703 Leiden edition.)

————. *The Praise of Folly*, trans. John Wilson, ed. P. S. Allen. Oxford: Clarendon, 1913.

Fowles, John. *The Collector*. Boston: Little, Brown, 1963.

Gogol, Nikolai V. "Diary of a Madman," in *The Collected Tales and Plays of Nikolai Gogol*, trans. Constance Garnett, ed. Leonard J. Kent. New York: Pantheon, 1964, pp. 453–73.

Gogol', N[ikolaj] V. "Zapiski sumasšedšego," in *Sočinenija*. New York: International Univ. Press, n.d. [1949?], pp. 217–26.

Grass, Günter. *Die Blechtrommel*. Darmstadt: Luchterhand, 1974.

————. *The Tin Drum*, trans. Ralph Manheim. New York: Pantheon, 1961.

Grimmelshausen, Hans Jakob Christoph von. *Der abenteuerliche Simplicissimus*. Munich: Winkler, n.d.

————. *Simplicius Simplicissimus*, trans. George Schulz-Behrend. Indianapolis: Bobbs-Merrill, 1965.

Hedayat, Sadegh. *The Blind Owl*, trans. D. P. Costello. New York: Grove, 1969.

Homer. *The Odyssey*, trans. Robert Fitzgerald. New York: Doubleday, 1961.

La vida de Lazarillo de Tormes y de sus fortunas y adversidades, ed. Joseph V. Ricapito. Madrid: Cátedra, 1976.

The Life of Lazarillo of Tormes, trans. Robert S. Rudder. New York: Ungar, 1973.

Mann, Thomas. *Die Bekenntnisse des Hochstaplers Felix Krull*. Frankfurt a.M.: S. Fischer, 1954.

————. *Confessions of Felix Krull, Confidence Man*, trans. Denver Lindley. New York: Knopf, 1955.

Nabokov, Vladimir. *Lolita*. New York: Putnam, 1955.

186

Poe, Edgar Allan. *Complete Stories and Poems*. Garden City, N.Y.: Doubleday, 1966.

Quevedo y Villegas, Francisco Gómez de. *Historia de la vida del buscón*, ed. Américo Castro. Madrid: La Lectura, 1911.

―――. *The Scavenger*, trans. Hugh A. Harter. New York: Las Américas, 1962.

Salinger, J[erome] D[avid]. *The Catcher in the Rye*. New York: Little, Brown, 1951.

Sterne, Laurence. *The Life and Opinions of Tristram Shandy, Gentleman*. New York: Norton, 1965.

Twain, Mark. [Samuel Langhorne Clemens.] *The Adventures of Huckleberry Finn*. New York: Harper & Brothers, 1912.

2. FIRST-PERSON NARRATION AND UNRELIABILITY

Allemann, Beda. *Ironie und Dichtung*. Tübingen: Neske, 1956.

Axthelm, Peter. *The Modern Confessional Novel*. New Haven, Conn.: Yale Univ. Press, 1967.

Baker, J. R. "From Initiation to Rhetoric." *Novel*, 6 (1973), 197–217.

Bašić, S. "Ivo Vidan: *Nepouzdani pripovjedač* (The Unreliable Narrator)." *Studia Romanica et Anglica Zagrebientia*, 33–36 (1972–73), 876–80. (Review.)

Booth, Wayne C. *The Rhetoric of Fiction*. Chicago: Univ. of Chicago Press, 1961.

―――. "*The Rhetoric of Fiction* and the Poetics of Fictions." *Novel*, 1 (1968), 105–117.

Brooks, Cleanth, and Robert Penn Warren. *Understanding Fiction*, 2nd ed. New York: Appleton-Century-Crofts, 1959.

Cruttwell, Patrick. "Makers and Persons." *Hudson Review*, 12 (1959–60), 487–507.

Edel, Leon. *The Modern Psychological Novel*. New York: Grosset & Dunlap, 1959.

Epstein, Edmund L. "The Irrelevant Narrator: A Stylistic Note on the Place of the Author in Contemporary Technique of the Novel." *Language and Style*, 2 (1966), 92–94.

Friedemann, Käte. *Die Rolle des Erzählers in der Epik*. Darmstadt: Wissenschaftliche Buchgesellschaft, 1969.

Friedman, Alan Warren. *Lawrence Durrell and the Alexandria Quartet: Art for Love's Sake*. Norman: Univ. of Oklahoma Press, 1970.

Friedman, Melvin J. *Stream of Consciousness: A Study in Literary Method.* New Haven, Conn.: Yale Univ. Press, 1955.

Friedmann, Norman. "Point of View in Fiction: The Development of a Critical Concept." *PMLA*, 70 (1955), 1160–84.

Frye, Northrop. *Anatomy of Criticism.* Princeton, N.J.: Princeton Univ. Press, 1957.

Gibson, Walker. "Authors, Speakers, Readers, and Mock Readers." *College English*, 11 (1950), 265–69.

Goldknopf, David. "The Confessional Increment: A New Look at the I-Narrator." *Journal of Aesthetics and Art Criticism*, 28 (1969), 13–21.

Hamburger, Käte. *The Logic of Literature*, trans. Marilyn J. Rose. Bloomington: Indiana Univ. Press, 1973.

Henning, Margrit. *Die Ich-Form und ihre Funktion in Thomas Manns "Doktor Faustus" und in der deutschen Literatur der Gegenwart.* Tübingen: Niemeyer, 1966.

Highet, Gilbert. *The Anatomy of Satire.* Princeton, N.J.: Princeton Univ. Press, 1962.

Humphrey, Robert. *Stream of Consciousness in the Modern Novel.* Berkeley: Univ. of California Press, 1954.

James, Henry. *The Art of the Novel: Critical Prefaces*, ed. Richard P. Blackmur. New York: Scribner's, 1934.

Kahler, Erich. "Die Verinnerlichung des Erzählens." *Neue Rundschau*, 70 (1959), 1–54, 177–220.

Kayser, Wolfgang. "Das Problem des Erzählers im Roman." *German Quarterly*, 29 (1956), 225–38.

Klotz, Günther. *Das Werturteil des Erzählers.* Halle: Niemeyer, 1960.

Lämmert, Eberhard. *Bauformen des Erzählens.* Stuttgart: Metzler, 1965.

Madden, David. "The Fallacy of the Subject-Dominated Novel." *English Record*, 18, iv (Winter 1968), 11–19.

Martini, Fritz, ed. *Probleme des Erzählens in der Weltliteratur: Festschrift für Käte Hamburger zum 75. Geburtstag.* Stuttgart: Klett, 1971.

Morrissette, Bruce. "Narrative 'You' in Contemporary Literature." *Comparative Literature Studies*, 2 (1965), 1–24.

Muecke, D. C. *Irony.* Vol. 13 in the series *The Critical Idiom*, ed. John D. Jump. Norfolk, Eng.: Methuen, 1970.

Pascal, Roy. *Design and Truth in Autobiography*. London: Routledge & Kegan Paul, 1960.

Pearce, Roy Harvey, ed. *Experience in the Novel*. New York: Columbia Univ. Press, 1968.

Romberg, Bertil. *Studies in the Narrative Technique of the First-Person Novel*, trans. Michael Taylor and Harold H. Borland. Stockholm: Almqvist & Wiksell, 1962.

Rubin, Louis D., Jr. *The Teller in the Tale*. Settle: Univ. of Washington Press, 1967.

Schaefer, Albert, ed. *Ironie und Dichtung*. Munich: Beck, 1970.

Scholes, Robert, and Robert Kellogg. *The Nature of Narrative*. London: Oxford Univ. Press, 1966.

Schorer, Mark. "Technique as Discovery." *Hudson Review*, 1 (1948), 67–87.

Schwarz, Daniel R. "The Self-Deceiving Narrator of Conrad's 'Il Conde.'" *Studies in Short Fiction*, 6 (1968–69), 187–93.

Shunami, Gideon. "The Unreliable Narrator in *Wuthering Heights*." *Nineteenth Century Fiction*, 27 (1973), 449–68.

Sosnosky, Theodor von. "Der 'Ich' im Roman." *Die Gegenwart*, 59 (1901), 347–48.

Spacks, Patricia M. "In Search of Sincerity." *College English*, 29 (1968), 591–602.

Thale, Jerome. "The Narrator as Hero." *Twentieth Century Literature*, 3 (1957), 69–73.

Todorov, Tzvetan. "De l'ambiguïté narrative." *Echanges et communication*, ed. Jean Pouillon and Pierre Maranda. The Hague: Mouton, 1970, Vol. 2, pp. 913–18.

Toenes, Sara. "Public Confession in *La Chute*." *Wisconsin Studies in Contemporary Literature*, 4 (1963), 305–318.

Warren, Austin, and René Wellek. *Theory of Literature*. New York: Harcourt, Brace & World, 1956.

Weinstein, Philip M. "The Exploitative and Protective Imagination: Unreliable Narration in *The Sacred Fount*," in *The Interpretation of Narrative: Theory and Practice*, ed. Morton W. Bloomfield. Cambridge, Mass.: Harvard Univ. Press, 1970.

Wright, Andrew H. "Irony and Fiction." *Journal of Aesthetics and Art Criticism*, 12 (1953), 111–18.

3. SECONDARY SOURCES

Abood, Edward F. *Underground Man*. San Francisco: Chandler & Sharp, 1973.

Adams, Richard P. "The Unity and Coherence of *Huckleberry Finn*." *Tulane Studies in English*, 6 (1956), 87–103.

Adler, Dorothea. "Sprachliche Zeichen ironischer Erzählweise: Zu Thomas Manns *Bekenntnisse des Hochstaplers Felix Krull*." *Wirkendes Wort*, 20 (1970), 86–102.

Alonso, Amado. "Das Pikareske des Schelmenromans," in *Pikarische Welt*, ed. Helmut Heidenreich. Darmstadt: Wissenschaftliche Buchgesellschaft, 1969, pp. 79–100.

Alter, Robert. *Rogue's Progress*. Cambridge, Mass.: Harvard Univ. Press, 1964.

Anderson, Howard. "*Tristram Shandy* and the Reader's Imagination." *PMLA*, 86 (1971), 966–73.

Appel, Alfred, Jr. "Backgrounds of *Lolita*," in *Nabokov: Criticism, Reminiscences, Translations, and Tributes*, eds. Alfred Appel, Jr., and Charles Newman. Evanston, Ill.: Northwestern Univ. Press, 1970, pp. 17–39.

———. "*Lolita*: The Springboard of Parody." *Wisconsin Studies in Contemporary Literature*, 8 (1967), 204–41.

Baader, Horst. "Noch einmal zur Ich-Form im *Lazarillo de Tormes*." *Romanische Forschungen*, 76 (1964), 437–46.

Bakhtin, Mikhail. *Problems of Dostoevsky's Poetics*, trans. R. W. Rotsel. Ann Arbor, Mich.: Ardis, 1973.

Bance, A. F. "The Enigma of Oskar in Grass's *Blechtrommel*." *Seminar*, 3 (1967), 147–56.

Bashiri, Iraj. *Hedayat's Ivory Tower: Structural Analysis of "The Blind Owl"*. Minneapolis: Manor House, 1974.

Bataillon, Marcel. *Le roman picaresque*. Paris: La Renaissance de Livre, 1931.

Baumbach, Jonathan. "The Saint as a Young Man: A Reappraisal of *The Catcher in the Rye*." *Modern Language Quarterly*, 25 (1964), 461–72.

Baumgart, Reinhard. *Das Ironische und die Ironie in den Werken Thomas Manns*. Munich: Winkler, 1964.

Beard, Michael Crowell. "Sadeq Hedayat's *Blind Owl* and the West: A

190

Study in the Transition of Genre." Diss., Indiana Univ., 1974.

Benardette, Jane Johnson. "*Huckleberry Finn* and the Nature of Fiction." *Massachusetts Review*, 9 (1968), 209–226.

Bercovitch, Sacvan. "Dramatic Irony in *Notes from the Underground*." *Slavic and East European Journal*, 8 (1964), 284–91.

Bleznick, Donald William. *Quevedo*. Boston: Twayne, 1972.

Booth, Wayne C. "Did Sterne Complete *Tristram Shandy?*" *Modern Philology*, 48 (1951), 172–83.

———. "*Tristram Shandy* and the Problem of Formal Coherence," in his *The Rhetoric of Fiction*. Chicago: Univ. of Chicago Press, 1961, pp. 221–40.

Branch, Edgar. "Mark Twain and J. D. Salinger: A Study in Literary Continuity." *American Quarterly*, 9 (1957), 144–58.

Brick, Allan. "The Madman in His Cell: Joyce, Beckett, Nabokov, and the Stereotypes." *Massachusetts Review*, 1 (1959), 40–55.

Brown, Clarence A. "*Huckleberry Finn*: A Study in Structure and Point of View." *Mark Twain Journal*, 12 (1964), 10–15.

Bryan, James. "The Psychological Structure of *The Catcher in the Rye*." *PMLA*, 89 (1974), 1065–74.

Butler, Diana. "Lolita Lepidoptera." *New World Writing*, 16 (1960), 58–84.

Carey, Douglas M. "Asides and Interiority in 'Lazarillo de Tormes.'" *Studies in Philology*, 66 (1969), 119–34.

Chandler, Frank Wadleigh. *Romances of Roguery*. New York: Franklin, 1961.

Clive, Geoffrey. "The Sickness unto Death in the Underworld: A Study of Nihilism." *Harvard Theological Review*, 51 (1958), 135–67.

Cohen, Hubert I. "'A Woeful Agony Which Forced Me to Begin My Tale': *The Catcher in the Rye*." *Modern Fiction Studies*, 12 (1966), 355–66.

Columbus, Robert R. "Conscious Artistry in *Moll Flanders*." *Studies in English Literature*, 3 (1963), 415–32.

Cook, Albert. *The Dark Voyage and the Golden Mean: A Philosophy of Comedy*. Cambridge, Mass.: Harvard Univ. Press, 1949.

Costello, Donald P. "The Language of *The Catcher in the Rye*." *American Speech*, 34 (1959), 172–81.

Cox, James M. "Edgar Poe: Style as Pose." *Virginia Quarterly Review*, 64 (1968), 67–89.

Cunliffe, W. Gordon. *Günter Grass*. Boston: Twayne, 1969.

Davidson, Edward H. *Poe: A Critical Study*. Cambridge, Mass.: Harvard Univ. Press, 1966.

Diederichs, Rainer. *Strukturen des Schelmischen im modernen deutschen Roman*. Düsseldorf: Diederichs, 1971.

Diller, Edward. *A Mythic Journey: Günter Grass's "Tin Drum"*. Lexington: Univ. of Kentucky Press, 1974.

Donoghue, Denis. "The Values of Moll Flanders." *Sewanee Review*, 71 (1963), 287–303.

Durand, Frank. "The Author and Lázaro: Levels of Comic Meaning." *Bulletin of Hispanic Studies*, 45 (1968), 89–101.

Durzak, Manfred. "Kunstfigur und Figur des Künstlers: *Die Blechtrommel*," in his *Der deutsche Roman der Gegenwart*, 2nd enl. ed. Stuttgart: Kohlhammer, 1973, pp. 138–49.

Dutton, Robert F. *Saul Bellow*. Boston: Twayne, 1971.

Dyson, A. E. "Huckleberry Finn and the Whole Truth." *Critical Quarterly*, 3 (1961), 29–40.

Elliott, Robert C. *Twentieth-Century Interpretations of "Moll Flanders."* Englewood Cliffs, N.J.: Prentice-Hall, 1970.

Enzensberger, Hans Magnus. "*Wilhelm Meister* auf Blech getrommelt," in his *Einzelheiten*. Frankfurt a.M.: Suhrkamp, 1962, pp. 221–27.

Erlich, Victor. *Gogol*. New Haven, Conn.: Yale Univ. Press, 1969.

Farrell, William J. "Nature Versus Art as a Comic Pattern in *Tristram Shandy*." *English Literary History*, 30 (1963), 16–35.

Fiedler, Leslie. "The Eye of Innocence," in *Salinger: A Critical and Personal Portrait*, ed. Henry Anatole Grunwald. New York: Harper & Row, 1962, pp. 218–45.

Field, Andrew. *Nabokov: His Life in Art*. Boston: Little, Brown, 1967.

Fitzmaurice-Kelly, James. "Quevedo's Art in *El buscón*." *Revue Hispanique*, 44 (1918), 1–9.

Fluchère, Henri. *Laurence Sterne: From Tristram to Yorick. An Interpretation of "Tristram Shandy"*, tr. Barbara Bray. London: Oxford Univ. Press, 1965.

Fowler, Douglas. *Reading Nabokov*. Ithaca, N.Y.: Cornell Univ. Press, 1974.

Frank, Joseph. "Nihilism and *Notes from Underground*." *Sewanee Review*, 69 (1961), 1–33.

Fraser, John. "In Defense of Culture: *Huckleberry Finn.*" *Oxford Review*, 6 (1967), 5–22.

Freedman, Ralph. "The Poet's Dilemma: The Narrative Worlds of Günter Grass." *Dimension*, Special Issue (1970), 50–63.

French, Warren. *J. D. Salinger.* Boston: Twayne, 1963.

Frohock, W. M. "The Failing Center: Recent Fiction and the Picaresque Tradition." *Novel*, 3 (1969), 62–69.

————. "The Idea of the Picaresque." *Yearbook of Comparative and General Literature*, 16 (1967), 43–52.

Gaffary, F. "*La chouette aveugle* et le cinéma." *Bizarre*, 1 (1953), 64.

Galloway, David D. *The Absurd Hero in American Fiction: Updike, Styron, Bellow, Salinger,* rev. ed. Austin: Univ. of Texas Press, 1970.

————. "The Absurd Man as Picaro: The Novels of Saul Bellow." *Texas Studies in Literature and Language*, 6 (1964), 226–54.

Gargano, James W. "The Question of Poe's Narrators." *College English*, 25 (1964), 177–81.

Garrison, Joseph M., Jr. "The Irony of 'Ligeia.'" *English Studies Quarterly*, 60 (1970), Supplement, 13–17.

Geismar, Maxwell. *American Moderns: From Rebellion to Conformity.* New York: Hill & Wang, 1958.

Gelley, Alexander. "Art and Reality in *Die Blechtrommel.*" *Forum for Modern Language Studies*, 2 (1967), 115–25.

Gerber, John C. "The Relation Between Point of View and Style in the Works of Mark Twain," in *Style in Prose Fiction*, ed. Harold C. Martin. New York: Columbia Univ. Press, 1959, pp. 142–71.

Gerstenberger, Donna. "Huckleberry Finn and the World's Illusion." *Western Humanities Review*, 14 (1960), 401–406.

Gilman, Stephen. "The Death of Lazarillo de Tormes." *PMLA*, 81 (1966), 149–56.

Goldberg, Gerald Jay. "Life's Customer: Augie March." *Critique*, 3, iii (Winter 1960), 15–27.

Green, Martin. "The Morality of *Lolita.*" *Kenyon Review*, 18 (1966), 352–77.

Guerard, Albert J. "Introduction" to *The Adventures of Augie March.* Greenwich, Conn.: Fawcett, 1971, pp. v–xviii.

Guillén, Claudio. "La disposición temporal del *Lazarillo de Tormes. Hispanic Review*, 25 (1957), 264–79.

————. *Literature as System*. Princeton, N.J.: Princeton Univ. Press, 1971.

Gukovskij, G. A. *Realizm Gogolja*. Moscow: n.p., 1959.

Gustafson, Richard F. "The Suffering Usurper: Gogol's *Diary of a Madman*." *Slavic and East European Journal*, 9 (1965), 268–80.

Gwynn, Frederick L., and Joseph L. Blotner. *The Fiction of J. D. Salinger*. Pittsburgh: Pittsburgh Univ. Press, 1958.

Harris, Harold J. "*Lolita* and the Sly Foreword." *Mad River Review*, 1, ii (Summer 1965), 29–38.

Harter, Hugh A. "Language and Mask: The Problem of Reality in Quevedo's *Buscón*." *Kentucky Foreign Language Quarterly*, 9 (1962), 205–209.

Heidenreich, Helmut, ed. *Pikarische Welt: Schriften zum europäischen Schelmenroman*. Darmstadt: Wissenschaftliche Buchgesellschaft, 1969.

Heilman, Robert B. "Variations of the Picaresque (*Felix Krull*)." *Sewanee Review*, 66 (1958), 547–77.

Heiserman, Arthur, and James E. Miller, Jr. "J. D. Salinger: Some Crazy Cliff." *Western Humanities Review*, 10 (1956), 129–37.

Heller, Erich. "Felix Krull oder die Komödie des Künstlers." *Wort und Wahrheit*, 11 (1956), 40–48.

Henze, Eberhard. "Die Rolle des fiktiven Erzählers bei Thomas Mann." *Neue Rundschau*, 76 (1965), 189–201.

Hermsdorf, Klaus. *Thomas Manns Schelme: Figuren and Strukturen des Komischen*. Berlin: Rütten & Loening, 1968.

Hesse, Everett W. "The Protean Changes in Quevedo's *Buscón*." *Kentucky Romance Quarterly*, 16 (1969), 243–59.

Hiatt, L. R. "Nabokov's *Lolita*: A 'Freudian' Cryptic Crossword." *American Imago*, 24 (1967), 360–70.

Higdon, David L. "Defoe's *Moll Flanders*." *Explicator*, 29 (1971), Item 55.

Hitchcock, Richard. "Lazarillo and 'Vuestra Merced.'" *Modern Language Notes*, 86 (1971), 264–66.

Hoffmann, Michael J. "Huck's Ironic Circle." *Georgia Review*, 23 (1969), 307–322.

Holdheim, W. Wolfgang. "Die Struktur von Dostojewskijs *Aufzeichnungen aus dem Kellerloch*." *Deutsche Vierteljahrsschrift für Literaturwissenschaft und Geistesgeschichte*, 47 (1969), 310–23.

Hollmann, Werner. "Thomas Mann's *Felix Krull* and *Lazarillo*." *Modern Language Notes*, 66 (1951), 445–51.

Holquist, James. "Plot and Counter-Plot in *Notes from Underground.*" *Canadian-American Slavic Studies*, 6 (1972), 225–38.

Hughes, Daniel J. "Reality and the Hero: *Lolita* and *Henderson the Rain King.*" *Modern Fiction Studies*, 6 (1960), 345–64.

Ivey, Frederick M. *"The Tin Drum"; or Retreat to the Word.* Wichita, Kans.: Wichita State Univ. Press, 1966.

Jackson, Robert L. *Dostojevskij's Underground Man in Russian Literature.* The Hague: Mouton, 1958.

Jauss, Hans Robert. "Ursprung and Bedeutung der Ich-Form im *Lazarillo de Tormes.*" *Romanistisches Jahrbuch*, 8 (1957), 290–311.

Josipovici, G. D. *"Lolita*: Parody and the Pursuit of Beauty." *Critical Quarterly*, 6 (1964), 35–48.

Juran, Sylvia. *"Zapiski sumasšedšego*: Some Insights into Gogol's World." *Slavic and East European Journal*, 4 (1961), 331–33.

Just, Georg. *Darstellung und Appell in der "Blechtrommel" von Günter Grass.* Frankfurt a.M.: Athenäum, 1972.

Kamshad, Hassan. *Modern Persian Prose Literature.* Cambridge: Cambridge Univ. Press, 1966.

Kaplan, Charles. "Holden and Huck: The Odysseys of Youth." *College English*, 18 (1956), 76–80.

Kearful, Frank J. "Spanish Rogues and English Foundlings: On the Disintegration of the Picaresque." *Genre*, 4 (1971), 376–91.

Kegel, Charles H. "Incommunicability in Salinger's *The Catcher in the Rye.*" *Western Humanities Review*, 11 (1957), 188–90.

Kermode, Frank. *Puzzles and Epiphanies.* London: Routledge & Kegan Paul, 1962.

Kinney, Arthur F. "The Theme of Charity in *The Catcher in the Rye.*" *Papers of the Michigan Academy of Science, Art and Letters*, 48, 691–702.

Kirk, Irene. "Dramatization of Consciousness in Albert Camus' *La chute* and Dostoevsky's *Notes from Underground.*" *Actes du Ve Congrès de l'Association Internationale de Littérature Comparée, Belgrade 1967*, ed. Nikola Bonašević. Belgrade: Univ. of Belgrade Press, 1969, pp. 609–615.

Klingmann, Ulrich. *"Bekenntnisse des Hochstaplers Felix Krull*: Ein moderner Schelmenroman?" *Acta Germanica*, 2 (1968), 63–73.

Koonce, Howard L. "Moll's Muddle: Defoe's Use of Irony in *Moll Flanders.*" *English Literary History*, 30 (1964), 377–94.

Kubíčková, Vera. "Persian Literature of the 20th Century," in Jan

Rypka's *History of Iranian Literature*, trans. P. van Popta, et al. Dordrecht: Reidel, 1968, pp. 355–418.

Lange, Victor. "Betrachtungen zur Thematik von *Felix Krull*." *Germanic Review*, 31 (1956), 215–24.

Lanham, Richard A. *"Tristram Shandy": The Games of Pleasure*. Berkeley: Univ. of California Press, 1973.

Laser, Marvin, and Norman Fruman, eds. *Studies in J. D. Salinger.* New York: Odyssey, 1963.

Lauber, John. "'Ligeia' and Its Critics: A Plea for Literalism." *Studies in Short Fiction*, 4 (1967), 28–32.

Laurenti, Joseph L. *Estudios sobre la novela picaresca española*. Madrid: Castalia, 1971.

Lehman, Benjamin H. *Studies in the Comic*. Berkeley: Univ. of California Press, 1941.

Lescot, Roger. "Le roman et la nouvelle dans la littérature iranienne contemporaine." *Bulletins d'Etudes Orientales*, 9 (1943).

Lethcoe, James. "Self-Deception in Dostoevskij's *Notes from the Underground*." *Slavic and East European Journal*, 10 (1966), 9–21.

Lettis, Richard. *J. D. Salinger: "The Catcher in the Rye"*. Great Neck, N.Y.: Barron, 1964.

Levine, Paul. "Saul Bellow: The Affirmation of the Philosophical Fool." *Perspective*, 10 (1959), 163–76.

Life and Letters and the London Mercury, 63, no. 148 (December 1949). (Persian Writers Issue.)

Lockridge, Ernest H. "A Vision of the Sentimental Absurd: Sterne and Camus." *Southern Review*, 72 (1964), 652–67.

Magarshack, David. *Gogol: A Life*. London: Faber & Faber, 1957.

Matlaw, Ralph E. "Structure and Integration in *Notes from Underground*." *PMLA*, 73 (1958), 101–109.

Maurer, Robert. "The End of Innocence: Günter Grass's *The Tin Drum*." *Bucknell Review*, 16, ii (May 1968), 45–65.

May, T. E. "Good and Evil in the *Buscón*." *Modern Language Review*, 45 (1950), 319–35.

Mayer, Hans. "Felix Krull und Oskar Matzerath: Aspekte des Romans," in his *Das Geschehen und das Schweigen: Aspekte der Literatur*. Frankfurt a.M.: Suhrkamp, 1969, pp. 35–67.

McNamara, Eugene. "Holden as Novelist." *English Jounal*, 54 (1965), 166–70.

Mengeling, Marvin, and Frances Mengeling. "From Fancy to Failure: A Study of the Narrators in the Tales of E. A. Poe." *University Review*, 33 (1966), 293–98, and 34 (1967), 31–37.

Merrill, Reed. "The Mistaken Endeavor: Dostoevsky's *Notes from Underground*." *Modern Fiction Studies*, 18 (1972–73), 505–516.

Miles, Keith. *Günter Grass*. New York: Barnes & Noble, 1975.

Miller, Stuart. *The Picaresque Novel*. Cleveland: Case Western Reserve Univ. Press, 1967.

Mitchell, Charles. "Mythic Seriousness in *Lolita*." *Texas Studies in Literature and Language*, 5 (1963), 329–43.

Mochulsky, Konstantin. *Dostoevsky: His Life and Work*, tr. Michael A. Minihan. Princeton, N.J.: Princeton Univ. Press, 1967.

Mohandessi, Menoutchehr. "Hedayat and Rilke." *Comparative Literature*, 23 (1971), 209–216.

Moteil, Vincent. *Sâdeq Hedâyat*. Tehran: Editions de l'Institut Franco-Iranien, 1952.

Morris, Cyril Brian. "The Unity and Structure of *El buscón: desgracias encadenadas*." *Occasional Papers in Modern Languages*, Univ. of Hull, 1 (1965).

Morrison, Claudia C. "Poe's 'Ligeia': An Analysis." *Studies in Short Fiction*, 4 (1967), 234–44.

Müller, Joachim. "Glücksspiel und Göttermythe: Zu Thomas Manns *Krull*," in *Vollendung und Größe Thomas Manns*, ed. Georg Wenzel. Halle: VEB, 1962, pp. 233–49.

Nelson, Donald F. "Felix Krull or: 'All the World's a Stage.'" *Germanic Review*, 45 (1970), 41–51.

Neuhäuser, Rudolf. "Observations on the Structure of *Notes from Underground* with Reference to the Main Themes of Part II." *Canadian-American Slavic Studies*, 6 (1972), 239–55.

Nevo, Ruth. "Towards a Theory of Comedy." *Journal of Aesthetics and Art Criticism*, 21 (1963), 327–32.

Novak, Maximillian. "Conscious Irony in *Moll Flanders*: Facts and Problems." *College English*, 26 (1964), 198–208.

———. "Defoe's 'Indifferent Monitor': The Complexity of *Moll Flanders*." *Eighteenth Century Studies*, 3 (1970), 351–65.

O'Nan, Martha. "Günter Grass's Oskar: The Rogue," in her *The Role of Mind in Hugo, Faulkner, Beckett, and Grass*. New York: Philosophical Library, 1969, pp. 36–49.

197

Opdahl, Keith Michael. *The Novels of Saul Bellow: An Introduction.* University Park: Pennsylvania State Univ. Press, 1967.

Paris, Bernard J. *A Psychological Approach to Fiction.* Bloomington: Indiana Univ. Press, 1974.

————. *"Notes from Underground*: A Horneyan Analysis." *PMLA*, 88 (1973), 511–22.

Parish, Charles. "The Nature of Mr. Tristram Shandy, Author." *Boston University Studies in English,* 5 (1961), 74–90.

Parker, Alexander Augustine. *Literature and the Delinquent: The Picaresque Novel in Spain and Europe 1599–1753.* Edinburgh: Edinburgh Univ. Press, 1967.

————. "The Psychology of the Pícaro in *El buscón*." *Modern Language Review,* 42 (1947), 58–69.

Paulsen, Ronald. "Picaresque Narrative: The Servant-Master Relation," in his *The Fictions of Satire.* Baltimore: Johns Hopkins Univ. Press, 1967.

Pearce, Richard. *Dostoevsky.* Cambridge: Cambridge Univ. Press, 1971.

————. *Stages of the Clown: Stages of Modern Fiction from Dostoevsky to Beckett.* Carbondale: Southern Illinois Univ. Press, 1970.

Perry, Ben Edwin. "An Interpretation of Apuleius' *Metamorphoses*." *Transactions and Proceedings of the American Philological Association,* ed. Joseph William Hewitt, 57 (1926), 238–60.

Phillips, Elizabeth. "The Hocus-Pocus of *Lolita*." *Literature and Psychology,* 10 (1960), 97–101.

Pilkington, John. "About This Madman Stuff." *University of Mississippi Studies in English,* 7 (1966), 65–75.

Piper, William Bowman. "Tristram Shandy's Digressive Artistry." *Studies in English Literature 1500–1900,* 1, iii (Autumn 1961), 65–76.

Proffer, Carl R. *Keys to "Lolita".* Bloomington: Indiana Univ. Press, 1968.

Raban, Jonathan. *Mark Twain: "Huckleberry Finn".* London: Arnold, 1968.

Rabassa, Gregory. "Lying to Athena: Cortázar and the Art of Fiction." *Books Abroad,* 50 (1976), 542–47.

Ricapito, Joseph V. "Introducción," in *Lazarillo de Tormes,* ed. Joseph V. Ricapito. Madrid: Cátedra, 1976, pp. 11–81.

————. "Towards a Definition of the Picaresque." Diss., UCLA, 1966.

Rico, Francisco. *La novela picaresca y el punto de vista.* Barcelona: Seix Barral, 1970.

Rocks, James E. "Conflict and Motive in 'The Cask of Amontillado.'" *Poe Studies*, 5, ii (December 1972), 50–51.

Rodnon, Stewart. "*The Adventures of Huckleberry Finn* and *Invisible Man:* Thematic and Structural Comparisons." *Negro American Literature Forum*, 4, 45–51.

Rogers, Franklin R. *Mark Twain's Burlesque Patterns as Seen in the Novels and Narratives in 1855–1885.* Dallas: Southern Methodist Univ. Press, 1960.

Rolle, Dietrich. *Fielding und Sterne: Untersuchungen über die Funktion des Erzählers.* Münster: Aschendorff, 1963.

Rousseaux, André. "Sadegh Hedayat et son chef-d'oeuvre." *Le Figaro Littéraire*, July 18, 1953, p. 2.

Rubenstein, E. "Approaching *Lolita.*" *Minnesota Review*, 6 (1966), 361–67.

Scarcia, Gianroberto. "*Hāǧī Āqā* e *Buf-e Kur*, i cosiddetti due aspetti dell'opera dello scrittore contemporaneo persiano Sādeq Hedāyat." *Annali Istituto Universitario Orientale de Napoli*, N.S., 8 (1958), 103–123.

Sheer-Schäzler, Brigitte. *Saul Bellow.* New York: Ungar, 1971.

Schmidt, Lothar. "Das Ich im *Simplicissimus.*" *Wirkendes Wort*, 10 (1960), 215–20.

Schroeter, James. "A Misreading of Poe's 'Ligeia.'" *PMLA*, 76 (1961), 397–406.

Schwarz, Wilhelm Johannes. *Der Erzähler Günter Grass.* Bern: Francke, 1969.

Seidlin, Oskar. "Picaresque Elements in Thomas Mann's Work." *Modern Language Quarterly*, 12 (1951), 183–200.

Seng, Peter J. "The Fallen Idol: The Immature World of Holden Caulfield." *College English*, 23 (1961), 203–209.

Sharfman, William L. "The Organization of Experience in *The Tin Drum.*" *Minnesota Review*, 6 (1966), 59–65.

Simmons, Ernest J. *Dostoevsky: The Making of a Novelist.* New York: Random House, 1940.

Smalley, Barbara. "The Compulsive Patterns of Dostoyevsky's Underground Man." *Studies in Short Fiction*, 10 (1973), 389–96.

Smith, Henry Nash. *Mark Twain: The Development of a Writer.* Cambridge, Mass.: Harvard Univ. Press, 1962.

Spilka, Mark. "Playing Crazy in the Underground." *Minnesota Review*, 6 (1966), 233–43.

Spitzer, Leo. "Zur Kunst Quevedos in seinem *Buscón*." *Archivum Romanicum*, 11 (1927), 551–80.

Stauffer, Donald Barlow. "Style and Meaning in 'Ligeia' and 'William Wilson.'" *Studies in Short Fiction*, 2 (1965), 316–30.

Stedmond, John M. *The Comic Art of Laurence Sterne*. Toronto: Univ. of Toronto Press, 1967.

Stegner, S. Page. *Escape into Aesthetics: The Art of Vladimir Nabokov*. New York: Dial, 1966.

Stone, Albert E., Jr. *The Innocent Eye: Childhood in Mark Twain's Imagination*. New Haven, Conn.: Yale Univ. Press, 1961.

Strandberg, Victor. "Poe's Hollow Men." *University Review*, 35 (1961), 203–212.

Strauch, Carl F. "Kings in the Back Row: Meaning through Structure. A Reading of Salinger's *The Catcher in the Rye*." *Wisconsin Studies in Contemporary Literature*, 2 (1961), 5–30.

Tank, Kurt Lothar. *Günter Grass*. Berlin: Colloquium, 1965.

Tanner, Tony. "Huck Finn and the Reflections of a Saphead," in his *The Reign of Wonder*. Cambridge: Cambridge Univ. Press, 1965, pp. 155–83.

———. *Saul Bellow*. New York: Barnes & Noble, 1965.

Tarr, F. Courtney. "Literary and Artistic Unity in the *Lazarillo de Tormes*." *PMLA*, 42 (1927), 404–421.

Thackeray, William Makepeace. "Sterne and Goldsmith," in his *The English Humourists of the Eighteenth Century*. London: Macmillan, 1910.

Thompson, G. R. *Poe's Fiction: Romantic Irony in the Gothic Tales*. Madison: Univ. of Wisconsin Press, 1973.

———. "'Proper Evidence of Madness': American Gothic and the Interpretation of 'Ligeia.'" *Emerson Society Quarterly*, 66 (1972), 30–49.

Tober, Karl. "Vom Schein: Anmerkungen zu Thomas Manns Schelmenroman." *Acta Germanica*, 3 (1968), 257–66.

Trascher, Isidore. "Dostoevsky's *Notes from Underground*." *Accent*, 16 (1956), 255–64.

Traugott, John. *Tristram Shandy's World: Sterne's Philosophical Rhetoric*. Berkeley: Univ. of California Press, 1954.

Trilling, Lionel. "The Last Lover: Vladimir Nabokov's *Lolita*." *Encounter*, 2, iv (October 1958), 9–19.

Truman, R. W. "Parody and Irony in the Self-Portrayal of Lázaro de Tormes." *Modern Language Review*, 63 (1968), 600–605.

Uphaus, Robert W. "Nabokov's Künstlerroman: Portrait of the Artist as a Dying Man." *Twentieth Century Literature*, 13 (1967), 104–110.

Van der Will, Wilfried. *Pikaro heute*. Stuttgart: Kohlhammer, 1967.

Walker, Herbert. "Observations on Fyodor Dostoevsky's *Notes from the Underground*." *American Imago*, 19 (1962), 195–210.

Wasiolek, Edward. *Dostoevsky: The Major Fiction*. Cambridge, Mass.: MIT Press, 1964.

Wells, Arvin R. "Huck Finn and Holden Caulfield: The Situation of the Hero." *Ohio University Review*, 2 (1960), 31–42.

Welsford, Enid. *The Fool: His Social and Literary History*. Gloucester, Mass.: Peter Smith, 1966. (Originally published in London: Faber & Faber, 1935.)

Wenzel, Georg, ed. *Vollendung und Größe Thomas Manns*. Halle: VEB, 1962.

Whitbourn, Christine J., ed. *Knaves and Swindlers: Essays on the Picaresque Novel in Europe*. London: Oxford Univ. Press, 1974.

Willis, Raymond S. "Lázaro and the Pardoner." *Hispanic Review*, 27 (1959), 267–79.

Woodward, L. J. "Author-Reader Relationship in the *Lazarillo de Tormes*." *Forum for Modern Language Studies*, 1 (1965), 43–53.

Wright, Andrew. "The Artifice of Failure in *Tristram Shandy*." *Novel*, 2 (1969), 212–20.

Wysling, Hans. "Archivalisches Gewühle: Zur Entstehungsgeschichte der *Bekenntnisse des Hochstaplers Felix Krull*," in *Quellenkritische Studien zum Werk Thomas Manns*, eds. Paul Scherrer and Hans Wysling. Bern: Francke, 1967, 234–57.

Zeller, Hildegard. *Die Ich-Erzählung im englischen Roman*. Breslau: Priebatsch, 1933.

Index

203